Instructional Supervision

Applying Tools and Concepts

Second Edition

Sally J. Zepeda

EYE ON EDUCATION
6 DEPOT WAY WEST, SUITE 106
LARCHMONT, NY 10538
(914) 833–0551
(914) 833–0761 fax
www.eyeoneducation.com

Library of Congress Cataloging-in-Publication Data

Zepeda, Sally J., 1956-
  Instructional supervision : applying tools and concepts / Sally J. Zepeda.
— 2nd ed.
     p. cm.
  ISBN 1-59667-041-X
  1. School supervision. I. Title.
  LB2806.4.Z44 2007
  371.2'03—dc22

                                                              2006031917

10 9 8 7 6 5 4 3

Editorial and production services provided by
Freelance Editorial Services

Also Available from Eye On Education

The Instructional Leader's Guide to
Informal Classroom Observations
Sally J. Zepeda

The Principal as Instructional Leader:
A Handbook for Supervisors
Sally J. Zepeda

Instructional Leadership
for School Improvement
Sally J. Zepeda

Supervision Across the Content Areas
Sally J. Zepeda and R. Stewart Mayers

School Leader Internship:
Developing, Monitoring, and Evaluating
Your Leadership Experience, 2nd ed.
Martin, Wright, Danzig, Flanary, and Brown

Lead with Me: A Principal's
Guide to Teacher Leadership
Gayle Moller and Anita Pankake

Transforming School
Leadership with ISLLC and ELCC
Neil J. Shipman, J. Allen Queen, and Henry A. Peel

Countdown to the Principalship:
A Resource Guide for Beginning Principals
O'Rourke, Provenzano, Bellamy and Ballek

Data Analysis for
Continuous School Improvement
Victoria L. Bernhardt

The Administrator's Guide to
School Community Relations, 2nd ed.
George E. Pawlas

Handbook on Teacher Evaluation:
Assessing and Improving Performance
James H. Stronge and Pamela D. Tucker

Effective Schooling for English Language Learners:
What Elementary Principals Should Know and Do
Patricia Smiley and Trudy Salsberry

The Principal's Purpose: A Practical
Guide to Moral and Ethical School Leadership
Leanna Stohr Isaacson

Smart, Fast, Efficient:
The New Principals' Guide to Success
Leanna Stohr Isaacson

What Great Principals Do Differently:
15 Things That Matter Most
Todd Whitaker

What Successful Principals Do!
169 Tips for Principals
Franzy Fleck

BRAVO Principal!
Sandra Harris

Creating the High Schools of Our Choice
Tim Westerberg

Improving Your School One
Week at a Time: Building the Foundation
for Professional Teaching and Learning
Jeffrey Zoul

Lead Me—I Dare You!
Managing Resistance to Change
Sherrel Bergmann and Judith Brough

Talk It Out! The Educator's Guide to
Successful Difficult Conversations
Barbara E. Sanderson

About the Author

Sally J. Zepeda has served as a high school teacher, director of special programs, assistant principal, and principal. A professor and graduate coordinator in the Program in Educational Administration and Policy at the University of Georgia, she teaches instructional supervision and other courses related to professional development. Dr. Zepeda has written widely about educational administration, supervision of teaching, and leadership. Her books include *The Instructional Leader's Guide to Informal Classroom Observations; Instructional Leadership for School Improvement; The Principal as Instructional Leader: A Handbook for Supervisors; Supervision Across the Content Areas* (with R. Stewart Mayers); *Staff Development: Practices That Promote Leadership in Learning Communities; The Call to Teacher Leadership* (with R. Stewart Mayers and Brad N. Benson); *Hands-on Leadership Tools for Principals* (with Raymond Calabrese and Gary Short); *The Reflective Supervisor: A Practical Guide for Educators* (with Raymond Calabrese); *Special Programs in Regular Schools: Historical Foundations, Standards, and Contemporary Issues* (with Michael Langenbach); and *Supervision and Staff Development in the Block* (with R. Stewart Mayers).

Dr. Zepeda has served in a variety of leadership roles that support the work of practitioners and scholars, including serving as the immediate past network facilitator for the Association of Supervision and Curriculum Development (ASCD) and as the book and audio review column editor for the *Journal of Staff Development* for 10 years. She chaired the American Educational Research Association's Supervision and Instructional Leadership SIG. Dr. Zepeda also is a member of the Council of Professors of Instructional Supervision (COPIS). She reviews submissions for several scholarly journals and serves on the Editorial Board for *Educational Administration Quarterly*. In 2005, Dr. Zepeda was recognized by the University Council of Educational Administration (UCEA) as a Master Professor.

Dedication

This book is dedicated to all the supervisors, mentors, coaches, and significant others who nurture the spirit by providing supervision that makes a difference in the lives of teachers.

SJZ

Acknowledgments

Revising a textbook for a second edition is a daunting task, but through the thoughtful comments of reviewers from the rank and file of higher education and the many graduate-level students, this task was a rewarding and manageable one. I am grateful to the many teachers, administrators, and professors who shared their insights about supervisory practices. Numerous colleagues read this manuscript while it was in process. These colleagues include Dr. Lea Arnau, director of professional learning for Gwinnett County Schools (GA), Dr. Jackie Adams, principal of West Hall High School (GA), and Dr. Bill Kruskamp, principal of Creekland Middle School (GA). Lea, Jackie, and Bill have taught sections of instructional supervision at the University of Georgia, and they have used the data collection methods and tools as both instructors and as instructional supervisors.

Several professionals adapted the tools appearing in the first edition of this book and shared their adaptations with me, and others gave permission to include original materials they developed. I have acknowledged these individuals throughout the text. My thanks go to Theresa L. Benfante, behavior interventionist at Central Alternative School, Cobb County School District (GA); Dr. Marcia Wilbur, head, World Languages and Cultures Professional Development at The College Board; Kevin Johnson, a doctoral student in the Music Education Department at the University of Georgia; Meredith A. Byrd from Clayton County Public Schools (Jonesboro, GA); and Ann G. Haughey, technology coordinator for Wilkes County Schools (Washington, GA).

Owen Ogletree, an instructional coach at Monroe Area High School, spent countless hours field-testing instruments and providing helpful suggestions. Philip Potter gave feedback to earlier drafts on the chapter on marginal teaching, and in addition to finding materials and resources that were instrumental in adding this chapter to the second edition. University of Georgia Research Assistants Fred Prasuhn, a doctoral student in the Adult Education Program Area, and Ed Bengtson, a doctoral student in the Program in Educational Administration and Policy, "chased down" numerous documents from the library and assisted in so many other ways.

No book is worth anything without expert reviewers. I was very fortunate to have focused feedback from several reviewers who teach instructional supervision and who are leaders in the field. These reviewers include

Mary Aspedon, Southwestern Oklahoma State University

Jerry Garrett, Indiana University-Purdue University, Fort Wayne

Robert Kirschman, University of Bridgeport

R. Stewart Mayers, Southeastern Oklahoma State University

Paul Terry, University of South Florida, Lakeland

Marcia Wilbur, The College Board

Donald Wise, California State University, Fresno

Thank you and I hope that this book reflects your collective wisdom.

Suzanne Hall, office manager in the Department of Lifelong Education, Administration, and Policy, provided much technical assistance, as did Denise Collins. Special thanks are due to Mark Ginsberg, English teacher at Cedar Shoals High School, Athens, Georgia.

I admire Richard Adin for his ability to visually portray words and for his adept layout skills. Richard, although you worked behind the scenes, know that I respect your contributions to this book.

As always, I value Bob Sickles for his vision about the importance of leadership and supervision and his determination to "leave no stone unturned" in the process of getting this second edition to press.

SJZ

Table of Contents

Downloads for Professors and Students

A large selection of the supervision tools discussed and displayed in this volume can be downloaded by students who have purchased this book. Book buyers have permission to print out these Adobe Acrobat documents and use them in course practicums and/or with actual teachers in real school settings.

In addition, downloadable transparency masters are available for instructors who have assigned this book to their students.

You can access these downloads by visiting Eye On Education's website: www.eyeoneducation.com Click on FREE Downloads. Or search or browse our website from our home page to find this book and then scroll down for downloading instructions.

You'll need your book-buyer access code: **INSTR-7041-X**

Supervision Tools for Students

Transparency Masters for Instructors

1

Thinking About Supervision That Makes a Difference

In This Chapter...

♦ The landscape of standards

♦ Issues of accountability and high stakes

♦ Supervision is not a linear, lockstep process

♦ Linking instructional supervision, professional development, and teacher evaluation

♦ Developing a Vision for Supervision

Supervision

Perhaps the most important work a supervisor does—regardless of title or position—is to work with teachers in ways that promote lifelong learning skills: inquiry, reflection, collaboration, and a dedication to professional growth and development. Educators today sense an urgency that stems not least from high-stakes expectations for students to perform well on standardized tests. In turn, these expectations focus attention on how teachers must improve their skills so that students can achieve more. Essentially, supervisors are teachers of teachers—adult professionals with learning needs as varied as those of the students in their classrooms.

Although there is debate on the value and emphasis placed on how well students do on standardized tests, there is little debate on the need for supervisors and others to foster the professional growth of teachers. For supervisors, this means they must examine the fundamental ways of linking support—supervision, professional development, and teacher evaluation. The accountability movement, although pushing for students to "bubble in" their knowledge on standardized tests, cannot reduce supervision and teacher evaluation to a standardized checklist filled out once a year. The challenge for supervisors is to extend learning opportunities for teachers through a more unified approach to professional development and growth. They ignore this challenge at their peril.

Developing a vision for supervision is a reflective and iterative process. In a culture built on a foundation of collaboration, collegiality, and trust, the supervisor is in a better position to promote the processes that support and actively engage adults in reflection and inquiry.

The Landscape of Standards

Although the focus is on high-stakes performance of students, the stakes should be equally high for teachers and for the supervisors, professional developers, and teacher-leaders who help to induct, mentor, and coach teachers throughout their careers. Instructional supervisors must gain familiarity with several standards—a daunting task, especially for new supervisors. Moreover, it is difficult to supervise and then provide developmentally appropriate professional development activities without the knowledge that the standards offer. Standards can illuminate what is called best practice across subject and content areas. Figure 1.1 (next page) outlines a sampling of the types of standards that our profession embraces.

The standards identified in Figure 1.1 are but a few of many; prospective supervisors are well-advised to think through the myriad disciplines (English, math, social studies), grade levels (elementary, middle, high school), and specialty personnel (school nurse, counselor, social worker, and others) that make up a school. The following descriptions may help supervisors understand how standards can frame their work with school personnel.

Figure 1.1. Selected Standards at a Glance

Type of Standard	Examples	Contact Information
Content standards	National Council of Teachers of English	http://www.ncte.org/standards/
	National Council of Teachers of Mathematics	http://www.nctm.org/standards/overview.htm
	National Council of Social Studies	http://www.socialstudies.org/standards/teachers/home.shtml
Grade-level standards	National Middle School Association	http://www.nmsa.org/conferences.htm
State department standards	Kentucky	http://www.kde.state.ky.us/otec/epsb/standards/new_teach_stds.asp
National	National Board for Professional Teaching Standards	http://www.nbpts.org/

Subject-Matter Standards

Often referred to as content standards, these exist for just about every discipline in which teachers are certified (e.g., English, social studies, mathematics). For example, the National Council of Teachers of Mathematics (NCTM) has established the *Principles and Standards of Mathematics*, which delineates six principles to guide school mathematics programs and ten standards that set content and process goals across grades Pre-K through 12. Inherent in the standards are pedagogical considerations that supervisors must recognize as they work with teachers to develop a coherent curriculum across grade levels. Regarding this, the NCTM states that teachers must

> Continue to learn new or additional mathematics content, study how students learn mathematics, analyze issues in teaching mathematics, and use new materials and technology. Teachers must develop their own professional knowledge using research, the knowledge base of the profession, and their own experiences as resources. Preservice education, therefore, needs to prepare teachers to learn from their own teaching, from their students, from curriculum materials, from colleagues, and from other experts. (p. 3)[*]

---

[*] Reprinted with permission from *Principles and Standards of Mathematics* (2000) by the National Council of Teachers of Mathematics. All rights reserved.

Organizations such as the National Science Teachers Association (NSTA) offer valuable information to assist supervisors in their work with teachers. For example, NSTA (1992) suggests that science supervisors should improve science education through leadership and support for the professionalism of science teachers (Figure 1.2).

Figure 1.2. NSTA Supports Instructional Supervision for Science Teachers

Science supervisors support the professionalism of science teachers by...

- Staying abreast of the latest research on the ways students learn and apply major concepts in science so as to help teachers understand and embrace the latest, most effective teaching strategies;
- Becoming an advocate for the special instructional needs of historically underrepresented students, including minorities, females, disabled and at-risk students;
- Promoting the maintenance of a safe laboratory environment by facilitating implementation of federal, state, and local laws and regulations, and by disseminating information that is part of an experiential science education program;
- Advocating manageable laboratory student–teacher ratios to increase safety, expand hands-on opportunities, and contribute to enhanced student–teacher interactions;
- Interpreting the current philosophies and approaches to science curriculum and instruction, especially through the knowledge of existing core and supplementary instructional materials;
- Providing access to instructional resources and professional development opportunities for teachers, students, and aides to improve science education for all students;
- Networking among a variety of professional associations, organizations, and agencies concerned with the improvement of science teaching and learning;
- Building consensus through involvement in various local and state constituency groups for science education, so that the most effective practices are shared among a wider segment of the science education profession;
- Accommodating the ever-growing assessment techniques within accountability systems designed to gauge the effectiveness of instructional materials, programs, teachers, and students toward achieving the goal of scientific literacy;
- Making the best possible use of telecommunications media as one of the tools for interacting with administrators, teachers, and students; and

◆ Recognizing the special work (both curricular and co-curricular) of science departments, teachers, and students through effective public relations outreach.

Source: National Science Teachers Association, 1992.

Grade-Level Standards

Standards for teaching across grades Pre-K through 12 are available for supervisors to consult as they work with teachers. Professional organizations, such as the National Middle School Association (NMSA), have been proactively supporting standards for both initial preparation and ongoing professional development of middle-level educators. For example, *Program Standards for Middle Level Preparation* (2000) calls for middle-level teachers who can work appropriately with middle-level students. Figure 1.3 details some of the program standards for middle-level preparation.

Figure 1.3. Sample Program Standards for Middle-Level Preparation

Middle-level teachers can...

1. Use a variety of teaching/learning strategies and resources that motivate young adolescents to learn.
2. Create learning experiences that encourage exploration and problem solving so all young adolescents can be actively engaged in learning.
3. Plan effective instruction individually and with colleagues.
4. Use a variety of formal and informal assessment techniques to improve teaching/learning strategies (e.g., evaluation of student learning).
5. Provide all young adolescents with opportunities to engage in independent and collaborative inquiry.
6. Participate in professional development activities that increase their knowledge of effective teaching/learning strategies.
7. Establish positive learning climates for all young adolescents.
8. Employ effective, developmentally responsive classroom management techniques.

Source: *Program Standards for Middle Level Preparation*, 2000. Used with permission. National Middle School Association. All rights reserved.

State Department Standards

All states that initially certify teachers require them to meet certain standards; many states also have standards for the ongoing certification of teachers. For example, Kentucky has standards both for initial teacher certification and for experienced teachers. Figure 1.4 illustrates these two sets of standards.

Figure 1.4. Kentucky Standards for Beginning and Experienced Teachers

Beginning Teachers

> Standard I: Designs/Plans Instruction
> Standard II: Creates/Maintains Learning Climates
> Standard III: Implements/Manages Instruction
> Standard IV: Assesses and Communicates Learning Results
> Standard V: Reflects/Evaluates Teaching/Learning
> Standard VI: Collaborates with Colleagues/Parents/Others
> Standard VII: Engages in Professional Development
> Standard VIII: Knowledge of Content
> Standard IX: Demonstrates Implementation of Technology

Source: http://www.kde.state.ky.us/otec/epsb/standards/new_teach_stds.asp

Experienced Teachers

> Standard 1: Demonstrates Professional Leadership
> Standard 2: Demonstrates Knowledge of Content
> Standard 3: Designs/Plans Instruction
> Standard 4: Creates/Maintains Learning Climate
> Standard 5: Implements/Manages Instruction
> Standard 6: Assesses and Communicates Learning Results
> Standard 7: Reflects/Evaluates Teaching/Learning
> Standard 8: Collaborates with Colleagues/Parents/Others
> Standard 9: Engages in Professional Development
> Standard 10: Demonstrates Implementation of Technology

Source: http://www.kde.state.ky.us/otec/epsb/standards/exp_teach_stds.asp

Familiarity with standards is essential, but many supervisors want to know which standards to use. Professionals aspiring to a supervisory position are encouraged to do some legwork first. This includes accessing state department teaching standards, professional standards from organizations such as the National Council of Teachers of English, grade-level standards from such organizations as the National Association for Middle Level Education, and the National Board for Professional Teaching Standards. Standards often overlap. The supervisor needs to become familiar with these standards and think of ways to frame supervisory support and professional development so that teachers can meet and then exceed standards. Central-office curriculum coordinators, directors of professional development, and assistant and associate superintendents can be valuable resources. Curriculum guides often reflect standards and, typically during textbook adoption and other work such as curriculum alignment, instructional guides include updates to standards. Local universities, especially those that prepare prospective teachers and administrators, are another good source.

Prospective supervisors and administrators can consult standards of practice for school leaders. Figure 1.5 lists resources that provide not only standards of practice, but also the knowledge and dispositions that supervisors need in their ongoing work with teachers.

Figure 1.5. Standards of Practice for School Leaders

Standards	Source
National Board for Professional Teaching Standards (NBPTS)	http://www.nbpts.org/
National Staff Development Council (NSDC)	http://www.nsdc.org/educator index.htm
Council of Chief State School Officers (CCSSO)	http://www.ccsso.org/index.html
Interstate New Teacher Assessment and Support Consortium (INTASC)— Model Standards for Beginning Teacher Licensing and Development	http://www.ccsso.org/intascst.html
The Personnel Evaluation Standards	http://ww.eval.org/Evaluation Documents/perseval.html
Interstate School Leaders Licensure Consortium— Standards for School Leaders	http://www.ccsso.org/pdfs/ isllcstd.pdf
National Council for Accreditation of Teacher Education (NCATE)	http://www.ncate.org/
Standards for Advanced Programs in Educational Leadership for Principals, Superintendents, Curriculum Directors, and Supervisors	http://www.nacate.org/ standard/new%20program% standards/ecll%202001.pdf

Beginning supervisors, once hired, attend formal (and in most cases mandatory) training on the use of formal evaluation procedures and processes tied to state statutes governing teacher evaluation. Such training usually covers legal issues surrounding evaluation, dismissal, nonrenewal, and due process. Supervision *per se* is usually not covered; most trainers assume that administrators know the difference between supervision (which is formative) and evaluation (which is summative and related to a final rating).

Site level and district level supervisors can find a wealth of materials to help their work with supervising the instructional program and the teachers who shape it.

Figure 1.6 lists some of these organizations. Readers are encouraged to discover whether there are subject-specific organizations, such as the Florida Council of Language Arts Supervisors (CLAS) (http://www.santarosa.k12.fl.us/clas/) and the Connecticut Science Supervisors Association (CSSA) (http://www.cssaonline.net/index.html), available in your locality. These organizations often hold meetings, sponsor workshops, and offer opportunities for supervisors to network with other subject-area supervisors.

Figure 1.6. Organizations for Supervisors

The National Science Education Leadership Association (NSELA) (formerly known as National Science Supervisors Association)	http://www.nsela.org/
The Council of State Science Supervisors (CSSS)	http://www.csss-science.org/index.shtml
National Social Studies Supervisors Association (NSSSA)	http://www.socialstudies.org/nsssa/
National Council of Supervisors of Mathematics (NCSM)	http://mathforum.org/ncsm/
National Association of District Supervisors of Foreign Language (NADSFL)	http://www.nadsfl.org/

Issues of Accountability and High Stakes

The issues of accountability and high-stakes learning environments are so broad and deep that a textbook on instructional supervision cannot cover them all; however, the high-stakes movement does carry implications for the types of supervision, professional development, and evaluation provided for teachers. The accountability movement rooted most directly to the publication, *A Nation at Risk* (1983) and the numerous reforms including "...academic standards for students and professional standards for what constitutes quality in teaching," has brought into focus more sharply, the need to support teachers and the work they do (National Association of Elementary School Principals [NAESP], 2002, p. 2).

The era of accountability presents thorny issues for schools—teachers, administrators, parents, central administrators, and students. First, it is unlikely that accountability initiatives based on standards will diminish. Central to this issue is the use of standardized testing as the benchmark of student success. Darling-Hammond (2002) reports that

> In recent years, the education reform movement in the United States has focused increasingly on developing new standards and assessments for students. In the last decade, 47 states have adopted new standards for student learning and most have created or adopted statewide testing systems as well. Some of these measure student learning through complex, open-ended performance assessments. Most rely primarily on the multiple-choice testing technology that has dominated large-scale U.S. assessments for nearly 50 years. (p. 2)

The second issue is that some states are linking student performance on standardized and other assessments to teacher evaluation; this practice has implications for the administrators who supervise and then evaluate teachers. For example, in Georgia, the *A Plus Education Reform Act* of 2000 provides "...a new roadmap for the improvement of teaching and learning" (Eady, 2002, p. 1). According to the language of the *Education Reform Act* of 2000, teachers are to be rated based, in part, on academic gains of students assigned to the teacher, and student achievement will be determined through a number of assessments, including standardized and criterion-referenced tests.

The provisions of *A Plus* stipulates that a teacher receiving an unsatisfactory evaluation will not be entitled to an increase in state salary, and teachers who received two unsatisfactory annual performance evaluations in a previous five-year period will not be eligible for recertification until deficiencies are remediated. These provisions "raise the stakes for student assessment by linking teacher salary—and, ultimately, continued teacher certification and employment—to student performance" (Eady, 2002, p. 28). The evaluative functions of *A Plus* signal that principals will need to supervise and evaluate teachers in new and different ways.

The third issue deals with the relationship between accountability, improved teaching, and the support that teachers need from those who supervise them. Accountability systems have essentially created a ripple effect between what students and teachers do, and according to the NAESP,

We've learned that it's meaningless to set high expectations for student performance unless we also set high expectations for the performance of adults. We know that if we are going to improve learning, we must also improve teaching. And we must improve the environment in which teaching and learning occurs. (p. 2)

For supervisors, the challenge is to recognize that the professional development of teachers is essential to creating learning environments—communities in which teachers learn from the work they do with students and other teachers.

This challenge can lead to new opportunities for supervisors to be proactive in their work with teachers. Too often, however, the hectic tempo of life in schools prevents supervisors and teachers from finding the time and other necessary resources to engage in learning opportunities that match the needs of adult learners. Sorely missing are opportunities to link instructional supervision, professional development, and evaluation as a cohesive plan for professional development. What makes it difficult to connect activities designed for adult learning? Here are a few possibilities to consider:

◆ Teacher evaluations must be completed by a certain date, usually in the spring, two or more months before the end of the year.

◆ A prescribed number of classroom observations must be completed before a summative rating is assigned, but this number can be as few as one. Moreover, in some states, the length of time mandated for observing a teacher is as little as 15 minutes per observation.

◆ Teachers leave the building to attend professional development seminars throughout the year but have no opportunities to share with others what they have learned. Moreover, follow-up is sparse, perpetuating professional development as "shotgun learning."

◆ Central administrators often book big-name consultants to address districtwide issues on teacher workdays, but follow-up activities cease when the consultant leaves.

◆ Mentoring and induction delivered by central office personnel do not necessarily reflect the context of the school; site- and district-level activities typically stress more global issues, whereas building-level programs stress more context-specific issues.

◆ The efforts of mentors are not factored into the equation of what supervisors do to assist beginning teachers or other teachers.

- Supervisors often focus their attention on the hot spots—a single grade level implementing a new program, or deficit areas (grade levels that performed poorly on standardized tests).

- Supervisory and professional development efforts are rarely differentiated by taking into account the differences of teachers across the career continuum. Too often beginning and veteran teachers are supervised and evaluated the same, and professional development activities follow a one-size-fits-all format.

As a result, unifying elements between and among activities are rare, the pace of activities is frenetic, teachers and administrators feel behind schedule, and opportunities for teachers to plan and work together in any systematic way are absent. Reflection, dialogue, inquiry, and collegiality are not embedded in the work needed to refine classroom practice.

Teachers need assistance, and they need a green light from supervisors and from each other to engage in professional learning. Teacher accountability will become a reality only when teachers can exercise leadership in the learning process and assume partnership responsibility for their own learning *with* supervisors. Because teachers are on the front-line daily, for the most part, they know what is needed to help them improve their practice, and given the formal and informal networks in schools, teachers know who needs mentoring and other assistance.

Given myriad contextual variables in schools, the diverse experiences and training of teachers, and the reality that teachers and school systems are being forced to be increasingly accountable, those who work with teachers must begin to unify efforts. Supervision (regardless of its form), professional development, and teacher evaluation must be unified at both the site and district levels.

Principals would be at odds with teachers who failed to deliver a curriculum that was unified, flexible, and adaptable to the needs of students. This same professional care and concern must apply to teachers if they are to be able to help their students learn. A unity of purpose must link supervision, professional development, and teacher evaluation.

Supervision Is Not a Linear, Lockstep Process

Instructional supervision, clinical supervision, or any other form of in-classroom supervision that aims to foster the professional growth of teachers cannot be reduced to a lockstep, linear process with a fixed beginning or end. The processes involved in supervision, professional development, teacher evaluation, and the like must be cyclical and ongoing. The process known as *clinical supervision* was originally designed to continue in cycles, with each cycle (preobservation, observation, and postobservation) informing future cycles and identifying the activities needed to help teachers meet their learning objectives. The *intents* of supervision (that is, its underlying purposes) are more thoroughly discussed in Chapter 2, and the processes of the clinical supervisory model are explored in Chapters 3 through 6.

Professional development and teacher evaluation must be linked to instructional supervision, embedded within and throughout the workday for teachers. What is needed is a model that connects the various forms of assistance available to teachers. However, no one model can ever be expected to fit the needs of every teacher and the contexts in which they work. There are ways to bridge supervision, professional development, evaluation, and other activities, such as peer coaching and mentoring. The real charge for prospective and practicing supervisors is to unify these efforts. One way to start is to scan a particular school building or organization. In addition to clinical supervision, what support systems are in place for teachers?

Extended Reflection

Identify the professional development and supervisory opportunities available to personnel in a school building. In the first column, list these opportunities. In the second column, describe how they are linked.

Professional Development and Supervisory Opportunities	How These Opportunities are Linked
Peer coaching	Numerous peer coaches serve as mentors, coaching teachers through direct classroom observation that includes both pre- and postobservation conferences.
Induction	The induction program includes mentoring, peer coaching, and study groups.
Study groups	Teachers form study groups and examine instructional issues; groups may read common materials; some teachers are involved in peer coaching; some teachers extend study group activities with teacher-directed action research.
Portfolio development	Action research teams are developing portfolios to track changes in practice.

Teachers are the central actors in the learning process. In the final analysis, they are the ones who internally *control* what is (or is not) learned through schoolwide efforts, such as peer coaching or portfolio development, as well as in the traditional clinical model of supervision.

Prospective supervisors should seek a wide range of methods to extend the original model of clinical supervision. Examples include portfolio development, action research, peer coaching and other forms of coaching, and other original site-specific activities. All need to be embedded in practice and linked as a unifying whole. A part of this unifying whole is professional development and the learning opportunities afforded to teachers. Because the original intents of the clinical supervision model included multiple cycles of conferencing and classroom observations, much information, namely data from the classroom observations and the insights gained by the teacher during extended discussions in pre- and postobservation conferences, it is logical to link ongoing professional development learning opportunities to supervisory efforts. Chapter 14 has a more purposeful discussion of professional development.

Linking Instructional Supervision, Professional Development, and Teacher Evaluation

In *The Centerless Corporation: A New Model for Transforming Your Organization for Growth and Prosperity*, Pasternack and Viscio (1998) describe a type of unity they call coherence:

> Coherence is what holds the firm together. It is the glue that binds the various pieces, enabling them to act as one. It includes a broad range of processes. It begins with a shared vision and shared set of values, and expands to include numerous linkages across the company. (p. 61)

This shared vision and set of values links supervision, professional development, evaluation and other learning opportunities, but more importantly, this shared vision relates and unifies them. Woven together in a holistic way, learning opportunities follow their own course while contributing to the overall development of the faculty and the organization.

To be truly valuable, an approach must be flexible, adaptable to a particular environment, and shaped by the people who apply it. Figure 1.7 (on the next page) presents one approach to linking supervision, professional development, evaluation, and other approaches (such as peer coaching, action research, and portfolio development) in a way that fosters coherence.

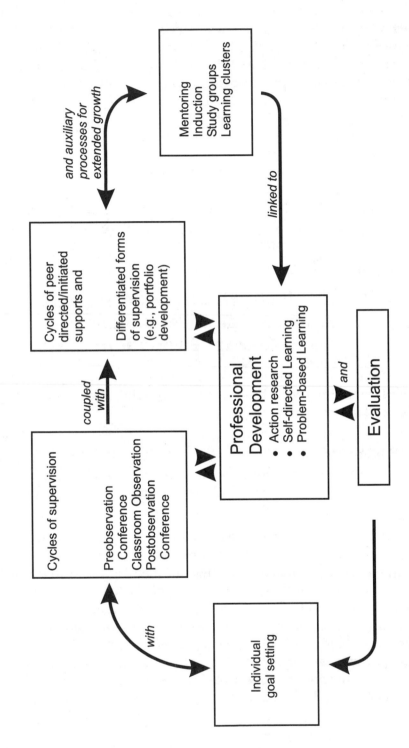

Figure 1.7. Linking Instructional Supervision, Professional Development, and Teacher Evaluation

Mentoring
Induction
Study groups
Learning clusters

and auxiliary processes for extended growth

linked to

Cycles of peer directed/initiated supports and

Differentiated forms of supervision (e.g., portfolio development)

coupled with

Cycles of supervision

Preobservation Conference
Classroom Observation
Postobservation Conference

Professional Development
• Action research
• Self-directed Learning
• Problem-based Learning

and

Evaluation

Individual goal setting

with

This approach offers a framework for unifying professional development and supervisory initiatives. Implicit assumptions are that the work of supervisors is recursive and that all approaches to supervision and professional development employ processes that promote growth, including reflection, inquiry, and dialogue. The basic premise is that supervision, professional development, teacher evaluation, and other efforts form a seamless web.

Developing a Vision for Supervision

The coherence of instructional supervision, professional development, and teacher evaluation portrayed in Figure 1.7 will not "just happen." The leadership of the supervisor is needed to promote and champion these connections and to work proactively with teachers supporting the development of more coherent and seamless approaches to professional learning. Prospective supervisors need to stand for something related to leading and learning. They need a vision for supervision to guide their work.

The field of instructional supervision continues to evolve and in 2005, the first set of codified standards for instructional supervision was developed. These standards can be found in the book, *Standards for Instructional Supervision: Enhancing Teaching and Learning*, edited by Dr. Stephen Gordon. This text opens the discussion for the field and includes chapters addressing a variety of standards for instructional supervision. Additionally, there are standards in place for the preparation of school leaders, most notably, the Interstate School Leaders Licensure Consortium Standards (ISLLC, 1996) and the Educational Leadership Constituent Council Standards (ELCC, 2002). These standards give insight for the practice of instructional supervision.

For the purposes of this discussion, attention is focused on selected aspects of the language of ELCC Standard 2 (Figure 1.8, on the next page) and the connections to supervision and professional development.

Although standards are critically important, standards alone are not enough for the implementation of supervision in schools. Developing a supervisory vision is an important first step. Why is a supervisory vision important to the work of supervisors? This question begs for reflection by professionals aspiring to a leadership position and especially for those positions that require supervision. Conley (1996) believes the vision acts as an internal compass, and Speck (1999) makes a compelling argument that "Vision is what separates the principals who are school leaders from those who are simply managers" (p. 117).

Figure 1.8. Selected Excerpts from ELCC Standard 2 and Targets

Elements	Meets Standards for School-Building Leadership
2.1 Promote Positive School Culture	a. Candidates assess school culture using multiple methods and implement context-appropriate strategies that capitalize on the diversity (e.g., population, language, disability, gender, race, socioeconomic) of the school community to improve school programs and culture.
2.2 Provide Effective Instructional Program	a. Candidates demonstrate the ability to facilitate activities that apply principles of effective instruction to improve instructional practices and curricular materials. c. Candidates demonstrate the ability to use and promote technology and information systems to enrich curriculum and instruction, to monitor instructional practices and provide staff the assistance needed for improvement.
2.3 Apply Best Practice to Student Learning	a. Candidates demonstrate the ability to assist school personnel in understanding and applying best practices for student learning.
2.4 Design Comprehensive Professional Growth Plans	a. Candidates design and demonstrate an ability to implement well-planned, context-appropriate professional development programs based on reflective practice and research on student learning consistent with the school vision and goals. b. Candidates demonstrate the ability to use strategies such as observations, collaborative reflection, and adult learning strategies to form comprehensive professional growth plans with teachers and other school personnel. c. Candidates develop and implement personal professional growth plans that reflect a commitment to lifelong learning.

Source: National Policy Board for Educational Administration. (2002). *Educational Leadership Constituent Council Standards for Advanced Programs in Educational Leadership for Principals, Superintendents, Curriculum Directors, and Supervisors.* Reston, VA: Author. Retrieved August 9, 2006, from http://www.npbea.org/ELCC/ELCCStandards%20_5–02.pdf.

Beliefs and Values Shape the Vision

A vision is shaped by beliefs and values about students, learning, and leading. These values and beliefs influence actions and motivation related to supervising instruction and the supervisory behaviors associated with working with teachers. Developing and enacting a vision is a process shaped by prior experiences, beliefs, values, and other factors that interact with each other over time. Because of this interaction, a vision about anything should be revisited periodically to check on how beliefs, attitudes, and subsequent actions and interactions change over time.

Because those who supervise instruction work with the most important resource in schools—teachers—and by extension, students—it is important to identify core values and beliefs that motivate supervisory efforts based on these values and beliefs. A starting point in the development of a supervisory vision is to identify what a person stands for as a leader. The following questions serve to guide this process:

- What do I stand for?
- What is my personal vision about teaching, students, and achievement?
- What does good teaching look like?
- What separates good teaching from excellent teaching, mediocre teaching?
- How does data about learning translate to teaching, professional development, and the needs of the community?
- What contextual factors (e.g., time, teaching schedules) affect supervision, professional development, and teacher evaluation at the site level?
- What types of support would teachers need to achieve good teaching as I envision this picture of good teaching?
- How does instructional supervision, evaluation, and professional development fit into this scheme of support?
- What types of teaching do students need to learn? Can all children learn?

Extended Reflection

As a prospective supervisor, develop a supervisory vision that will serve as the road map for your approach to instructional supervision, leadership, and learning. Share this with your instructor.

A personal vision for instructional supervision unfolds at the school site, and there are important workplace conditions, such as culture and norms of collegiality and collaboration, that are important to consider.

School Culture

According to Peterson (2002),

> School culture is the set of norms, values and beliefs, rituals and ceremonies, symbols and stories that make up the "persona" of the school. These unwritten expectations build up over time as teachers, administrators, parents, and students work together, solve problems, deal with challenges and, at times, cope with failures. (p. 10)

Leonard (2002) indicates that positive cultures are marked by professional collaboration that is "evidenced when teachers and administrators, share their knowledge, contribute ideas, and develop plans for the purpose of achieving educational and organizational goals" (¶ 4). In healthy school cultures, principals work with teachers; they focus on student learning; and they work under a common set of assumptions about learning for both students and adults.

A healthy culture does not magically occur. Strong cultures emerge, in part, by the efforts of the principal to support and nurture the conditions that teachers need to collaborate. Fiore (2001) believes that there are key behaviors of principals in schools that reinforce healthy or unhealthy cultures (Figure 1.9, on the next page).

Figure 1.9. Principal Behaviors—
Healthy and Unhealthy Cultures

Principals in Healthy Cultures

♦ Are visible to all stakeholders

♦ Communicate regularly and purposefully

♦ Never forget that they are role models

♦ Are passionate about their work

♦ Accept responsibility for the school's culture

♦ Are organized

♦ Exhibit a positive outlook

♦ Take pride in the physical environment of the school

♦ Empower others appropriately

♦ Demonstrate stewardship—they protect their school and its people

Principals in Unhealthy Cultures

♦ Are rarely seen outside their office

♦ Find little time for communication

♦ Feel that other people are responsible for their school building's physical needs—they take passive roles in decorating and furnishing their schools

♦ See themselves as the lone leader, or "boss", of the school—they never empower teachers to lead

♦ Are poorly organized

♦ Habitually make excuses for their school's shortcomings, blaming inadequacies on outside influences

Source: Fiore, 2001. Used with permission.

Healthy school cultures thrive in environments built through collaboration, trust, and care for the members of the school. Kruse, Louis, and Bryk (1994) assert that collaborative school cultures are dependent on

♦ *Critical elements of school communities*: reflective dialogue, deprivatization of practice, collective focus on student learning, collaboration, and shared norms and values.

♦ *Structural conditions*: time to meet and talk, physical proximity, interdependent teaching roles, communications structures, and teacher empowerment.

♦ *Social and human factors*: openness to improvement, trust and respect, supportive leadership, and socialization of teachers. (pp. 4–5)

An important aspect of understanding the culture of a school is to know the faculty and the types of learning opportunities available to them vis-à-vis professional development, supervision, leadership opportunities, and the relationships that teachers have with each other and the administration. Figure 1.10 can serve as a way to identify the programs for teachers that shape the school culture.

Figure 1.10. Identifying Programs for Teachers that Shape the School Culture

◆ What types of professional development activities are available for teachers?

◆ How many teachers participate in these activities?

◆ What types of programs would teachers like to see initiated?

◆ Are teachers provided time during the day to observe each other teach and talk about what they learn from one another?

◆ What types of leadership activities are available for teachers?

◆ How many teachers are involved in formal and informal leadership activities?

◆ What types of teacher recognition programs are in place?

Source: Adapted from Calabrese, Short, & Zepeda, 1996.

Building a collaborative school culture and positive school climate are dependent on several variables, including, most notably, norms.

Norms

Norms are unwritten rules of behavior that serve as a guide to the way people interact with one another (Chance & Chance, 2002). Saphier and King (1985) identify 12 norms of school culture, which, if strong, contribute to the instructional effectiveness of a school. The norms that "grow" a strong school culture include

1. *Collegiality*: How people interact with one another, the openness members of the community have toward one another.
2. *Experimentation*: Risk-taking.
3. *High expectations*: Do people have high expectations for themselves, for each other, and for students?
4. *Trust and confidence*: Do people trust one another?
5. *Tangible support*: Resources—time, support.
6. *Reaching out to the knowledge bases*: Information is available.
7. *Appreciation and recognition*: People feel important, respected, and part of the school. They feel that what they do is important

and those colleagues, administrators, and the larger community hold the work they accomplish in high esteem.

8. *Caring, celebration, and humor*: People thrive when they feel emotionally supported. Communities take the time to celebrate—the big and small accomplishments of each other and students.

9. *Involvement in decision making*: Decision making spans the school environment and is not just a function of the administration.

10. *Protection of what is important*: Principals and others identify what is important, and then protect time and secure resources to support priorities.

11. *Traditions*: Traditions shape the culture and traditions are upheld as part of the community.

12. *Honest, open communication*: People talk to one another; they share ideas openly without fear.

Collegiality and Collaboration

Supervisors dedicated to fostering the conditions for improved instruction promote collegial and collaborative relationships with and among teachers. The norms of collegiality are promoted in an environment that supports

1. *Interaction and participation.* People have many opportunities and reasons to come together in deliberation, association, and action.

2. *Interdependence.* These associations and actions both promote and depend on mutual needs and commitments.

3. *Shared interests and beliefs.* People share perspectives, values, understandings, and commitment to common purposes.

4. *Concern for individual and minority views.* Individual differences are embraced through critical reflection and mechanisms for dissent and lead to growth through the new perspectives they foster.

5. *Meaningful relationships.* Interactions reflect a commitment to caring, sustaining relationships. (Westheimer, 1998, p. 17, emphasis in the original)

Collaboration in schools has been marked as the "key schooling process variable for increasing the norms of student achievement" (Lunenburg, 1995, p. 41). Similarly, Hargreaves (1997) reports that

Cultures of collaboration among teachers seem to produce greater willingness to take risks, to learn from mistakes, and share successful strategies with colleagues that lead to teachers having positive senses of their own efficiency, beliefs that their children can learn, and improved outcomes....(p. 68)

Collaboration is about altering relationships and is dependent on the feeling of interdependence (*we are in this together*) and opportunity. When teachers collaborate, they share ideas and problem-solve solutions to the thorny issues they face in the classroom.

Through collaboration, teachers are able to support their own growth and development while improving instructional practices. Collaboration includes such activities as coplanning and teaching lessons, brainstorming ideas, conducting action research, and interclassroom observations (peer coaching), and the reflection and dialogue that follow. To break the prevalent patterns of teacher isolation, time and the commitment of the supervisor are needed. Collaborative cultures send strong messages to teachers and students about the seriousness of the work accomplished in the classroom. Students benefit in collaborative cultures when teachers work toward the betterment of instructional practices.

Trust

Trust is a prerequisite for building a positive school culture. Without trust, efforts to build a healthy culture will be diminished. Without trust, relationships will flounder. Trust and respect build a strong foundation for the work and efforts of teachers. Bryk and Schneider (2002) identify "relational trust" as the core ingredient for school improvement. Relational trust rests on a foundation of respect, personal regard, and integrity. Relational trust flourishes when all members of the school are encouraged to contribute, to learn, and to be part of the discussion about teaching and student learning.

Building and maintaining trust evolves over time. Trust is built on its history in the organization, and the history of trust between teachers and administrators. A leader must ask several questions, including the following:

- ◆ Do teachers trust me?
- ◆ Do teachers have confidence in my actions?
- ◆ Do my words and actions align with each other?
- ◆ Do teachers believe I hold them in high regard?
- ◆ Do I exhibit integrity in the way I make decisions, communicate expectations, and allocate resources?
- ◆ What behaviors have in the past eroded trust in the leadership of the school?

The answers to these questions can serve as a guide to self-discovery about the patterns of trust, and the work needed to build more trusting relationships with teachers.

Extended Reflection

Think back to your own experiences with instructional supervision. What did your supervisor do to signal that trust was present or absent in the supervisory relationship?

Summary

Many believe that hyperbole permeates the discussion on standards, student assessment, and the high-stakes propositions found in state statutes. Perhaps this belief is warranted; however, what is not hyperbole is the absolute need for supervision that makes a difference in the professional lives of teachers. Teachers need opportunities to grow and develop, and there must be coherence in the work, efforts, and programs designed to help teachers excel in the classroom.

Prospective and practicing administrators face many competing tasks, but none is as important as the work that centers on teacher development and growth. Although often snowed under by their complex responsibilities, supervisors need not travel this road alone. Professional teachers will grow and thrive if the conditions are right. The real work of supervisors is to get things right so teachers can work in a culture that promotes collaboration and collegiality.

Suggested Activities

From Theory to Practice

Consult the State Department of Education Web site in the state in which you work. Identify the Standards for Teacher Performance and Certification. Then access the Web site for the formal organization that sets standards for teaching and accountability in your field (e.g., for English consult the National Council of Teachers of English). Download these sets of standards and identify their similarities and differences.

Group Processing

In a small group, share the various standards for the subject areas in which group members teach. What are the commonalities for instruction? As prospective supervisors, develop a rubric—an assessment form—for supervisors and other leaders such as lead teachers and department chairs—to use as they work with teachers to assess their instructional practices. What types of information would be important for teachers and supervisors to have on this form?

Reflection

Is it possible for a supervisor to be familiar with all the professional standards that dictate professional performance?

References

A Plus Education Reform Act of 2000. O. C. G. A. §20–2-200(a)(8).

Bryk, A. S., & Schneider, B. (2002). *Trust in schools: A core resource for improvement.* New York, NY: Russell Sage.

Calabrese, R. L., Short, G., & Zepeda, S. J. (1996). *Hands-on leadership tools for principals.* Larchmont, NY: Eye on Education.

Chance, P. L., & Chance, E. W. (2002). *Introduction to educational leadership and organizational behavior: Theory into practice.* Larchmont, NY: Eye on Education.

Conley, D. T. (1996). *Are you ready to restructure? A guidebook for educators, parents, and community members.* Thousand Oaks, CA: Corwin Press.

Connecticut Science Supervisors Association (CSSA). Retrieved August 9, 2006, from http://www.cssaonline.net/index.html

Council of State Science Supervisors. Retrieved August 9, 2006, from http://www.csss-science.org/index.shtml

Darling-Hammond, L. (2002). What's at stake in high stakes testing? (Standardized testing.) *The Brown University Child and Adolescent Behavior Letter.* January, 2002, sponsored by Manisses Communications Group, Inc. and the Gale Group. Retrieved June 3, 2002, from http://www.findarticles.com/cf_dls/m0537/1_18/83139498/p1/article.jhtml?term=

Eady, C. K. (2002). *Rural middle school principals' perspectives of supervision and evaluation as they implement Georgia's A PLUS Education Reform Act of 2000.* Unpublished doctoral dissertation, University of Georgia, Athens.

Fiore, D. J. (2001). *Creating connections for better schools: How leaders enhance school culture.* Larchmont, NY: Eye on Education.

Florida Council of Language Arts Supervisors. Retrieved August 9, 2006, from http://www.santarosa.k12.fl.us/clas/

Gordon, S. P. (Ed). (2005). *Standards for instructional supervision: Enhancing teaching and learning.* Larchmont, NY: Eye on Education.

Hargreaves, A. (1997). Cultures of teaching and educational change. In M. Fullan (Ed.), *The challenge of school change* (pp. 57–84). Arlington Heights, IL: Skylight Training and Publishing.

Interstate School Leaders Licensure Consortium (1996). *Standards for school leaders.* Council of Chief State School Officers. Washington, DC: Author. Retrieved on August 7, 2006, from http://www.ccsso.org/content/pdfs/isllcstd.pdf

Kentucky Education Professional Standards Board, The (1999). *New teacher standards for preparation and certification*. Louisville, KY: Author. Retrieved March 5, 2002, from http://www.kde.state.ky.us/otec/epsb/standards/new_teach_stds.asp

Kruse, S., Louis, K. S., & Bryk, A. (1994). *Building professional community in schools. Issues in restructuring schools* (pp. 6, 3–6). Madison, WI: Center on Organization and Restructuring of Schools, Wisconsin Center for Education Research, School of Education, University of Wisconsin-Madison.

Leonard, L. J. (2002). Schools as professional communities: Addressing the collaborative challenge. *International Electronic Journal for Leadership in Learning, 6*(17). Retrieved September 9, 2006, from http://www.ucalgary.ca/~iejll/

Lunenburg, F. C. (1995). *The principalship: Concepts and applications*. Englewood Cliffs, NJ: Merrill.

National Association of District Supervisors of Foreign Language. Retrieved August 9, 2006, from http://www.nadsfl.org/

National Association of Elementary School Principals (2002). *Leading learning communities: Standards for what principals should know and be able to do*. Alexandria, VA: Author.

National Commission on Excellence in Education (1983). *A nation at risk: The imperative for educational reform*. Washington, DC: Author.

National Council of Supervisors of Mathematics (NCSM). Retrieved August 9, 2006, from http://mathforum.org/ncsm/

National Council of Teachers of Mathematics (2000). *Principles and standards of mathematics*. Reston, VA: Author.

National Policy Board for Educational Administration, (2002). *Educational Leadership Constituent Council standards for advanced programs in educational leadership for principals, superintendents, curriculum directors, and supervisors*. Reston, VA: Author. National Policy Board for Educational Administration.

National Science Education Leadership Association. Retrieved August 9, 2006, from http://www.nsela.org

National Science Teachers Association (1992). *NSTA position statements on science education supervisors*. Arlington VA: Author. Retrieved March 5, 2002, from http://www.nsta.org/159&id=36

National Social Studies Supervisors Association. Retrieved August 9, 2006, from http://www.socialstudies.org/nsssa/

Pasternak, B. A., & Viscio, A. J. (1998). *The centerless corporation: A new model for transforming your organization for growth and prosperity*. New York: Simon & Schuster.

Peterson, K. D. (2002). Positive or negative? *Journal of Staff Development, 23*(3), 10–15.

Professional Preparation Committee of the National Middle School Association (2000). *Program standards for middle level preparation*. Westerville, OH: Author.

Saphier, J., & King, M. (1985). Good seeds grow in strong cultures. *Educational Leadership, 42*(6), 67–74.

Speck, M. (1999). *The principalship: Building a learning community*. Upper Saddle River, NJ: Prentice-Hall.

Westheimer, J. (1998). *Among school teachers: Community autonomy and ideology in teachers' work*. New York, NY: Teachers College Press.

2

Understanding Instructional Supervision

In This Chapter...

- ◆ The intents of instructional supervision
- ◆ The intents of teacher evaluation
- ◆ Differentiated supervision
- ◆ Developmental supervision
- ◆ Styles that support differentiated and developmental supervision

Introducing Instructional Supervision

Never before has the field of instructional supervision faced such an urgent need to help teachers thrive in the classroom. The complexities of schools, the many ways in which teachers prepare to enter the field, the varying experience levels of the adults in any given school, and higher calls for accountability as mandated by state boards of education now present administrators with the crucial task of providing learning opportunities that meet the needs of teachers (Zepeda, 2006).

Learning opportunities can be formal, through such processes as instructional supervision and professional development, or informal, through interactions with peers and independent study. Formative approaches to supervision include more than just a classroom observation at the end of the year. Figure 2.1 (on the next page) illustrates the formative and cyclical nature of supervision.

Figure 2.1. The Formative and Cyclical Nature of Instructional Supervision

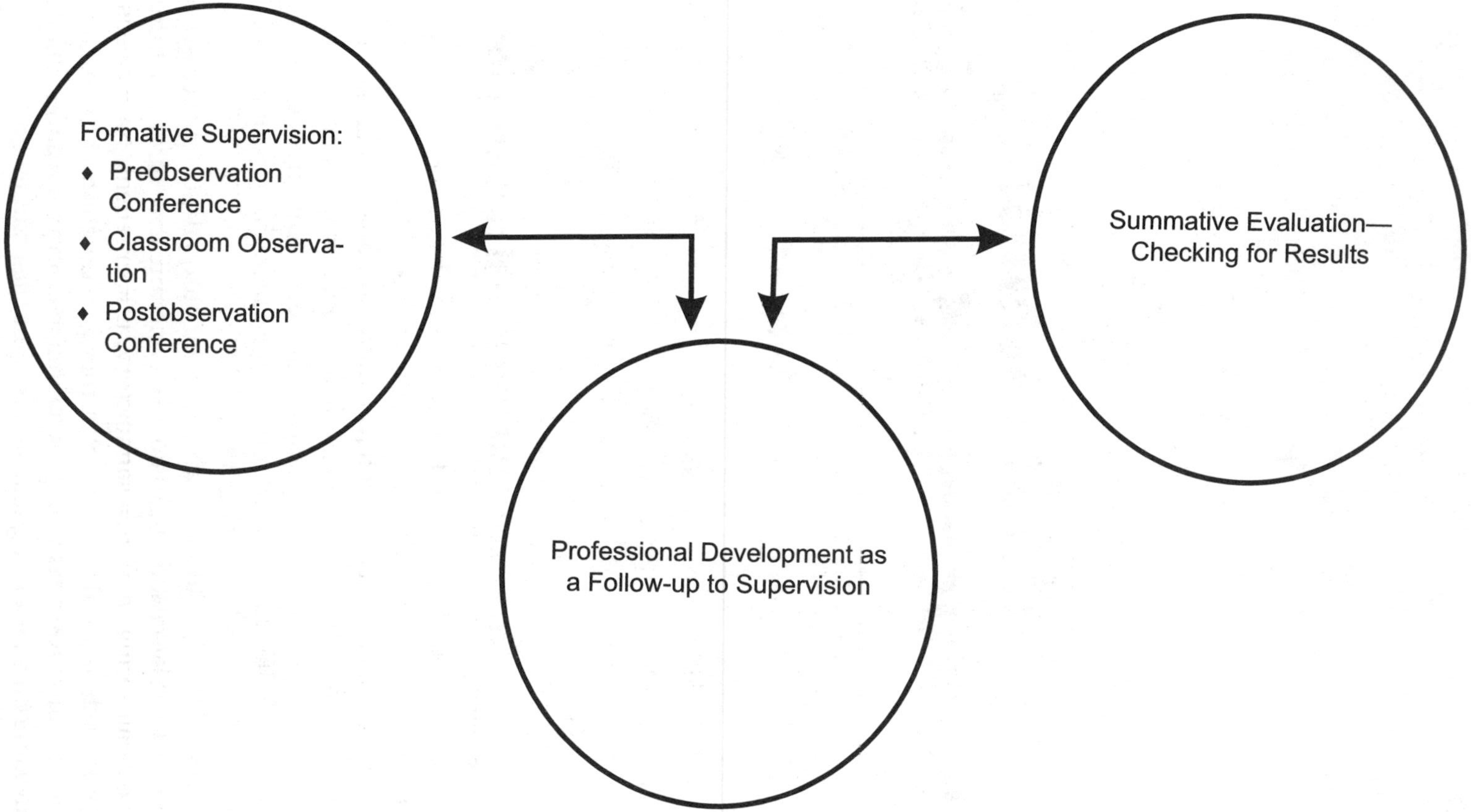

Summative Evaluation—
Checking for Results

Professional Development as
a Follow-up to Supervision

Formative Supervision:
- Preobservation
  Conference
- Classroom Observa-
  tion
- Postobservation
  Conference

Instructional supervision is the focus of this book, and this chapter examines the purposes and intents of instructional supervision, as well as differentiated and developmental aspects of supervision. Learning how to become a supervisor or how to refine existing supervisory skills is an ongoing practice that continually evolves as experience is gained and working relationships with teachers are nurtured. Thus this chapter begins with an extended reflection.

Extended Reflection

♦ From your perspective as an active or prospective supervisor, define the terms instructional supervision and teacher evaluation.

♦ Keep these definitions at hand and modify them as you read this chapter and others.

The Intents of Instructional Supervision

Instructional supervision aims to promote growth, development, interaction, fault-free problem solving, and a commitment to build capacity in teachers. Cogan (1973) and Goldhammer (1969), the early framers of clinical supervision, envisioned practices that would position the teacher as an active learner. Moreover, Cogan asserted that teachers were able to be professionally responsible and more than able to be "analytical of their own performance, open to help from others, and self-directing" (p. 12).

Unruh and Turner (1970) saw supervision as "a social process of stimulating, nurturing, and appraising the professional growth of teachers" (p. 17) and the supervisor as "the prime mover in the development of optimum conditions for learning" for adults (p. 135). When teachers learn from examining their own practices with the assistance of peers or supervisors, their learning is more personalized and therefore more powerful.

The intents of instructional supervision are formative, concerned with ongoing, developmental, and differentiated approaches that enable teachers to learn from analyzing and reflecting on their classroom practices with the assistance of another professional (Glatthorn, 1984, 1990; Glickman, 1990). In contrast, the intents of evaluation are summative; classroom observations and other assessments of professional performance lead to a final judgment or overall rating (e.g., S = satisfactory, E = excellent, NI = needs improvement). McGreal (1983) made clear that all supervisory roads lead to evaluation and that supervisors cannot evaluate teachers until they have spent considerable time observing teachers *in* their classrooms.

Research on the practice of supervision reveals that most K–12 schools shortchange the original intents of instructional supervision by supplanting it with evaluation (Sullivan & Glanz, 2000). The intents of evaluation are to meet state statutes and district policies, assign teachers a rating at the end of the year, and determine whether a teacher will return to work. Supervision for the sake of evaluation does not support teacher growth and development.

The intents of supervision promote

♦ Face-to-face interaction and relationship building between the teacher and supervisor (Acheson & Gall, 1997; Bellon & Bellon, 1982; Goldhammer, 1969; McGreal, 1983);

♦ Ongoing learning for the teacher and the supervisor (Mosher & Purpel, 1972);

♦ The improvement of students' learning through improvement of the teacher's instruction (Blumberg, 1980; Cogan, 1973; Harris, 1975);

♦ Data-based decision making (Bellon & Bellon, 1982);

♦ Capacity building of individuals and the organization (Pajak, 1993);

♦ Trust in the processes, each other, and the environment (Costa & Garmston, 1994); and

♦ Change that results in a better developmental life for teachers and students and their learning (Sergiovanni & Starratt, 1998).

Glatthorn (1984) believed clinical supervision was not "hitting the mark" and that a differentiated approach to supervision was necessary because

♦ The standard supervisory practice of administrators and supervisors is often both inadequate and ineffective.

♦ It is neither feasible nor necessary to provide clinical supervision to all teachers—it is so time-consuming that it is not practical to use with all teachers, and there is no conclusive evidence that clinical supervision improves the performance of competent, experienced teachers.

♦ Teachers have different growth needs and learning styles—they differ in the type of interaction they prefer, the supervisory relationships they prefer, and the kinds of environments in which they work. (pp. 2–3)

Glatthorn (1990) concludes, "Too often clinical supervision is offered from a 'one-up' vantage point: the supervisor, who knows the answer, is going to help the teacher, who needs to be improved" (p. 17).

Extended Reflection

Consider how you are supervised and evaluated. Given your own experiences with supervision and evaluation

♦ What changes would make sense and why?

♦ What would supervision that is developmental and differentiated look like?

♦ What would need to change in your work environment for a supervisor to implement the changes identified?

School districts typically use the same supervision methods for all teachers regardless of whether they are beginning, mid-career, or late-career teachers. This one-size-fits-all approach to supervision is bureaucratic, relies on inspectional methods, and is more concerned with administrative efficiency (Sullivan & Glanz, 2000). Supervision in this vein goes against the grain of what can be achieved by professionals working together, "in helping relationships that are authentic, mutual, and individualized" (Glatthorn & Shields, 1983, p. 80).

Although there is recognition that learning to teach is an ongoing process, rarely does instructional supervision give individual teachers authority to select professional development and supervisory options that best fit their needs.

This contradiction in the theory and intents of supervision occurs when supervision is practiced as evaluation, and when supervision is limited to only one model such as the clinical model of supervision. The principles of adult learning and teacher career stages are examined in detail in Chapter 7. Thinking ahead, it makes good sense to reflect about teachers and their unique learning needs while reading this chapter and then reading Chapter 7.

The Intents of Teacher Evaluation

Teacher evaluation is summative and ideally occurs as a complement to formative supervision. The purposes of evaluation and supervision need not be in direct opposition; both can support the improvement of instruction. At the end of every quarter, semester, and school year, teachers assign students a final grade based on the work accomplished during that time. In the same vein, teacher evaluation leads to a rating for the year. Like students who receive input throughout the year, teachers receive input about their performance through professional activities such as multiple cycles of supervision, and then they receive an overall rating. The rating serves as a benchmark.

Much of the inherent conflict and tension between supervision and evaluation stems from the intent or final outcome of evaluation. Acheson and Gall (1997) highlight the conflict between evaluation and supervision as follows:

> One of the most persistent problems in supervision is the dilemma between (a) evaluating a teacher in order to make decisions about retention, promotion, and tenure, and (b) working with the teacher as a friendly critic or colleague to help develop skills the teacher wants to use and to expand the repertoire of strategies that can be employed. (p. 209)

Admitting an enduring struggle with the dynamics described above, Acheson and Gall argue that supervision and evaluation ultimately serve the same purpose: "the improvement of instruction" (p. 48).

Darling-Hammond (1986) summarizes that "evaluation of teaching is conducted largely to ensure that proper standards of practice are being employed" (p. 532). Given the hectic nature of the work of teachers and administrators, supervision and evaluation are often practiced as one and the same; a single classroom observation toward the end of the year yields an immediate rating. Most teachers experience evaluation as "a principal's report of teacher performance, usually recorded on a checklist form, and sometimes accompanied by a brief meeting" (Peterson, 2000, p. 18). Through such practice, it is little wonder that teachers do not easily see the distinctions between supervision and evaluation.

McGreal (1983) suggests that when teachers receive their summative rating for the year—S, E, or NI—growth ceases. Perhaps a contributing factor is the variety of outcomes linked to teacher ratings: promotion, retention, termination, and pay raise. Evaluation becomes a "big club" (although one that can be used to help nudge teachers, especially marginal ones, toward improvement). Peterson (2000) suggests 12 new directions for teacher evaluation that can bridge the gulf between supervision and evaluation:

1. Emphasize that the function of teacher evaluation should be to seek out, document, and acknowledge the good teaching that already exists.
2. Use good reasons to evaluate.
3. Place the teacher at the center of evaluation activity.
4. Use more than one person to judge teacher quality and performance.
5. Limit administrator judgment role in teacher evaluation.
6. Use multiple data sources to inform judgments about teacher quality.
7. When possible, include actual pupil achievement data.
8. Use variable data sources to inform judgments [about teaching]
9. Spend the time and other resources needed to recognize good teaching.
10. Use research on teacher evaluation correctly.
11. Attend to the sociology of teacher evaluation.
12. Use the results of teacher evaluation to encourage the development of a personal professional dossier, publicize aggregated results, and support teacher promotion systems. (pp. 4–12)

Extended Reflection

Peterson (2000) indicates that evaluators, and by extension supervisors, need to, "when possible, include actual pupil achievement data" and to "use variable data sources to inform judgments [about teaching]" as two future directions for teacher evaluation.

From a formative perspective, what beside pupil achievement data can and should be used to promote teacher development and growth? After identifying other data points:

   ◆ How would you engage teachers in examining such items as artifacts of teaching (e.g., student work, lesson plans, etc.)?

   ◆ What types of administrative support would be needed?

   ◆ How would you help teachers to monitor the impact of these efforts on their practices? Student achievement?

Supervision can become "the heart of a good teacher evaluation system" (Acheson & Gall, 1997, p. 60), especially if supervision is differentiated and teachers become the central actors in the process.

Differentiated Supervision

Glatthorn (1997) describes differentiated supervision as "an approach to supervision that provides teachers with options about the kinds of supervisory and evaluative services they receive" (p. 3). Differentiated supervision operates on the premise that teaching is a profession; teachers should have a degree of control over their professional development and the power to make choices about the support they need.

Effective schools support collegiality in communities built on a foundation of cooperation, mutual assistance, and trust among faculty and staff. Without collegial relationships between teachers and supervisors, it is unlikely that either can be nurtured toward ongoing growth and development. As Kindred indicated in 1952, all teachers share common needs; they want

- ◆ Security;
- ◆ Desirable working conditions;
- ◆ Fair treatment;
- ◆ The feeling that they are an integral part of the school;
- ◆ Recognition for their work; and
- ◆ A voice in administration. (pp. 158–159)

Differentiated supervision can unfold only in an environment in which collegial relationships are built through "cooperation and mutual assistance" (Glatthorn, 1990, p. 177).

Differentiated supervisory approaches allow supervisors to concentrate on teachers who need their time and effort most, rather than conducting perfunctory classroom observations of all teachers merely to satisfy district policies. Glatthorn's differentiated system was built on the assumption that "regardless of experience and competence, all teachers will be involved in three related processes for improving instruction: teacher evaluation, staff development, and informal observations" (1990, p. 179). According to Glatthorn, teachers must be involved in "two or more" of the following:

- ◆ *Intensive development* (mandatory use of the clinical supervision model);
- ◆ *Cooperative development* (developmental, socially mediated activities such as peer coaching or action research); or
- ◆ *Self-directed development* (developmental activities teachers direct on their own).

Glatthorn's differentiated approach was not meant to be prescriptive, but rather "a process approach, in which each school district or school develops its own homegrown model, one responsive to its special needs and resources" (1990, p. 179).

Fieldwork

Ask a Supervisor...

Interview a person (e.g., principal, assistant principal, department chair) who supervises teachers on a regular basis. Ask this person:

◆ How do you differentiate supervision?

◆ Why do you differentiate supervision?

◆ How do you know when to differentiate supervision?

◆ Are there instances where it is not advisable to differentiate supervision?

After this informal interview, identify the major points you learned about differentiating supervision. What did you learn?

Developmental Supervision

Glickman (1981) asserts that "the goal of instructional supervision is to help teachers learn how to increase their own capacity to achieve professional learning goals for their students" (p. 3), and a supervisor's style either enhances or diminishes teachers' abilities to engage in learning that is developmentally appropriate. The success of developmental supervision rests on the supervisor's ability to assess the conceptual level of the teacher or a group of teachers and then to apply a supervisory approach that matches this level.

Diagnosing the conceptual level of teachers is central to the success of developmental supervision. Ham's findings (1986), cited by Waite (1998), suggest, "The most effective supervisors were those able to match appropriate models or strategies to the specific needs and developmental levels of their teachers" (1998, p. 300). Given the diversity of the teaching force and the varied experience levels of any given faculty, supervisors need to be aware of the principles of adult learning (Chapter 7).

A Case Study

As principal of Highland High School, Suzanne Franklin has just hired 14 new teachers. Eight of these teachers just graduated from college, and 6 are new to the system, Highland Community School District 092. Both groups of teachers have been assigned mentors, all veteran teachers within their departments. What considerations should Suzanne and the administrative team consider as they develop a strategy to supervise the new teachers?

Glickman (1981) identified supervisory orientations as directive, nondirective, and collaborative. These orientations portray the kind of approaches a supervisor would choose based on the developmental stage of the teacher; "effective supervision must be based on matching orientations of supervision with the needs and characteristics of teachers" (p. 40). Chapter 7 details the career stages and the principles of adult learning.

Styles that Support Differentiated and Developmental Supervision

Glickman (1990) identified four interpersonal approaches parallel to situational leadership theory:

1. The directive control approach;
2. The directive informational approach;
3. The collaborative approach; and
4. The nondirective approach.

Figure 2.2, on the next page, describes the four supervisory approaches, with suggestions of when and under what conditions a supervisor might use them.

Figure 2.2. Supervisory Styles

Supervisory Style	Audience	Range of Supervisory Behaviors
Directive control approach: Supervisor directs all aspects of the supervisory process.	Beginning teachers; teachers on formal plans of improvement; teachers struggling with learning to use new but essential instructional strategies.	Inform, direct, show, lecture, and mandate.
Directive informational approach: Supervisor shares information with an emphasis on what must be achieved.	Beginning teachers; teachers struggling with learning to use new but essential instructional strategies.	Inform, lecture, generate alternatives between the teacher and supervisor.
Collaborative approach: Open, two-way problem solving; teacher and supervisor are equals searching for understanding of practice and its impact on student learning. Collaborative decision making with the teacher taking the lead in framing questions, posing solutions, and making the final decision about what course of action to take next.	Experienced teachers; teachers with expertise and refined skills.	Guide, keep the focus during discussions, link teachers with similar needs.
Nondirective approach: Self-directing; the teacher develops solutions and ongoing activities to assist with examining practices.	Master teachers.	Listen in a nonjudgmental manner; ask open-ended questions; provide clarification to questions; extend inquiry through reflection, role-playing scenarios, and dialogue.

Source: Glickman, 1981.

Note that there are no hard-and-fast rules about which style to use, and as Glickman (1981) asserted, "unless all teachers in a staff are remarkably homogeneous, no single approach will be effective for all" (p. 40).

A Case Study

Franklin Adams, Science Department chair at Reynolds High School, just completed a 45-minute classroom observation of Jack Bradford, a first-year chemistry teacher. Franklin is sitting at his desk thinking through how to approach the postobservation conference. Going through his notes, Franklin looks at the data:

1. Fourteen of the 22 students were on task less than 50 percent of the time.

2. Bradford spent approximately 30 percent of his time redirecting off-task behaviors.

3. Students were "less than respectful" to Bradford (mumbling under their breaths, ignoring his directives).

4. During the last 15 minutes of class, students who were generally on task, began to become off task (Stacy turned to Rob and they chatted; Jim pulled out his lunch; Peter was selling candy bars; Tina was reading *To Kill a Mockingbird*; Franklin put his head down and pulled his jacket over his head; Kat applied makeup).

5. When the bell rang, students "bolted" while Bradford was explaining the homework assignment.

6. Two students were directed to report to Bradford after school.

In the preobservation conference, Jack revealed he was having a "miserable" time with the students. He shared that students were off task and talked among themselves to the point where the "better" students were complaining. Franklin sets the tempo and explains that he will focus his "observation eye" overall on classroom management. He explains to Jack that he will track interactions with students, students' on-task and off-task behaviors, and the verbal cues that Jack gives to students who appear to be off-task.

Jack entered teaching as a second career. Prior to teaching, Jack worked for 17 years as a chemist with a major pharmaceutical company. For the past two years, Jack attended school part-time to earn his teaching credentials at a local university.

After reviewing Glickman's Supervisory Styles presented in Figure 2.2 (previous page), discuss an approach to the postobservation conference. In pairs, role play, assuming the roles of Franklin and Jack. Where does Franklin start with the feedback?

Supervisors do more than merely observe teachers in the classroom; they engage in a wide range of activities that focus on the instructional lives of teachers. These activities include linking professional development to the efforts of supervision. Activities could include promoting peer coaching, action research, the development of teaching portfolios, study groups, critical friends, and other initiatives that make sense for the context of the school site. The role of the supervisor is a very complex one; Wiles and Bondi (1996) list several roles that require competence:

♦ *Supervisors are developers of people.* Supervisors need to be sensitive to the fact that schools are diverse learning communities.

♦ *Supervisors are curriculum developers.* Curriculum development is a cycle that begins with clarifying goals and objectives and ends with the evaluation of the curriculum effort.

♦ *Supervisors are instructional specialists.* The instructional role of supervision has three dimensions: research, communication, and teaching.

♦ *Supervisors are human relations workers.* Multiple human relations skills are called for in the daily interaction with diverse groups.

♦ *Supervisors are staff developers.* Planning staff development is a major method of improving instruction.

♦ *Supervisors are administrators.* Administrators need a very specialized set of skills.

♦ *Supervisors are managers of change.* Systemic reform movements require supervisors to manage and implement change.

♦ *Supervisors are evaluators.* The evaluative role is constant. (1996, pp. 18–22)

Extended Reflection

Wiles and Bondi (1996) indicate that "supervisors are administrators. Administrators need a very specialized set of skills."

♦ Is there an inherent conflict in the first part of the statement "supervisors are administrators?" Be prepared to share your thoughts in a small group.

♦ What are the "very specialized set(s) of skills" that supervisors (who are very often administrators by title) need to work with teachers? Be prepared to share your thoughts in a small group, and then in a larger discussion across groups.

Regardless of the work, tasks, or roles that supervisors assume, the supervisor's style (e.g., directive, collaborative) will have impact on the relationship between the teacher and supervisor. Teachers have unique needs across the career continuum, which are examined in Chapter 7. Some experienced, competent teachers will prefer to work on their own to foster their professional development (Glatthorn, 1997). These teachers have the ability to direct a program of study that addresses their own personal and professional learning needs. In self-directed supervision, the teacher takes the initiative to select an area of interest or need, locate available resources for meeting goals, and develop and carry out a plan for learning and development. The supervisor acts as a supporter, not the omnipotent director.

Extended Reflection

Reflect on your most recent experience with instructional supervision.

♦ How would you classify the administrator's supervisory style?

♦ What behaviors led you to this conclusion?

♦ What supervisory style, if any, would have been more appropriate? Why?

It is important for a building-level supervisor to conscientiously reflect about what kind of supervisory practices would best suit teachers. Effective supervisors

♦ Provide teachers with a supportive environment that emphasizes risk taking;

♦ Motivate teachers to continuously seek optimum performance;

♦ Encourage the use of sound instructional principles; and

♦ Provide multiple opportunities for professional growth.

There are many approaches to supervision. When the differentiated approach was in its early stages, peer coaching was just emerging as a staff development model, and Glickman's (1981) developmental approach to supervisory leadership and subsequent approaches had gained acceptance in K-12 schools. Differentiated approaches to supervision have since expanded to include, for example,

♦ Peer coaching (Chapter 9);

♦ Action research (Chapter 10); and

- The portfolio as a means to expand the clinical supervisory process (see Chapter 11).

Summary

The intents of the original clinical supervisory model rested on providing opportunities for teachers to examine and then reflect on their practices with the assistance of an instructional supervisor. Moreover, the intents supported the growth and development of teachers.

The hallmark of a differentiated approach to supervision is that it centers on the needs of teachers (career stages and adult learning are addressed in Chapter 7). Any approach linked to clinical supervision includes the preobservation conference, the observation, and the postobservation conference. Each approach has a unique design and application; however, all approaches champion practices rooted in constructivism and social learning theory—modeling, dialogue, reflection, inquiry, and active problem solving.

Suggested Activities

From Theory to Practice

For an earlier activity in this chapter, you obtained a copy of the policies and procedures that govern teacher evaluation and supervision in the school system where you work. Now locate state statutes that govern the supervision, evaluation, and professional development of teachers. In these documents, find the intersections governing the supervision, evaluation, and professional development of teachers. What are the discrepancies? Report your findings to the class.

Group Processing

The Interstate School Leaders Licensure Consortium (ISLLC) has developed a series of standards for school leaders. To read the standards in their entirety, go to http://www.ccsso.org/content/pdfs/isllcstd.pdf. Figure 2.3 (on the next page) shows ISLLC Standard 2. In a small group, examine ISLLC Standard 2 and identify how the intents of supervision can be linked to this standard across the domains of knowledge, dispositions, and performances. Report your analysis to the class.

Figure 2.3. ISLLC Standard 2

Standard 2: A school administrator is an educational leader who promotes the success of all students by advocating, nurturing, and sustaining a school culture and instructional program conducive to student learning and staff professional growth.

Knowledge

The administrator has knowledge and understanding of

- Student growth and development
- Applied learning theories
- Applied motivational theories
- Curriculum design, implementation, evaluation, and refinement
- Principles of effective instruction
- Measurement, evaluation, and assessment strategies
- Diversity and its meaning for educational programs
- Adult learning and professional development models
- The change process for systems, organizations, and individuals
- The role of technology in promoting student learning and professional growth
- School cultures

Dispositions

The administrator believes in, values, and is committed to

- Student learning as the fundamental purpose of schooling
- The proposition that all students can learn
- The variety of ways in which students can learn
- Lifelong learning for self and others
- Professional development as an integral part of school improvement
- The benefits that diversity brings to the school community
- A safe and supportive learning environment
- Preparing students to be contributing members of society

Performances

The administrator facilitates processes and engages in activities ensuring that

- All individuals are treated with fairness, dignity, and respect
- Professional development promotes a focus on student learning consistent with the school vision and goals
- Students and staff feel valued and important

- The responsibilities and contributions of each individual are acknowledged
- Barriers to student learning are identified, clarified, and addressed
- Diversity is considered in developing learning experiences
- Lifelong learning is encouraged and modeled
- There is a culture of high expectations for self, student, and staff performance
- Technologies are used in teaching and learning
- Student and staff accomplishments are recognized and celebrated
- Multiple opportunities to learn are available to all students
- The school is organized and aligned for success
- Curricular, co-curricular, and extracurricular programs are designed, implemented, evaluated, and refined
- Curriculum decisions are based on research, expertise of teachers, and the recommendations of learned societies
- The school culture and climate are assessed on a regular basis
- A variety of sources of information is used to make decisions
- Student learning is assessed using a variety of techniques
- Multiple sources of information regarding performance are used by staff and students
- A variety of supervisory and evaluation models is employed
- Pupil personnel programs are developed to meet the needs of students and their families

Source: The Interstate School Leaders Licensure Consortium Standards for School Leaders http://www.ccsso.org/content/pdfs/isllcstd.pdf

Reflection

1. Consider this statement: Given the size of schools, differentiated supervision is just not possible.
2. If you developed a Vision for Supervision (see Chapter 1), return to this vision. Make modifications as desired.

References

Acheson, K. A., & Gall, M. D. (1997). *Techniques in the clinical supervision of teachers: Preservice and inservice applications* (4th ed.). White Plains, NY: Longman.

Bellon, J. J., & Bellon, E. C. (1982). *Classroom supervision and instructional improvement: A synergetic process* (2nd ed.). Dubuque, IA: Kendall/Hunt.

Blumberg, A. (1980). *Supervisors and teachers: A private cold war* (2nd ed.). Berkeley, CA: McCutchan.

Cogan, M. (1973). *Clinical supervision*. Boston: Houghton-Mifflin.

Costa, A. L., & Garmston, R. J. (1994). *Cognitive coaching: A foundation for renaissance schools*. Norwood, MA: Christopher-Gordon.

Interstate School Leaders Licensure Consortium Standards for School Leaders. (1996). Retrieved July 7, 2006, from http://www.ccsso.org/standrds.html

Darling-Hammond, L. (1986). Teaching knowledge: How do we test it? *American Educator, 10*(3), 18–21, 46.

Glatthorn, A. A. (1997). *Differentiated supervision* (2nd ed.). Alexandria, VA: Association for Supervision and Curriculum Development.

Glatthorn, A. A. (1990). *Supervisory leadership: Introduction to instructional supervision*. New York: HarperCollins.

Glatthorn A. A. (1984). *Differentiated supervision*. Alexandria, VA: Association for Supervision and Curriculum.

Glatthorn, A. A., & Shields, C. R. (1983). Credo for supervision in Catholic schools. In J. J. Ciriello (Ed.), *The principal as managerial leader: Expectations in the areas of personnel management, institutional management, finance, and development* (pp. 76–89). Washington, DC: U.S. Catholic Conference.

Glickman, C. D. (1990). *Supervision of instruction: A development approach* (2nd ed.). Boston: Allyn and Bacon.

Glickman, C. D. (1981*). Developmental supervision: Alternative practices for helping teachers improve instruction*. Alexandria, VA: Association for Supervision and Curriculum Development.

Goldhammer, R. (1969). *Clinical supervision: Special methods for the supervision of teachers*. New York: Holt, Rinehart and Winston.

Harris, B. M. (1975). *Supervisory behavior in education* (2nd ed.). Englewood Cliffs, NJ: Prentice-Hall.

Interstate School Leaders Licensure Consortium. (1996). *Standards for school leaders*. Washington, DC: Author. Retrieved July 7, 2006, from http://www.ccsso.org/content/pdfs/isllcstd.pdf

Kindred, L. W. (1952). How can the principal promote professional growth in the staff? *National Association of Secondary Principals Bulletin, 185*(2), 156–162.

McGreal, T. (1983). *Effective teacher evaluation*. Alexandria, VA: Association for Supervision and Curriculum.

Mosher, R. L., & Purpel, D. E. (1972). *Supervision: The reluctant profession*. Boston: Houghton-Mifflin.

Pajak, E. F. (1993). *Approaches to clinical supervision: Alternatives for improving instruction*. Norwood, MA: Christopher-Gordon.

Peterson, K. D. (2000). *Teacher evaluation: A comprehensive guide to new direction and practices* (2nd ed.). Thousand Oaks, CA: Corwin Press.

Sergiovanni, T. J., & Starratt, R. J. (1998). *Supervision: A re-definition* (6th ed.). Boston: McGraw-Hill.

Sullivan, S., & Glanz, J. (2000). Alternative approaches to supervision: Cases from the field. *Journal of Curriculum and Supervision, 15*(3), 212–235.

Unruh, A., & Turner, H. E. (1970). *Supervision for change and innovation.* Boston: Houghton-Mifflin.

Waite, D. (1998). Anthropology, sociology, and supervision. In G. R. Firth, & E. F. Pajak (Eds.), *Handbook of research on school supervision* (pp. 287–309). New York: Simon & Schuster.

Wiles, J., & Bondi, J. (1996). *Supervision: A guide to practice.* Columbus, OH: C. E. Merrill.

Zepeda, S.J. (2006). High stakes supervision: We must do more. *The International Journal of Leadership in Education, 9*(1), 61–73.

3

Informal and Formal Instructional Supervision

In This Chapter...

♦ Informal classroom observations

♦ Formal classroom observations

♦ The clinical supervision model and its components

Introducing Informal and Formal Instructional Supervision

The overall intents of instructional supervision are teacher growth and development. The instructional supervisor needs to work with teachers on a daily basis. Effective supervisors do not wait to be invited into classrooms; they find opportunities to drop in for informal visits in addition to the more formal, mandated classroom observations tied to evaluation. They constantly scan the learning environment, looking for ways to help teachers develop further. Effective supervisors get out of the main office to pay attention to the pulse of the school.

Teachers want supervisors to be accessible—but not just by having an open-door policy. Teachers want supervisors to be visible—but not just by walking the halls during passing periods. In short, teachers want supervisors to visit their classrooms, and it is the supervisor's responsibility to do so.

Figure 3.1, on the next page, outlines how a supervisor might approach the task of getting supervision out of the main office and into the classroom.

Figure 3.1. Getting Supervision Out of the Main Office

To create the conditions for effective informal and formal supervision, the supervisor needs to examine the history and context of instructional supervision in the school. Issues include:

+ The framework of the clinical supervision process:
+ What is the history of supervision and evaluation at the site?
+ What are the experience levels and other defining features of the faculty?
+ What is done with information collected before, during, and after the observation?
+ At what time of year does the cycle (preobservation conference, extended classroom observation, and postobservation conference) occur?
+ Does the cycle continue with another round?
+ The intent of classroom observations:
+ Why am I observing a particular teacher?
+ How often do I observe teachers?
+ What is the length of an observation?
+ Do I observe certain teachers more than others?
+ If so, what factors motivate me to do so?
+ The nature of the interaction:
+ Do I merely report what I observed?
+ Do I try to link other activities such as professional development to the supervisory process?
+ Are postobservation conferences conducted? In a timely manner?
+ Where are pre- and postobservation conferences conducted? (In the teacher's classroom? The main office?)

Regardless of their form (formal, informal, peer), supervisory practices are bound by the context of the school site, the culture and climate of the school, the characteristics of teachers and administrators, and the values that the school community embraces.

Informal Classroom Observations

The informal classroom observation has evolved in the literature and in practice. Recently, there has been a resurgence in attention to the informal classroom observation (Downey, Steffy, English, Frase, & Poston, 2004; Zepeda, 2005). Historically the informal classroom observation's popularity emerged in the 1980s and can be tied to the *Management By Wandering Around*

(MBWA) movement, which was popularized with the publication of the Peters and Waterman (1982) book, *In Search of Excellence: Lessons From America's Best Run Companies.*

Executives who embraced MBWA promoted informal communication and personal involvement with employees by getting out of the office. Through this accessibility and visibility, executives were able to ensure accountability and affirm the work of employees. The practice of informal classroom observations also embraces getting supervision and evaluation out of the main office, situating principals as active participants in the instructional lives of their teachers by promoting visibility and accessibility.

Walking Around Supervision and Short Visits

In the supervision and teacher evaluation literature, informal classroom observations have been tied to both formative and summative evaluation practices. Manning (1988) asserted that information about teachers gleaned from "walking around supervision" and "short visits" should be included as summative samplings in the overall evaluation of teaching. Although both are similar, Manning makes a sharp distinction between walking-around supervision and short visits. Walking-around supervision promotes the visibility of the principal but primarily "in the halls…before and after the first bell in the morning, and immediately before the dismissal bell in the afternoon" (p. 145) and in the lunchrooms. During these times and others, the principal takes in information about instruction and plans short visits if there is a need (e.g., a teacher who is having difficulties with classroom management or a teacher who is regarded as having an exemplary instructional method). According to Manning, short visits last longer, "less than a full class period." Also, "it is important to always follow up a short visit with a brief conference" especially "if a problem is noted, the principal can discuss this…and plan for an additional evaluation" (p. 146). The reader is reminded that Manning's assessment of informal classroom observations developed in the 1980s, a period in which instructional supervision was evolving to include developmental forms of supervision (Glickman, 1981) and differentiated supervision (Glatthorn, 1984).

We have learned much about the perspective of teachers related to supervision (Zepeda & Ponticell, 1998). Above all else, the supervision of instruction should not be viewed as a means to find fault with teaching. Supervision and evaluation processes that do so, situate teachers in a deficit mode.

Catch Teachers in the Act of Teaching

The principal conducts informal classroom visitations neither to catch the teacher off guard or by surprise, nor to interrupt classroom activities. Informal classroom observations allow principals to affirm what teachers are doing right, encouraging them to keep up the momentum. Moreover, informal observations allow the principal and teacher to celebrate successes in teaching and student learning.

By observing teacher's work in their classrooms, principals can exert informed effort and energy to assist teachers beyond formally scheduled observations. Informal observations provide opportunities for supervisors to

♦ Motivate teachers.

♦ Monitor instruction.

♦ Be accessible and provide support.

♦ Keep informed [about instruction in the school]. (Blase & Blase, 1998, pp. 108–109)

An Observation By Any Other Name

Sometimes referred to as pop-ins, walk-ins, or drop-ins, informal classroom observations

♦ Are brief, lasting approximately 15 to 20 minutes (perhaps longer).

♦ Can occur at the beginning, middle, or end of a period.

♦ Can occur at any time during the school day.

♦ Focus on a variety of aspects, including instruction, use of time, classroom management, transitions between learning activities, the clarity of instructions, etc.

The informal classroom observation is a strategy to get into classrooms with the intent to focus on teaching, learning, and the interactions between teachers and students as the events of instruction unfold.

Informal observations are not intended to supplant formal ones; they do not include a preobservation conference. Too often informal classroom observations forgo postobservation conferences. The principal is reminded that the value of the informal observation that culminates with an opportunity to talk with teachers is that principals can strengthen their relationships with teachers by communicating something about what was observed. In fact, a majority of informal observations should include some type of follow-up conversation about teaching and learning.

Informal observations do not necessarily include a postobservation conference, but supervisors can strengthen their relationships with teachers by communicating something about what was observed. Although face-to-face interaction with a teacher is the best way to do this, Figures 3.2 and 3.3 (pages 51 and 52, respectively) offer sample forms for written comments after an informal classroom observation. Perhaps the most important aspect of communicating what was observed in a teacher's classroom is to be as specific as possible and to avoid platitudes such as "good job." Teachers will benefit more from specific information about their teaching, the ways in which they interact with students, or an approach used to deal with a classroom event. Timeliness is also important; just like students, teachers respond to immediate feedback.

Figure 3.2. Sample Informal Observation Note

Dear Mary,

I enjoyed my informal observation on September 9 during your Honors English class. The overheads used to illustrate the proper uses of dependent clauses kept students focused on the common mistakes they made in their own essays.

Clear directions kept students on task when they broke into small groups to proofread their essays. The small group size (three) kept all students engaged. Perhaps you might want to share these techniques with other freshman Honors teachers?

Thanks, and I hope to see you at the faculty tailgate party tonight!

Source: Zepeda (2003). Used with permission.

Extended Reflection

Dr. Raul Lopez, principal of Johnston Middle School, will conduct a series of informal classroom observations starting with the teachers on the sixth grade teams. Dr. Lopez believes he can help this team of teachers as they implement the new statewide curriculum in language arts and mathematics. After he has conducted several informal classroom observations, he plans to meet with the sixth grade teachers as a team to share insights about instruction and the new curriculum.

What suggestions would you give to Dr. Lopez before he starts conducting informal classroom observations?

Figure 3.3. Sample Informal Observation Form

Teacher: _Nancy Young_   Date of Observation: _January 8, 2007_
Time: _9:05–9:20_   Class Period: _3_   Subject: _English I_
Number of students present: _23_

Students were:

- ☐ working in small, cooperative groups
- ☐ making a presentation
- ☐ taking a test
- ☑ working independently at their desks
- ☐ viewing a film
- ☐ other_____

Teacher was:

- ☐ lecturing
- ☐ facilitating a question and answer sequence
- ☑ working independently with students
- ☐ demonstrating a concept
- ☐ introducing a new concept
- ☐ reviewing for a test
- ☐ coming to closure
- ☐ other_____

Comments: Nancy:

- ♦ Students were working independently at their desks.
- ♦ The rearrangement of the room (desk, podium, table) allowed you to work independently with students on their essays *and* to keep an eye on students working at their desks.

Perhaps you should hold the next freshman-level meeting in your room so others can see your room arrangement.

Thanks for letting me visit your room and see the work you do to help our students become better writers. I appreciate your efforts.

Marcie Stiso

Source: Zepeda (2003). Used with permission.

Special care must be taken to ensure that informal classroom observations do not become disruptive or send mixed messages to teachers. This is especially true if the supervisor is new or if informal classroom observations have not been conducted in the past. Sergiovanni and Starratt (1998) believe that

> Successful informal supervision requires that teachers accept certain expectations. Otherwise it will likely be viewed as a system of informal surveillance. Principals and other supervisors need to be viewed as *principal teachers* who have a responsibility to be a part of all the teaching that takes place in the school. (p. 258, emphasis added)

Is Three Minutes Enough?

The Downey Informal Observation method, in which principals spend three to five minutes observing a classroom, has piqued interest in informal classroom observations (Downey et al., 2004). Although that method will certainly get supervision out of the main office, the principal is encouraged to spend more than three to five minutes in the classroom during an informal observation to ensure a meaningful experience for the teacher. The egg-timer approach to classroom observation of this duration is a "blitz" in which the observation's brevity minimizes data collection. It is preferable to conduct fewer but longer informal observations on a daily basis to connect with teachers and derive a more accurate sense of the classroom activities observed.

The principal's daily struggle is to find time for mandatory formal classroom observations and for informal classroom visits. Although no clear-cut solution to this problem applies across all school systems, many principals find creative ways to make the most of available human resources and provide a supervisory program centered on teachers' needs. A commitment to being more visible to teachers will be strengthened by the impact classroom visitations can have on the instructional program; the dividend is movement toward high-quality learning for the teachers entrusted to educate children.

Guidelines for Informal Classroom Observations

The following guidelines for informal classroom observations are offered as a starting point for framing this important work.

Guidelines for Informal Classroom Observation*

Informally Observe All Teachers

All teachers can benefit from the informal classroom observation. Refrain from "over" observing teachers (e.g., only teachers who are having difficulty, beginning teachers, teachers who teach subject areas that are heavily tested). Given the suggestion that the informal classroom observation should last between 15 and 20 minutes, conduct only as many observations a day that you can follow up with teachers either on the same day as the observation or the very next day. Teachers need and deserve some type of feedback that is immediate.

Informally Observe as Often as You Can

The principal's presence in classrooms sends a positive message to teachers: the principal cares. Including the informal classroom observation as a schoolwide initiative requires consistency and frequency. Become opportunistic in finding time in the day to observe teachers, and vary the time of the day in which you observe teachers. What occurs in the morning is much different than what occurs in the afternoon.

Watch, Listen, and Write but Focus on One or Two Areas

Although there is no predetermined focus established in a preobservation conference, find a focus based on the instruction, events, or discussions that are occurring in the classroom. Avoid having a predetermined focus in which teachers know how to teach to the hot spot of the observer. For example, if the principal is a proponent of cooperative learning, teachers might be tempted to transition to cooperative learning activities once the principal enters the room.

Given that informal observations are relatively brief (15–20 minutes) as compared to an extended classroom observation (30–45 minutes), data from a single focus will make for richer conversation during the follow-up discussion.

Have Fun

Check your demeanor—let your body language and facial expressions communicate that you are enjoying the time in the classroom. A principal's demeanor sends strong messages—either the principal enjoys being out and about or the principal grudgingly engages in informal classroom observations. Think about how you want teachers and students to view you.

(Figure continues on next page)

---

* Adapted from *Twelve Guidelines for Managing By Walking Around* (MBWA) at FutureCents. Retrieved February 14, 2005, from http://www.futurecents. com/mainmbwa.htm

Catch Them in the Act of Doing Something Right and Applaud Efforts

Look for victories rather than failures, and applaud them. Work to create an ethos of sharing. Teachers who are especially adept at a strategy or technique need time and opportunities for sharing their expertise with others. For example, a certain amount of time at weekly or monthly faculty meetings could be set aside for teachers to share insights or techniques with one another.

Make the Time to Follow Up

Follow-up communication to informal classroom observation is a critical component. Through conversations and reflection, teachers better understand the complexities of their work. Feedback and dialogue form the cornerstone of all supervisory activities.

Follow Up with Resources

After feedback, the effective principal follows up with resources that teachers need to refine practice. The principal's efforts at returning to do a follow-up informal observation might very well be a resource to provide.

Make Informal Observations Invitational

Encourage teachers to invite you to observe them. Teachers who are experimenting with unique or novel instructional approaches or whose students are making presentations would welcome the opportunity for the principal to be present.

A Case Study

Richard Monroe, a first-year principal at Drake Middle School, was eager to get to know his teachers. As a teacher, he had enjoyed having his principal come into his classroom. Monroe decided to make three to five informal classroom observations, beginning the first week of the school year. At the end of the first week, he received a phone call from the assistant superintendent asking him to hold off from informal observations until they could meet.

♦ If you were Monroe, what questions would you want to ask the assistant superintendent?

♦ What do you believe the issues are?

To ensure positive responses to informal classroom observations and to foster an environment that supports them, supervisors need to take certain steps:

- Publish procedures for observations at the beginning of the year.
- Conduct informal classroom visitations regularly (one or two per week).
- Remind teachers to ask you in to see something new and innovative. Harry Wong (1998) believes that learning is invitational.
- Avoid using informal observation to check on a teacher when you have received complaints from parents or others.
- Know when to leave if you sense that a personal teaching moment is in progress. (Zepeda, 1995)

Fieldwork

Ask a building administrator for permission to informally observe a teacher. Conduct a pop-in observation and spend 15 to 20 minutes in the classroom. After you leave the teacher's classroom, write a follow-up note (see Figures 3.2, p. 51, and 3.3, p. 52) that details the highlights of what you observed.

Follow up with a brief conversation with the teacher you observed informally. What was the teacher's reaction to the informal observation and the follow-up note?

Informal classroom observations at the start of the year can be especially beneficial for first-year teachers and for teachers new to a school. The start of the year marks a period of transition, and the presence of a supervisor signals that teachers are not alone. Informal supervision can help assess what teachers need to thrive in the classroom.

In response to teacher retirement and shortages in critical subject areas, a school may well hire 15 or more teachers a year. With increased hiring, principals will need help making informal classroom observations. If the school has more than one administrator, dividing informal observations among supervisors can offer a useful solution. Figure 3.4, on the next page, provides an example of how supervisors can track informal observations.

Figure 3.4. Tracking Informal Observations

Teacher	Supervi-sor	Informal Observa-tion	Formal Observation	Period(s)/ Time(s)	Follow-Up
Adams	Schmidt	09/01	10/05	1 (8:15–8:30) 5 (11:10–11:20)	Cooperative learning grouping
Baker	Marlowe	11/08	03/20	1 (8:15–8:25) 1 (8:15–8:25)	Instructional pacing
Beatty	Linton	09/05; 09/08; 10/18; 11/07	10/07; 10/14; 11/02; 12/05	1 (8:30–8:45) 3 (10:10–10:25) 1 (8:15–8:25) 6 (1:05–1:15)	Classroom management; beginning and ending of period proce-dures
Burton	Schmidt	09/07	10/31	1 (8:00–8:15) 8 (2:15–2:30)	Classroom management

By reviewing the record of informal classroom observations, supervisors can determine whether any teachers have been missed, whether observations are spread evenly throughout a portion of the school year or the day (indicated by period or time of the observation), and what follow-up has been or should be made. Supervisors can also look for patterns. For example, in Figure 3.4, above, Marlowe did not observe Baker at all for four months; Linton is balancing formal and informal observations. The supervisor should interpret these patterns in the context of the school and the characteristics of the teachers being supervised.

Formal Classroom Observations

During a formal classroom observation, the supervisor typically spends an extended period of time in the classroom. In the state of Georgia, current legislation calls for formal classroom observations to last approximately 20 minutes, and in Illinois, many school districts require 2 or more formal observations of at least 30 minutes before an end-of-the-year rating can be issued. Common sense suggests that extended visits are needed if the observer is to get more than a snapshot of the classroom environment. Only extended classroom observations can provide teachers with detailed information about their teaching and interactions with students.

Regardless of its length, a formal observation requires a preobservation conference and a postobservation conference. Why are these necessary? The answer is not simple, but its core is that to omit these steps makes the visit a waste of time for the supervisor and useless to the teacher. Consider the following case study.

A Case Study

Principal Mark Adams enters Dr. Lori Quincy's first-period algebra class 15 minutes into the period. For five minutes, Adams watches students sit at their desks copying notes from the overhead. Then some students begin working problems at the blackboard, others leave their desks to work at the computer stations, and others gather around Dr. Quincy's desk as she works with a student in the back of the room.

Adams is confused; he leaves the room unsure of what he saw, and his observation notes are sparse.

It is not surprising that Adams is confused. Adams entered the room clueless about Quincy's

- Learning objectives;
- Lesson content;
- Overall placement in the lesson or unit (beginning, middle, end);
- Long-term plan; and
- Students' ability levels (e.g., perhaps the students were struggling with a concept, and this was a review for them).

In short, Adams is not on the same page as Quincy. Like a person walking into a movie 30 minutes late, he has to guess where to focus his attention, who the major players are, where the story line is going, and how earlier events influence the action. Without a preobservation conference, Adams lacks the clarity, focus, and perspective that give meaning to what he sees.

But Adams and Quincy face yet another issue: What will they talk about in the postobservation conference? How meaningful will Adams' notes be as he reviews the lesson with Quincy? The preobservation conference readies the supervisor to collect data focused on an aspect of the lesson that the teacher wants more information about. The postobservation conference presents these data in a way that helps the teacher reflect about classroom practices. Teachers need and want opportunities to talk about their teaching—as McGreal states, "The more teachers talk about teaching, the better they get at it" (1983, p. 63)—but the talk must be based on objective data derived from a properly conducted classroom observation. There is no substitute.

The preobservation and postobservation conferences are explored in greater detail in Chapters 4 and 6. The key point here is that a formal and extended classroom observation without preobservation and postobservation conferences is a waste of time and effort for both the supervisor and the teacher.

Many new principals and other supervisors freeze at the thought of observing a class on subject matter they are not certified to teach or in an area they do not know and understand (e.g., physics, special education, drafting). Furthermore, classroom observation calls for skills other than subject-matter knowledge. Other sources of concern for supervisors faced with the task of talking about teaching with another professional include

- Insecurity about capturing data in a fast-paced lesson in a way that will make sense;
- Unfamiliarity with the processes of clinical supervision (perhaps because they were never supervised in this way); and
- Insufficient knowledge of grade levels (elementary, middle, high school), the characteristics of students at a particular level, or a range of instructional practices.

The following guide for talking about teaching (Figure 3.5, pages 60 and 61) has evolved from the author's work at the University of Oklahoma, at the University of Georgia, and with administrators in the field. The guide presents broad categories (e.g., knowledge of subject matter) and possible indicators reflecting activity within each category (e.g., relates content to prior and future information). The categories and the possible indicators offer a point of departure for supervisors seeking to capture the work of the teacher during the observation and to frame thoughts while preparing for the postobservation conference. The supervisor may well add other indicators that reflect what was observed in the teacher's classroom.

Figure 3.5. Criteria for Talking about Teaching

Criterion	Possible Indicators
Knowledge of subject matter	◆ Transfers content/concepts to everyday life. ◆ Relates content to prior and future information. ◆ Communicates content in a logical and sequential manner. ◆ Uses words and content appropriate to subject area and students' abilities. ◆ Demonstrates subject knowledge. ◆ Actively pursues lifelong learning, especially in subject area.
Effectiveness of instructional strategies	◆ Cooperative learning. ◆ Demonstrations. ◆ Guided and independent practice. ◆ Modeling. ◆ Specific feedback. ◆ Appropriate wait time. ◆ Age-appropriate competition, inclusive of individuals and groups. ◆ Instructional methodologies include all learning styles. ◆ Multiple intelligences. ◆ Questions asked at multiple cognitive levels. ◆ Technology incorporated as an instructional tool.
Classroom management	◆ Routines are evident. ◆ Rules and procedures are posted. ◆ Rules and procedures are enforced. ◆ Beginning and ending class procedures are in place. ◆ Teacher monitors student behavior. ◆ Rewards and consequences are in place. ◆ Physical environment is conducive to orderliness. ◆ Teacher ensures a safe environment.

Variety of assessment methods	◆ Written, verbal, and nonverbal assessment may include
	  • tests/quizzes/written exams
	  • teacher observation
	  • participation
	  • portfolios
	  • feedback
	  • projects
	  • barometer, thumbs up/down—checking for continued understanding and application
	  • peer teaching
	  • homework

	◆ Assessments are frequent.
	◆ Assessment instruments are teacher/student-driven.
	◆ Accommodations are made for alternative assessments and individualized where needed.
	◆ Assessments are based on curriculum objectives.
High expectations for all students	◆ Teacher establishes expectations and communicates them by words and actions.
	◆ Gives varying opportunities for success.
	◆ Encourages each student to function at an appropriate level.
	◆ Begins instruction at level of the learner and plans for cognitive growth.
	◆ Provides enrichment opportunities as well as remediation.
Teacher/student rapport	◆ Student-centered.
	◆ Open climate.
	◆ Interactions with students are positive.
	◆ Teacher demonstrates tact, patience, and understanding, fosters growth in student self-esteem.
	◆ Uses specific praise.
	◆ Demonstrates enthusiasm.
	◆ Generates excitement for learning.
Technology	◆ Basic computer skills:
	• keyboardingcomputer applications (e.g., Word, Excel, Power Point, Internet, and E-mail)
	• record-keeping programs
	• required and supplemental programs in specific areas of expertise
	◆ Multimedia:
	• use of various media equipment (e.g., VCR, laser disk, overhead projector)
	◆ Integration of technology within subject matter
Communication	◆ Uses standard English in written and spoken communication.
	◆ Reflects all learning styles and levels of functioning
Gender, race, and culture	◆ Teacher is sensitive to students' cultural backgrounds and the effect on learning.
	◆ Communication (oral and written) is free of bias.
	◆ Female and male students are treated equally. Calling patterns and other practices reflect this.

The Clinical Supervision Model and Its Components

The clinical supervisory model comprises the preobservation conference, an extended classroom observation, and a postobservation conference. Figure 3.6 portrays the phases of the original clinical supervisory model.

Figure 3.6. The Phases of the Original Clinical Supervisory Model

Basic Phase	Cogan (1973)	Goldhammer, Anderson, and Krajewski (1993)	Acheson and Gall (1997)
Clarifying the supervisory relationship	Establishing the relationship		
Planning	Planning with the teacher Planning for the observation	Holding the preobservation conference	Holding the planning conference
Observing	Making the classroom observation	Making the classroom observation	Making the classroom observation
Analyzing	Analyzing the teaching/learning process Planning the conference strategy	Making the analysis and planning strategy	
Conferencing	Holding the conference	Holding the supervisory conference	Holding the feedback conference
Evaluating	Doing renewed planning	Holding the postconference analysis	

Source: Acheson & Gall, 1997; Cogan, 1973; Goldhammer, Anderson, & Krajewski, 1993.

The current clinical supervisory model is much more streamlined than the original model, and the focus has shifted from the supervisor's leadership to the teacher's initiative and response. This view is more empowering; the teacher has a greater voice in the process and is in a better position to construct knowledge.

Although more streamlined, instructional supervision is still a time-intensive proposition, and supervisors face many dilemmas as they try to deliver a supervisory program that is responsive to the needs of teachers in their schools. Consider the following case study.

A Case Study

The administrative team of Panola High School—Principal Inga Fox and three assistant principals—meets in early August to develop a long-term plan for supervising and evaluating the 135 teachers in their building. The district policy mandates that each teacher be formally observed at least twice, with each observation lasting at least 40 minutes. The math is simple:

135 teachers × 2 classroom observations each = 270 observations

270 observations ÷ 4 administrators = 67 observations per administrator

At 40 minutes per observation, this amounts to more than 45 hours each—not including the pre- and postobservation conferences. Added to this are the informal observations, which are a priority for Fox because a directive from the superintendent states that he wants "teachers to feel supported and administrators to be visible in classrooms—both formally and informally."

Every K-12 supervisor faces this dilemma, and there are no clear answers. As a prospective supervisor, brainstorm possible approaches that Fox and the administrative team might consider.

The perennial struggle to find time for mandatory formal classroom observations and for informal classroom visits is exacerbated in schools where many teachers are in their first year or new to the system. Although no clear-cut solution to this problem can be applied across all school systems, many supervisors have found creative ways to make the most of available human resources and provide a supervisory program that centers on teachers' needs.

The following ideas offer a point of departure for identifying proactive measures to empower teachers while reducing the burden on principals. First, supervisors can cast the net wide, framing a comprehensive system that includes department chairs, lead teachers, instructional coordinators, and other school leaders as peer coaches and mentors. Although formal authority to evaluate teachers is vested in administrators, teacher leaders can multiply the impact of the administrator's efforts. Other sources of supervisory assistance include district-level subject-area coordinators and directors who are specialists in areas such as English, foreign language, social studies, health, and math. Second, supervisors must provide resources to train and support teachers who are willing to coach and mentor their colleagues. The investment will yield rewards not only in the professional development of teachers, but also in the correlated gains in student achievement.

Chapters 4, 5, and 6 explore in depth the preobservation conference, the extended classroom observation, and the postobservation conference. These form the baseline of all models of supervision (e.g., peer coaching, peer supervision, and the clinical model of supervision).

Summary

Instructional supervision can occur through formal or informal classroom observations. Informal classroom visits, although brief, are important to the program of instructional supervision. Teachers need feedback more than once or twice a year; informal classroom observations provide valuable opportunities for more frequent interaction between the supervisor and the teacher. However, informal classroom observations lose value if they are predicated on fault finding or triggered by an unfavorable report from a parent or colleague.

New supervisors should determine the history of supervision at the site before making informal classroom observations. At first, the school's culture might not support such interaction between teachers and their supervisors. It takes time to establish trust and build a culture that embraces informal observations.

Formal, scheduled observations include preobservation and postobservation conferences that engage teachers in sustained discussion about their teaching. Optimally, teachers will participate in at least one formal and extended classroom observation each year. Keeping a log of observations by various school personnel (e.g., department chair, assistant principal, or principal) helps the supervisor identify patterns and determine the instructional needs of particular teachers.

Effective supervisors take advantage of a range of opportunities to become involved in the instructional lives of their teachers. A purposeful combination of formal and informal observations will help build a culture that supports this path toward professional development and growth.

Suggested Activities

From Theory to Practice

Arrange to interview two building-level administrators who conduct formal and informal classroom observations. Ask each administrator to share perspectives about these observations. Given the content of this chapter, construct four or five open-ended questions to guide the interview. After completing these interviews, write a summary of what the administrators shared with you.

Group Processing

After completing the above project, discuss in a small group the results of your findings and what these findings mean to the practice of formal and informal supervision.

Reflection

What does this mean to you? How will these findings influence your approach to conducting formal and informal supervision?

References

Acheson, K. A., & Gall, M.D. (1997). *Techniques in the clinical supervision of teachers: Preservice and inservice applications* (4th ed.). New York: Longman.

Blase, J. R., & Blase, J. (1998). *Handbook of instructional leadership: How really good principals promote teaching and learning.* Thousand Oaks, CA: Corwin Press.

Cogan, M. (1973). *Clinical supervision.* Boston: Houghton-Mifflin.

Downey, C.J., Steffy, B.E., English, F. W., Frase, L.E., & Poston, W.K., Jr. (2004). *Changing school supervisory practices one teacher at a time: The three-minute classroom walk-through.* Thousand Oaks, CA: Corwin Press.

FutureCents. (n.d.). *Twelve guidelines for managing by walking around* (MBWA). Retrieved February 14, 2005, from http://www.futurecents.com/mainmbwa.htm

Goldhammer, R., Anderson, R., & Krajewski, R. (1993). *Clinical supervision: Special methods for the supervision of teachers* (3rd ed.). Fort Worth, TX: Harcourt Brace Jovanovich College Publishers.

Glatthorn A. A. (1984). *Differentiated supervision.* Alexandra, VA: Association for Supervision and Curriculum.

Glickman, C. D. (1981). *Developmental supervision: Alternative practices for helping teachers improve instruction.* Alexandria, VA: Association for Supervision and Curriculum Development.

Manning, R. C. (1988). *The teacher evaluation handbook: Step-by-step techniques and forms for improving instruction.* Paramus, NJ: Prentice Hall.

McGreal, T. (1983). *Effective teacher evaluation.* Alexandria, VA: Association for Curriculum and Supervision.

Peters, T. J., & Waterman, R. H., Jr. (1982). *In search of excellence: Lessons from America's best run companies.* New York: Harper and Row.

Sergiovanni, T. J., & Starratt, R. J. (1998). *Supervision: A re-definition* (6th ed.). Boston: McGraw-Hill.

Wong, H. K., & Wong, R. T. (1998). *The first days of school: How to be an effective teacher* (2nd ed.). Mountain View, CA: Harry K. Wong Publications.

Zepeda, S.J. (2005). *The Instructional leaders guide to informal classroom observations.* Larchmont, NY: Eye on Education.

Zepeda, S.J. (2003). *The principal as instructional leader: A handbook for supervisors.* Larchmont, NY: Eye on Education.

Zepeda, S.J. (1995). *How to ensure positive responses in classroom observations. Tips for principals: National Association of Secondary School Principals.* Reston, VA: National Association of Secondary School Principals.

4

The Preobservation Conference

In This Chapter...

- ◆ Attributes of the preobservation conference
- ◆ Focus and the preobservation conference
- ◆ The Johari Window and the preobservation conference
- ◆ How to prepare for the classroom observation

Given their fast-paced workday and myriad extracurricular activities (e.g., club moderator, member of the school improvement team), teachers rarely have time to talk with adults about their classroom practices. The pre- and postobservation conferences of the clinical supervisory model give teachers this valuable opportunity.

Acheson and Gall (1997) indicate that the supervisor's main responsibility is to serve as "another set of eyes," holding up the "mirror of practice" in which the teacher can examine specific classroom behaviors. Supervisors who collect stable data during the observation provide a clearer reflection. During the conference that precedes a formal classroom observation, the supervisor determines what kinds of data to gather. The supervisor can also use this time to cultivate the supervisory relationship and to learn more about the teacher's classroom. The preobservation conference opens the door to the teacher's world.

Attributes of the
Preobservation Conference

During the preobservation conference, teacher and supervisor establish the focus for the classroom observation. In talking about concerns or areas of practice, the teacher should take the lead (though the teacher's career stage naturally makes a difference here). This conversation supports decisions about what data will provide useful information for the postobservation conference and what tools the supervisor will use to gather that data. Ideally, the preobservation conference

- ◆ Strengthens the professional relationship between the supervisor and the teacher;
- ◆ Is held within 24 to 48 hours prior to the observation;
- ◆ Takes place in the classroom where the observation will occur;
- ◆ Defines a clear focus for the observation, with the teacher taking the lead;
- ◆ Gives the teacher the opportunity to "talk through" teaching; and
- ◆ Illuminates the context, characteristics, climate, and culture of the classroom.

The preobservation conference sets the stage for all that follows.

Extended Reflection

Think of the most hectic teaching period or segment you have had this year. Imagine that your supervisor walked into your classroom during this time and stayed for 50 minutes.

What do you think the outcome would have been (a) with a preobservation conference and (b) without a preobservation conference?

Most school systems have their own preobservation form. The teacher might want to complete this form in advance, although the supervisor and teacher should work together to determine the focus during the conference. The preobservation form presented in Figure 4.1, on the next page, can help the supervisor to

- ◆ Better understand the classroom during the extended observation;
- ◆ Identify the focus of the observation; and

◆ Get teachers to talk about their classroom practices.

Understanding the classroom environment and the teacher's instructional objectives positions the supervisor to collect the specific data that can help teachers understand the dynamics of their work.

Figure 4.1. Preobservation Conference Form (With Explanations)

Teacher: _____ Date of Observation: _____

Observer:_____

Class: _____ Period of the Day: _____

Time of Observation: Start: _____   End: _____

Total Time Spent in Observation: _____

Number of Students Present: _____

Topic of the Lesson: _____

Date of Postobservation Conference: _____

1. Learning Objectives
    ◆ *Content:* What will the students learn?

    Ask the teacher to walk you through the lesson for the observation (this is sometimes called preplanning, an original process in the first clinical supervisory model). Make sure that you understand what topics (subject matter) will be covered during the class you will be observing. The teacher should make clear the objectives for the class.

    ◆ *Process:* What will instruction look and sound like?

    What will the teacher be doing and what will the students be doing? Probe the teacher to articulate a "cause-and-effect" between what he/she will be doing and what it is anticipated that the students will be doing.

    What instructional strategies will be used?

    Ask the teacher to talk you through the method so that you understand it. Try to discover why the teacher has chosen specific instructional strategies. Probe so that you understand both the content and the instructional method.

    ◆ *Resources:* What resources and materials will the teacher use throughout the lesson?

    With the advent of technology, teachers have a variety of equipment available to enhance instruction. Technology can serve both as a resource and as an instructional method.

(Figure continues on next page)

2. Understanding the Classroom Environment

Schools are diverse. It is unlikely that every math teacher who teaches Algebra I follows the same plan. This part of the preobservation form focuses on the *characteristics, culture,* and *climate* of the classroom learning environment.

♦ *Characteristics of the learners:* What are the students like? Are students on an even playing field in relation to performances, motivational levels, and abilities? Are there students with special learning needs that require modifications in instruction or assessment?

♦ *Culture and climate:* How do you characterize the atmosphere in the room? Invite the teacher to talk about how things are run, the roles students assume in the learning process, the ways students communicate with one another and you, the levels of cooperation, student attitudes, and student behavior and hot spots.

3. Looking for Results

This portion of the preobservation focuses on how the teacher will determine whether objectives have been met, how the teacher will monitor for learning and application of concepts, and what types of assessments will be used in the class or later.

♦ *Assessment:* What teaching behaviors assist you in assessing student learning? Query the teacher to identify what students will be able to demonstrate and what artifacts (test or quiz grades, portfolio artifact, project, essay) will be used to demonstrate mastery.

4. Focusing for the Observation

The focus is perhaps the most important aspect of the preobservation conference. The focus allows the observer to

♦ "Zoom" into the area in which the teacher wants objective data describing teaching behavior; and

♦ Collect better data because the supervisor will know what type of observation tool to use to collect more stable data.

Source: Zepeda, 1995.

Figure 4.2, on the next page, provides a blank preobservation conference form and Figure 4.3 (pages 72 and 73) shows a typical completed form.

Figure 4.2. Preobservation Conference Form (Blank)

Teacher: _____ Date of Observation:

Observer:_____

Class: _____ Period of the Day: _____

Time of Observation: Start: _____ End: _____

Total Time Spent in Observation: _____

Number of Students Present: _____

Topic of the Lesson: _____

Date of Postobservation Conference: _____

1. Learning Objectives
    ♦ *Content:* What will the students learn?

    ♦ *Process:* What will instruction look and sound like?

    ♦ *Resources:* What resources and materials will the teacher use throughout the lesson?

2. Understanding the Classroom Environment
    ♦ *Characteristics of the learners:* What are the students like?

    ♦ *Culture and climate:* How do you characterize the atmosphere in the room?

3. Looking for Results
    ♦ *Assessment:*

4. Focusing for the Observation

Figure 4.3. Preobservation Conference Form (Completed)

Teacher: <u>Rita Sanchez</u>   Date of Observation: <u>September 28, 2006</u>

Observer: <u>Connie Elliot</u>

Class: <u>Language Arts—3rd Graders</u>   Period of the Day: <u>Morning Language Arts Block</u>

Time of Observation: Start: <u>8:05</u>   End: <u>8:55</u>

Total Time Spent in Observation: <u>50 Minutes</u>

Number of Students Present: <u>11</u>

Topic of the Lesson: <u>Similes and the words "Like" and "As"</u>

Date of Postobservation Conference: <u>September 28, 2006 (after school)</u>

1. Learning Objectives

    ♦ *Content:* What will the students learn?

    Students will learn about the words "like" and "as" and how these words are used in similes to compare two things.

    ♦ *Process:* What instructional strategies will be used?

    A mini-lesson on similes will begin with students working in groups of three finding the words "like" and "as" in the short story "Annie Goes to the Bank." Each group will prepare a list of the similes in the story. Each small group will share the similes they found with the class. Teacher will lead a whole-class discussion, asking students to describe the characteristics of the words found. Students will brainstorm aloud with the teacher in analyzing the characteristics of the comparisons used in the story. Students will be asked to write two paragraphs that contain similes.

    ♦ *Resources:* What resources and materials will the teacher use throughout the lesson?

    The short story "Annie Goes to the Bank," poster boards to write similes.

2. Understanding the Classroom Environment

    ♦ *Characteristics of the learners:*

    Students range in ability from below grade level to above grade level. The class has 11 students. One student is partially deaf and sits close to the teacher.

    ♦ *Culture and climate:*

    The classroom atmosphere is student centered, and the students are sensitive to the special needs of the partially deaf student. Generally, the students work well together in small groups, but they are still learning the social skills needed to work as members of a group.

3. Looking for Results

   ♦ *Assessment:*

   Quality of responses during the discussion of the similes found in the story. The teacher will monitor student participation in the small group. The teacher will assess student paragraphs for the similes they write; a follow-up discussion will include the presentation of the similes written by students in their paragraphs. Students will also read and proof each other's work before turning in the assignment to the teacher.

4. Focusing for the Observation

   Ms. Sanchez wants to focus on (a) the way she breaks students into groups; (b) the clarity of directions she gives to students; (c) the way she monitors students working in small groups; and (d) the transitions between class activities (e.g., small group work to large group sharing).

Fieldwork

Conducting a Preobservation Conference

Ask a teaching colleague if it would be possible to conduct a preobservation conference using Figure 4.2 (p. 71). The preobservation conference can be held before school, during either a mutual plan period or a lunch period, or after school. It might be helpful to provide the teacher with a blank copy of the preobservation form found in Figure 4.2, or you might want to use a form that the school system in which you work uses.

After the preobservation conference is over, reflect on:

♦ The length of the preobservation conference.

♦ The amount of talking you did versus the amount the teacher talked.

♦ Artifacts shared (e.g., seating chart, teaching materials, samples of student work).

Reconstruct the experience and identify what went well and what you would do differently the next time you conduct a preobservation conference.

Focus and the Preobservation Conference

Perhaps the most important feature of the preobservation conference is the focus for the upcoming classroom observation. Why is the focus so important? This is a complex question with a multifaceted answer. The focus serves to

♦ Promote dialogue between the supervisor and the teacher;

♦ Help the teacher identify a growth area; and

♦ Help the supervisor identify what concrete data to gather and what observation tools to use.

Who should direct the focus portion of the preobservation conference? The teacher? The supervisor? Both? Opinions vary, and there are no universal truths. Ideally, the supervisor and the teacher mutually agree on a focus for the observation. Here are some guiding thoughts.

Teacher-Directed Focus   As professionals capable of thinking critically about instruction, students, curriculum content, and methods, teachers are able to make informed decisions about the development of their practices and thus direct their own learning. The teacher can identify the observation focus area based on

♦ Interest in a target area;

♦ Perceived need to improve in a specific area;

♦ Follow-up on professional development areas; and

♦ Areas under construction (e.g., trying a new technique).

When the teacher assumes responsibility for directing the observation focus, the supervisor takes a more indirect approach, perhaps helping the teacher to flesh out an area of focus.

Supervisor-Directed Focus   The supervisor perceives a particular need and guides the teacher to focus on this target. Supervisors tend to take a directive approach with certain groups of teachers (such as first-year teachers or those on a plan of remediation). A supervisor-directed focus can certainly be positive and fruitful; however, teachers often feel greater autonomy when they have authority to determine the observation focus.

A Case Study

Mrs. Sweeney, a 17-year veteran language arts teacher at Arlington Middle School, teaches a districtwide professional development course on cooperative learning. Teachers in her building often observe her cooperative learning lessons.

Mr. Brown, the new assistant principal at Arlington Middle School, has been assigned to supervise Mrs. Sweeney. During the preobservation conference, Mr. Brown asks Mrs. Sweeney what she would like the focus of the observation to be. She responds, "How I monitor cooperative learning groups as they work."

Should Mr. Brown try to get Mrs. Sweeney to choose a different focus? What additional information does Mr. Brown need from Mrs. Sweeney to be clear on the focus? How should Mr. Brown proceed and why?

Regardless of who sets the focus, it must be realistic. If the focus is too broad, the supervisor and teacher will be unclear about the data to be gathered. If the focus is too ambitious, the observer will need to collect too much data scattered across too many areas. Return to Figure 4.3 (pages 72 and 73) for information. Has Rita Sanchez asked Ms. Elliot to focus the observation too broadly? If you were Ms. Elliot, would you try to work with Rita to narrow the focus? If so, what approach would you take?

Negotiating Boundaries for the Observation Focus

Experience First-year teachers might need guidance in developing the observation focus. Consider the following sequence:

- For the first formal observation, let the first-year teacher guide the focus with minimal input from the supervisor.
- Based on the first observation, exert more influence, if necessary, on the focus of the second formal observation.
- Link the focus of all subsequent observations to data from prior observations and the discussions in postobservation conferences.

Extenuating Circumstances Teachers on formalized plans of improvement will need a more directed focus

- To remediate a particular deficiency within a certain time; or
- To comply with other policies and procedures specified by the board of education, the bargaining unit, or state statutes.

Implications About Focus and the Observation

The focus steers the observer through the steps of the observation to

♦ Identify the instrument to collect useful data that will, for example, portray teacher and student activities or words, classroom procedures, instructional methods (pedagogy), and classroom management strategies.

♦ Focus intently on instructional behavior(s), record events, and present the teacher with a rich portrayal of practice to discuss and analyze during the postobservation conference.

♦ Assist as the teacher identifies an area to examine in detail.

Teaching does not occur in a vacuum; unexpected incidents may unfold during the observation. The supervisor may well notice events that fall outside the focus, and may choose to discuss them—but with caution. Trust is at stake. Letting unanticipated incidents clutter the postobservation conference can smack of "snoopervisory" or "gotcha" tactics. Consider these questions:

♦ Did the incident (e.g., unruly students) completely overshadow all instruction or student activities?

♦ If the event (e.g., unclear or incomplete directions, lack of classroom routines) is not discussed, will the teacher continue to encounter problems?

♦ Is the teacher even aware of the incident (e.g., were the students out of sight)?

♦ Will calling attention to the event diminish the teacher–supervisor relationship?

Extended Reflection

During his classroom observation of Mrs. Sweeney, Mr. Brown notes that two students in one of the cooperative groups are doing homework for a different class and a student in another group is reading a magazine. In a third group, three of five students do not have their books.

The focus agreed on in the preobservation conference was monitoring group work, not off-task behavior of students. If you were Mr. Brown, what would you do?

Fear to Focus

If you asked a group of teachers why they hesitate to ask their supervisors to focus on an area of concern, the answer would more than likely be fear—specifically, the belief that their supervisors are out to get them. This fear—now practically a tradition in Pre-K-12 schools—grows whenever a supervisor supplants supervision with summative evaluation that serves only to comply with state mandates. In the book *Supervisors and Teachers: A Private Cold War*, Blumberg (1980) concludes that clinical supervision is irrelevant in a teacher's professional life; it has become merely an organizational ritual. The only way to combat this fear is to build trust between teachers and supervisors.

The Johari Window and the Preobservation Conference

Teachers may hesitate to admit a weakness—especially if they have experienced evaluation as supervision, have not engaged in open, fault-free discussions, or fear that their jobs are on the line. However, many teachers will ask for help if they know they need it, especially if they believe their supervisors will provide useful insight and resources.

One tool for exploring communication between supervisors and teachers is the Johari Window. According to the Mallan Group Training and Management, Inc. (Tucson, Arizona), Luft and Ingham (1955) developed the Johari Window at the Western Training Laboratory. The Johari Window describes personal knowledge and interactions in terms of four panes: the open pane, the hidden pane, the blind pane, and the unknown pane. According to Luft and Ingham, the open pane and the hidden pane represent aspects of a person that are known to the self; the blind pane and the unknown pane represent aspects unknown to the self. Furthermore, the open pane and the blind pane represent aspects known to others; the hidden pane and the unknown pane represent aspects unknown to others.

The Mallan Group Training and Management, Inc. developed the Disclosure/Feedback model (Figure 4.4, on the next page) to help people assess awareness of communication patterns using the principles of the Johari Window.

Figure 4.4. The Johari Window

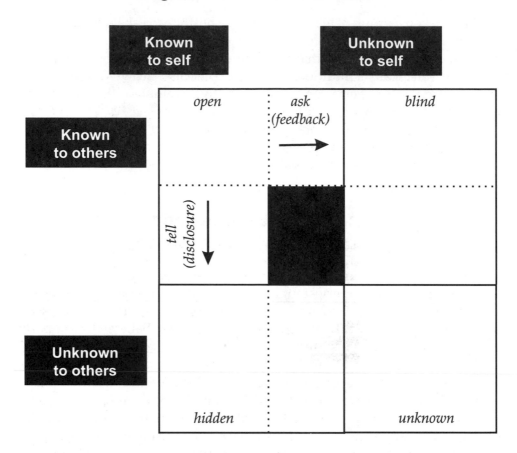

Source: Mallan Group Training and Management, Inc. KnowMe™. Retrieved May 30, 2001, from http://www.knowmegame.com/Johari_ Window/johari_ window.html. Used with permission.

The Mallan Group describes the four panes of the Johari Window as follows:

Open The open area is that part of our conscious self—our attitudes, behavior, motivation, values, way of life—that we are aware of and that is known to others. We move within this area with freedom. We are "open books."

Hidden   Others cannot know our hidden area unless we disclose it. Some aspects we freely keep within ourselves; others we retain behind a "closed" window out of fear. The degree to which we share ourselves with others (disclosure) is the degree to which we can be known.

Blind There are things about ourselves that we do not know but others can see more clearly, or things we imagine to be true of ourselves for a variety of reasons but others do not see at all. When others say what they see (feedback) in a supportive, responsible way, and we are able to hear it, we can test the reality of who we are and open ourselves to growth.

Unknown We are richer and more complex than the aspects we and others know, but from time to time something happens that is felt, read, heard, or dreamed that reveals something from our unconscious. Then we "know" what we have never "known" before.*

The known and unknown sides of a person affect communication, the ability to be open to feedback, and the willingness to recognize a weakness or an area that is not readily known to the person.

Implications for Supervision

Supervisors can use the Johari Window to consider how teachers feel about being observed and to interpret what teachers say or do not say in the pre- and postobservation conferences. While working with teachers to frame a focus for the classroom observation, for example, the supervisor may be asking them to disclose a weakness that lies behind the hidden pane. Likewise, after the observation, the type of feedback chosen and its intensity will depend on how much teachers already know about their practices. The following discussion of the Johari Window continues in Chapter 6, which addresses the postobservation conference.

Teachers who are comfortable with their Johari Window need very little prompting to identify a focus for the classroom observation. Teachers with little experience—first-year teachers, or those unfamiliar with the intents of supervision—might be more reluctant. The supervisor's job is to coach teachers in this aspect of professional growth.

The Open Pane Some teachers are (or appear to be) very open when discussing their teaching, readily sharing both the triumphs and the trials of their efforts in the classroom. Such teachers often are willing to have others (teachers, supervisors) visit their classrooms to observe, gather ideas, and give feedback. These visits are good learning opportunities—if the teacher is, indeed, effective. However, such classroom observations could be disastrous if the teacher's practices and self-image are not congruent.

---

* Used with permission of the Mallan Group Training and Management Inc.

The Hidden Pane Teachers who operate mainly in the hidden or secret part of the window say little about what goes on in their classrooms. Their reticence arises not from incompetence, but from insecurity or fear of not meeting expectations. The supervisor's job is to coach teachers into talking about their work. One approach is to engage the teacher in a general discussion of classroom practices and the learning objectives for a particular lesson. From this platform, the supervisor can guide the conversation with more specific questions. As trust develops between the teacher and supervisor, the discussion will arrive at a focus that the teacher wants to explore. It may take time to discover—or even uncover—what really matters.

The Blind Pane We do not always see ourselves as others see us. The supervisor at the back of the room may observe an aspect of a teacher's classroom practices that needs attention, though the teacher is unaware of it. Bringing such aspects into the open can be a difficult task, especially if the teacher resists recognizing or acknowledging them. On the other hand, teachers may also be blind to their own strengths (although such news is usually welcome). In framing effective feedback, the supervisor should rely on objective data gathered during the observation.

The Unknown Pane The unknown pane is the most difficult for people to open. This area hides information that only the individual can discover. Reflection, disclosure, and feedback can lead to this discovery, freeing the potential that lies behind the unknown pane. This aspect of the Johari Window offers perspectives that apply particularly to the postobservation conference, which is discussed in Chapter 6.

How to Prepare for the Classroom Observation

The primary tool for the preobservation conference is some type of preobservation conference form (see Figure 4.2, page 71). However, conducting a classroom observation requires other preparation as well. Effective supervisors arrive at the teacher's classroom ready to work. The following are some additional tools they use for an extended classroom observation.

Familiarity with the Teacher's Classroom   One way to become familiar with the classroom environment is to hold the preobservation conference in that classroom.

Establishment of Boundaries Effective supervisors enter the classroom without disrupting the class. During the preobservation conference, the teacher and supervisor agree on the details: when and how to enter, where to sit, how long to stay, and how to leave. These boundaries frame the observation and put the teacher at ease.

Artifacts In addition to paper and pencil, the prepared supervisor brings relevant artifacts, such as instructional materials (handouts, textbooks) or multiple copies of the teacher's seating chart (an effective way to track calling patterns or chronicle other events).

Tools One supervisor might use a laptop computer to track data related to the focus of the observation. Another might record events with a video camera. Using technology in classroom observations requires special care. For example, many school systems require parent permission to videotape children. Other district policies or union agreements might regulate videotaping teachers. Prospective and practicing supervisors need to be aware of district policies governing informal and formal observations, acceptable pre- and postobservation forms, and the method of communicating what they observed. To establish and maintain credibility with teachers and central administrators, the supervisor must know the school system's policies and procedures.

Summary

The formal supervision process includes the preobservation conference, the extended classroom observation, and a postobservation conference. During the classroom observation, the supervisor's responsibility is to collect accurate, objective data that reflect events. As Sergeant Friday used to say on Dragnet, "Nothing but the facts, ma'am." These data underpin the teacher's reflection and growth during the postobservation conference and beyond.

The preobservation conference can be a learning opportunity for teachers; successful conferences promote dialogue about teaching, with the teacher in the lead. The supervisor's goal should be to extend the dialogue by asking questions that invite reflection and further analysis. Actively planning instruction in company with the supervisor can enhance the teacher's learning. The supervisor also learns—about the teacher, the students, and the upcoming lesson. A key component of the preobservation conference is determining a focus for the classroom observation. In a sense, the focus serves as a guide for the teacher and the supervisor; it positions the supervisor to collect useful data for the teacher to analyze later.

In developing the focus of the classroom observation, teachers open one or more panes of their Johari Window. How much teachers disclose about their practices during the preobservation conference depends on their experience and the degree of trust between supervisor and teacher. Effective supervisors are proactive; they encourage teachers to look deeply at their practices with an eye to improvement and further development. The preobservation sets the stage for the classroom observation. The next chapter details the classroom observation and the tools that a supervisor can use to collect data.

Suggested Activities

From Theory to Practice

In the school where you work, enlist the cooperation of a professional colleague whom you may or may not know very well. In this chapter, you learned about the preobservation conference. The next two chapters cover the extended classroom observation and the postobservation conference. The activities that put these three chapters into practice are interlocking, so take care to enlist someone who will work with you through a preobservation conference, an extended classroom observation, and a postobservation conference.

Using the form presented in Figure 4.2 (page 71), conduct and videotape a preobservation conference. Then watch the tape by yourself, with your colleague, or with another interested person.

Group Processing

In small groups, debrief about the experience of conducting a preobservation conference. Ask the professor to consider seeking two volunteers to conduct a mock preobservation conference and have the class give feedback on preobservation conferencing skills.

Reflection

This chapter leads prospective supervisors through the preobservation conference process. Identify the bumps you encountered along the road. What have you learned about yourself and the process? How will you handle things in the future?

References

Acheson, K. A., & Gall, M.D. (1997). *Techniques in the clinical supervision of teachers: Preservice and inservice applications* (4th ed.). New York: Longman.

Blumberg, A. (1980). *Supervisors and teachers: A private cold war*. Berkeley, CA: McCutchan.

Mallan Group Training and Management Inc. *KnowMe*. Retrieved May 30, 2001, from http://www.knowmegame.com/Johari_Window/johari_window.html

Zepeda, S. J. (1995). *How to ensure positive responses in classroom observations. Tips for principals*. Reston, VA: National Association of Secondary School Principals.

5

The Classroom
Observation

In This Chapter...

♦ The intents of data collection

♦ Types of data

♦ Wide-angle and narrow-angle data collection techniques

♦ Tips from the field

♦ Overview and application of observation tools and methods

Introducing the
Classroom Observation

The preobservation conference underpins the formal classroom observation. It provides an opportunity for teachers to talk about teaching, but more crucially, it identifies a focus for the upcoming observation. The focus guides the supervisor's choice of a data collection tool. The quality and quantity of the data collected and how the supervisor presents it will significantly influence the quality of the postobservation conference.

Many tools and techniques enable the supervisor to collect stable, informative data in a systematic way. The supervisor, with input from the teacher, chooses one or more of these. At the end of the classroom observation, the key question is, "Do these data make sense?" Supervisors and teachers who invest time and effort in learning to use a variety of data collection tools can anticipate a rich return.

The Intents of Data Collection

According to McGreal (1983), data collection has four intents. The table below outlines the intents of data collection during each phase of the clinical supervision model.

Data Collection Intents in the
Phases of the Clinical Supervision Model

Clinical Supervision	Phase Data Collection Intent
Preobservation conference	The reliability and usefulness of classroom observation is related to the amount and type of information supervisors have before the observation.
Extended classroom observation	The narrower the focus supervisors use in observation observing classrooms, the more likely they will be able to describe the events related to that focus.
	The impact of observational data is related to the way the data are recorded during the observation.
Postobservation conference	The impact of observational data on supervisor–teacher relationships is related to the way feedback is presented to the teacher.

Source: McGreal, 1983.

Implications for Supervisors

These intents can guide the supervisor not only in collecting data during the observation, but also in framing discussions during the pre- and postobservation conferences. Supervisors need to work at collecting reliable data, free of value judgments and speculation. Consider the following two statements:

♦ *Statement 1* "While you were giving instructions for the small-group activity, one girl left her seat to sharpen a pencil."

♦ *Statement 2* "Because you were incapable of holding the students' attention, one girl sauntered to the pencil sharpener. From the smile on the girl's face, I believe she was mocking your shotgun approach to giving instructions."

The first statement presents the facts without editorial speculation. The second statement is value laden; even its wording ("incapable," "sauntered," "shotgun approach") sends a negative message. How is the teacher likely to respond to each statement? What impact might the second statement have on the relationship between the supervisor and the teacher?

The primary objective of collecting data is to promote teacher analysis, reflection, and ongoing planning. The classroom is a complex setting, but the focus established in the preobservation conference positions the supervisor to collect data that will make sense to the teacher. What technique will yield data that shed light on the focus? Figure 5.1 outlines the possibilities.

Figure 5.1. Classroom Observation Data Collection Methods

Method	Description
Behavior category	A narrow set of behaviors is determined and then tracked. Focus is more on the teacher than on the student.
Checklist	Supervisor uses a standardized form to identify activities and/or behaviors as present, absent, or in need of improvement (often disparagingly called "pencil whipping").
Classroom diagramming	Supervisor tracks and records certain behaviors or movement of teachers and students in short increments of time.
Selected verbatim	Supervisor records words, questions, or interactions notes exactly.
Open narrative	Supervisor takes anecdotal notes, with or without a focus.
Teacher-designed instrument	Teacher develops an instrument to audit certain teaching and/or learning behaviors.
Audiotape	Teacher and/or supervisor can audiotape classroom events and listen to them later.
Videotape	May require the assistance of another person. Teacher can review the lesson alone or with a supervisor or peer.

Types of Data

Data may be quantitative, qualitative, or a combination of both. Quantitative data include frequencies, distributions, and other counts or tallies of information. Checklists are quantitative because they do not use words to describe what occurred, how, or why.

For example, the observer could use a checklist to tally how many questions were asked of children in the front row, or how many times the teacher called on students whose hands were raised and those whose hands were not raised. Quantitative data have strengths; consider the following scenario:

> In the postobservation conference, Mr. Cranston tells Mr. Jones, "During the first 10 minutes of class, you didn't call on any students in the first row." Mr. Jones, who thought his lesson went smoothly, responds with consternation—I can't believe I could have completely ignored the whole front row!" However, Mr. Cranston has used multiple copies of the seating chart to track calling patterns in 10-minute increments. He invites Mr. Jones to examine the page for the first 10 minutes of class (Figure 5.2, next page).

Figure 5.2. Quantitative Data Sample

Date: <u>December 21, 2006</u>   Beginning Time: <u>8:15</u>   Ending Time: <u>8:45</u>
Teacher: <u>Martin Jones</u>   Observer: <u>Adam Cranston</u>
Lesson Topic: <u>Fractions</u>   Grade/Level: <u>Grade 7</u>
Date of Postobservation Conference: <u>December 22, 2006 (after school)</u>

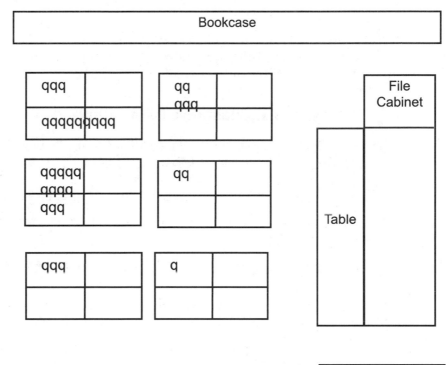

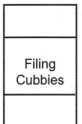

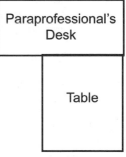

Other classroom observation data may be qualitative. Qualitative classroom observation would include the scripted notes of the supervisor or peer coach. Figure 5.3 shows an example of qualitative observation data.

Figure 5.3. Qualitative Data Sample

Date: <u>November 7, 2006</u>   Beginning Time: <u>8:15</u>   Ending Time: <u>8:45</u>
Teacher: <u>Jack Eliason</u>   Observer: <u>Oliver Campbell</u>
Lesson Topic: <u>Subject-Verb</u>   Grade/Level: <u>Grade 9</u>
Date of Postobservation Conference: <u>November 29, 2006 (before school)</u>

10:10:   T (teacher, Mr. Eliason) asks Marcie to repeat the question. Marcie repeats: "What is the subject?"

10:11:   T: "OK, so ask 'who' or 'what' of the verb." Taps chalk on the board to get Marcie's attention.

10:12:   T writes sentence on the board: *After the storm, several students left the roller rink.* T: "Try to ask 'who' or 'what' against the verb, 'left.'"

10:13:   T: "Marcie, answer the question, 'Who left the rink?'" Marcie stares at the sentence on the board. Two students raise their hands; 3 students write on paper; 3 students in back reading grammar book; 5 other students speaking with one another.

10:16:   Marcie blurts out, "several left."

10:17:   T: "Go back to the sentence, examine the word 'several'—check to see if the word is an adjective, 'How many students?'"

10:18:   Marcie: "Several—it's an adjective."

Although qualitative data record information in words, the patterns of activities, words, and other events observed and then recorded offer insights about the classroom environment. Whether data are quantitative or qualitative, accuracy is essential. The credibility of the process and the supervisor is at stake.

Even in the qualitative report in Figure 5.3 (page 90), certain observations can be quantified. For example, Mr. Eliason interacted for eight minutes with only one student (Marcie), while other students were off-task.

Wide-Angle and Narrow-Angle Data Collection Techniques

Data collection may focus on a single aspect (or a few aspects) of instruction (e.g., specific types of questions the teacher asks) or on a wide range of circumstances in the classroom (e.g., how things are going in general). Acheson and Gall (1997) developed a series of data collection techniques that they categorize—analogizing to camera lenses—as wide-angle or narrow-angle. Wide-angle techniques enable the supervisor to capture a large picture; narrow-angle techniques "zoom in" to collect data focused on a single aspect or two.

For example, if a teacher asked the supervisor to focus on the types of questions asked of students, the supervisor might decide to record, verbatim, the questions asked—a narrow-angle technique. The supervisor could expand the lens to track student responses as well; this decision would be a judgment call based on the level of trust between the teacher and the supervisor.

A Case Study

Mrs. Ortiz, a first-year assistant principal, is in Mr. Martin's classroom observing a lesson on subject–verb agreement. The focus they agreed on in the preobservation conference was to track calling patterns. Specifically, Martin wanted to know if he favored any students over others or called on students evenly to answer questions.

About 15 minutes into the observation, a few students in the front of the room begin talking and swapping what appear to be their lunch bags. Mrs. Ortiz stops collecting data on Mr. Martin's calling patterns; instead, she takes notes on these students and what they are doing.

At the end of class, Mrs. Ortiz returns to her office to review the classroom observation. She sees that almost half her notes deal with the students who were off-task, swapping lunches with each other.

♦ How should Mrs. Ortiz handle this situation?

♦ What factors should guide Mrs. Ortiz in making her decision?

Figure 5.4 summarizes the six most commonly used data collection tools developed by Acheson and Gall (1997).

Figure 5.4. Data Collection Tools: An Overview of Types

Type of Lens	Method to Collect Data	Focus
Narrow	Selective verbatim	Records words that were actually said by the teacher or the students.
Narrow	Verbal flow	Details the frequency of who spoke—how often and when.
Narrow	Class traffic	Tracks the teacher's (or students') physical movement.
Narrow	Interaction analysis	Provides detail about the types of statements made by either the teacher or the students.
Narrow	At-task	Provides detail, noting periodically over time what appears to be at-task.
Wide	Anecdotal notes	Notes overall what was occurring in the classroom. This can become more judgmental unless the supervisor records "Just the facts, Ma'am."

Source: Adapted from Acheson & Gall (1997).

Data collected during classroom observations tend to describe teacher and student behaviors using a series of snapshots with each piece of data depicting isolated events occurring during a teaching episode. It is the analysis of the data that permits the teacher and the supervisor to identify patterns through which a holistic image of teaching can be created. The key for success is to observe not only the teacher but also to observe students. Effective observation involves keeping one eye on the teacher and the other on the students, tracking the effect of teaching behaviors on student response and learning.

Data Collection Tools

Each data collection tool has its strengths and limitations and yields different types of information capturing the events of the classroom observation. The following illustrates what data would look like using select data collection tools as described in Figures 5.4 (page 92).

Selective Verbatim focuses on specific words, questions, or responses of the teacher, students, or both. The first example focuses on the questions a teacher asks.

T: What were the events leading up to the crime?
T: Of these events, which event motivated the main character the most?
T: Why was this event the most important?
T: How would the ending of the book have changed if this event did not occur?

The next example displays both the teacher's questions and the student's responses to questions.

Teacher Questions	Student Responses
1. What were the events leading up to the crime?	1. The man was desperate, he had to feed his children; he lost his job; his oldest son was diagnosed with a life-threatening disease.
2. Of these events, which event motivated the main character the most?	2. The son's life-threatening disease.
3. Why was this event the most important?	3. He had no money to pay the doctor.

Another way in which the selective verbatim technique can be used is to examine the teacher's responses categorized in the following example as either, "praise," "correction," or "preventive prompt," followed with the time noted in the following example.[1]

The data in Figure 5.5 sheds light not only on the teacher's statements but also on the patterns and routines for the beginning of the class period.

Figure 5.5. Selective Verbatim: Praise vs. Correction

Teacher: <u>Bob Bennet</u>   Date of Observation: <u>October 25, 2006</u>
Observer: <u>Pat Montalvo</u>
Class: <u>Study and Life Skills</u> Period of the Day: <u>Morning</u>
Time of Observation: Start: <u>9:40</u> End: <u>9:50</u>
Total Time Spent in Observation: <u>10 minutes</u>
Number of Students Present: <u>11</u> Grade Level: <u>Sophomores</u>
Topic of the Lesson: <u>Teacher was readying the class to begin work</u>
Date of Postobservation Conference: <u>October 27, 2006</u>

Teacher Comment/ Response	Time	Praise	Correction	Preventive Prompt
Please come in and get seated.	9:40		X	
Bob, close the door and come in.	9:41		X	
Your pencils need to be sharpened before class.	9:42		X	
Looks like Jeff is ready to get started.	9:43	X		
Jack needs to stop talking and follow along.	9:45		X	
Louise is patiently waiting for us to begin.	9:46	X		
Guys, you need to get paper out and follow along.	9:47		X	
I see Martin is ready!	9:48	X		
I can't begin until everyone's' attention is up here.	9:49		X	

---

1 Developed by Theresa L. Benfante, behavior interventionist at Central Alternative School, Cobb County School District (GA). Used with permission.

Teacher Comment/ Response	Time	Praise	Correction	Preventive Prompt
Tony, take your hood off your head please.	9:49		X	
We have wasted 10 minutes waiting for some of you to get ready.	9:50		X	
Leslie is ready to go.	"	X		
Bob and Jack, we are waiting for you to pay attention.	"		X	
Thanks Steve, I see you are ready.	"	X		
When you come to class prepared, we can begin on time.	"		X	X
Ratio of Praise to Correction: 5:9				
Preventive Prompts: 2				

Global Scan/Anecdotal focuses on events, actions, or words of the teacher, students, or both. Data that are scripted can take many forms. To chronicle the events, only a blank sheet of paper, an eye, and ear are needed to capture the events of the class. Anecdotal notes can focus events as they unfold by time or just by events.

Anecdotal Data Sample—By Time

9:05: Teacher asked student (male, red shirt) to elaborate on the "yes" response....How S. E. Hinton developed the symbol of the Siamese Fighting Fish.
9:06: Student: "at the end of the story...he sets the rumble fish free and then he dies...the characters fight like the rumble fish."
9:07: Teacher asks a general question: "Are there are other examples throughout the book?" (several hands go up...teacher calls on student who is fidgeting with her backpack)

Anecdotal Data Sample—Series of Events, No Time

- ◆ Teacher at door when students entered the room.
- ◆ Students knew the routine: they went to their seats, pulled out books, notebooks, and the homework assignment due (the agenda on the blackboard cued students on what to do to get ready for the period).
- ◆ When the bell rang, a student turned on the overhead projector; teacher pointed to the math problem—students began working on solving the word problem.
- ◆ Teacher took attendance, spoke briefly with a student at her desk, and walked up and down the aisles collecting homework assignments.
- ◆ Teacher focused students on the word problem—asked for the properties of the word problem before asking for the solution.
- ◆ Student in the back of the room (arm in cast) gave the answer to the word problem—320 pounds of coffee beans.
- ◆ Teacher asked student in front of the room to write the formula she used to get a different answer (285 was her response).
- ◆ As the student wrote the formula, teacher asked questions of another student who had the same answer.
- ◆ Student at the board "talked through" her answer and the steps she took to derive the answer.
- ◆ The teacher enlisted other students for answers to questions.
- ◆ Teacher transitioned the class to a page in their books—modeled how to analyze the word problem—wrote numbers on the board, enlisted students with helping her with the computations.

Checklists

A more narrow data collection method is the checklist approach in which data are usually tallied at the end so that patterns can be inferred from the data; however, checklist data can also be descriptive. Figure 5.6 (next page) details a sample of checklist data.

Figure 5.6. Sample Checklist Classroom Observation Form

Teacher: <u>Nancy Chandley</u>   Date of Observation: <u>November 13, 2006</u>
Observer: <u>Martine Orozco</u>
Class: <u>English I</u> Period of the Day: <u>Block 2</u>
Time of Observation: Start: <u>10:25</u>   End: <u>10:45</u>
Total Time Spent in Observation: <u>20 Minutes</u>
Number of Students Present: <u>26</u> Grade Level: <u>Freshman</u>
Topic of the Lesson: <u>Writing Narrative Essays</u>
Date of Postobservation Conference: <u>November 15, 2006</u>

Students were:

    ☐ Working in small, cooperative groups

    ☐ Making a presentation

    ☐ Taking a test

    ☑ Working independently at their desks

    ☐ Viewing a film

    ☐ Other _____

Teacher was:

    ☐ Lecturing

    ☐ Facilitating a question-and-answer sequence

    ☑ Working independently with students

    ☐ Demonstrating a concept

    ☐ Introducing a new concept

    ☐ Reviewing for a test

    ☐ Coming to closure

    ☐ Other

Comments: Nancy:

    ♦ Students were working independently at their desks.

    ♦ The rearrangement of the room (desk, podium, table) allowed you to work independently with students on their essays and to keep an eye on students working at their desks.

Perhaps you should hold the next freshman level meeting in your room so others can see your room arrangement.

Thanks for letting me visit your room and see the work you do to help our students become better writers. I appreciate your efforts.

Martine Orozco

The strength of the checklist method is its ease of use; the principal takes in information and checks off what was observed or heard during the observation period. A weakness is that it is often difficult to reduce words or actions to a predetermined category on a checklist form. Moreover, checklist data—although easy to tally or to look for patterns of occurrence of events (e.g., how many times students raised their hands, the number of questions asked)—can limit room available for describing or giving specific detail about the events observed. The checklist has its place and enables the principal to be more efficient when making observations.

Mixed-Method Data Collection Techniques

Combining scripted (anecdotal) and checklist methods provide both qualitative and quantitative data about what was observed. Figure 5.7 (below and next page) offers a sample of how both open-ended (scripted) and narrow (checklist) data can be combined to chronicle the events of the classroom.

Figure 5.7. Anecdotal and Checklist
Data Collection Method

Teacher: Janie Adams   Date of Observation: November 14, 2006
Observer: Antonio Tanuta
Class: U.S. History Period of the Day: 2nd Period
Time of Observation: Start: 9:05 End: 9:25
Total Time Spent in Observation: 20 Minutes
Number of Students Present: 26 Grade Level: Juniors
Topic of the Lesson: Examining How a Bill is Passed
Date of Postobservation Conference: November 16, 2006

Focus on Cooperative Learning	Presence or Absence	Notes
Objectives for the cooperative learning group	X	♦ Objective for the activity was written on the whiteboard ♦ Teacher referred to the objective as students asked questions ♦ Teacher returned to the objective during closure of group activity
Clarity of directions	X	♦ Before breaking students into groups, teacher gave directions ♦ Teacher distributed directions for each group once students moved into their groups

Focus on Cooperative Learning	Presence or Absence	Notes
Movement into groups	X	◆ 6 minutes for students to move into groups ◆ Materials were bundled for each group in advance of movement
Monitoring and intervening strategies	X	◆ Teacher turned lights on and off to get attention ◆ Teacher broke into group time 3 times with clarifying directions ◆ Teacher visited each group 4 times
Evaluation Strategies		
Interaction with students	X	◆ Asked questions and gave feedback to groups while monitoring ◆ Clarified directions ◆ Became a member of each group
Follow-up instruction —large-group processing	X	◆ After 23 minutes, teacher called end to group work ◆ Students moved desks and chairs back in order ◆ Group reporter gave report ◆ Teacher asked and answered questions

Figure 5.8, on the next page, presents an open-ended form for collecting data in a foreign language classroom.

Figure 5.8. Foreign Language Observation Checklist[2]

Teacher: <u>Mary Smith</u>   Date of Observation: <u>November 14, 2006</u>
Observer: <u>Fred Jones</u>
Class: <u>French 2</u> Period of the Day: <u>4</u>
Time of Observation: Start <u>12:30</u> End: <u>12:50</u>
Total Time Spent in Observation: <u>20 Minutes</u>
Number of Students Present: <u>28</u> Grade Level: <u>9 & 10</u>
Topic of the Lesson: <u>French teenagers</u>
Date of Postobservation Conference: <u>November 16, 2006</u>

1. Are all language modalities evident in the lesson (speaking, writing, listening, and reading), as well as culture?
   - Students heard a passage read by the teacher, then spoke either with a partner, or in a group of three, to collectively summarize (in writing) the gist of the reading.
   - Because the passage was about French teens, culture was evident.

2. Does the teacher use a wide variety of prepared and authentic materials at appropriate levels?
   - The reading was taken from an authentic French source—a Parisian teen magazine.
   - Students were able to re-create the gist, so the level was apparently suitable for these learners.

3. Is the purpose of each activity clearly explained to the students?
   - The activity had already begun when I entered. However, students seemed to have a clear understanding of what they were doing.

4. Does the teacher model activities when giving directions and check for comprehension afterwards?
   - Mary gave directions before and after each of the two times she read the passage.
   - When students had finished rewriting the passage summaries, three groups shared their summaries aloud with the class, and class members commented on the accuracy of information, making suggestions to augment, improve, and/or clarify the content of each.
   - Mary validated the information given, praised the students for their good work, and made suggestions for improvement as well.

---

2 Developed by Marcia Wilbur, PhD, head, World Languages and Cultures Professional Development at The College Board, based on her work at Gull Lake High School Foreign Language Department, Richland, MI. Used with permission.

5. Are the transitions between activities smooth?
   - I only observed the passage summary activity.
   - The class was preparing to move to a new activity when I left the room.
   - The steps in the summary activity went smoothly from one to the next.
6. Are the students on-task and actively involved in the learning process?
   - Most students worked cooperatively with their partners.
   - I noticed that there were three groups of three. In two of the groups, one student appeared to be much less involved than the other two students in the grouping.
   - Because only one student was writing per group, I suggest breaking up the groups of three and sticking to pairs for this particular activity so that as many students as possible are actively engaged in the process.
7. Is there an appropriate use of partner-pair and/or small-group activities?
   - Yes, students worked in pairs (or groups of three as described above) with some brief moments of teacher-centered talk for the reading, directions, and feedback.

The Seating Chart

An efficient way to collect data is by use of the seating chart. Generic seating charts can be made in advance, or teachers can be asked to provide a general seating chart of their rooms at the beginning of the year. Several techniques for observing student and teacher behaviors make good use of the seating chart to collect data. Advantages for using the seating chart to chronicle data include

- *Ease of use:* A seating chart can be drawn within a half minute from entering the room.
- *Amount of data:* A large amount of information can be recorded on a single chart. (Consider breaking up the observation into five-minute increments—it is easy to get five minutes worth of data on a single seating chart.)
- *Focus on the events:* Important aspects of student behavior can be recorded while observing the teacher and the class as a whole.

A range of data can be chronicled on a seating chart, including teacher and student classroom traffic patterns (movement), teacher-calling patterns, teacher feedback patterns, and the use of praise. Likewise, data recorded on the seating chart can show a range of information, including what students are doing during instruction and classroom activities.

If using the seating chart, it makes sense to have 15 to 20 copies available. Figure 5.9 is a generic seating chart that will assist you in collecting data.

Figure 5.9. Seating Chart

Teacher:_____ Date of Observation: _____

Class: _____ Period of the Day:_____

Observer: _____

Time of Observation: Start: _____ End: _____

Total Time Spent in Observation: _____

Number of Students Present: _____ Grade Level:_____

Topic of the Lesson: _____

Date of Postobservation Conference: _____

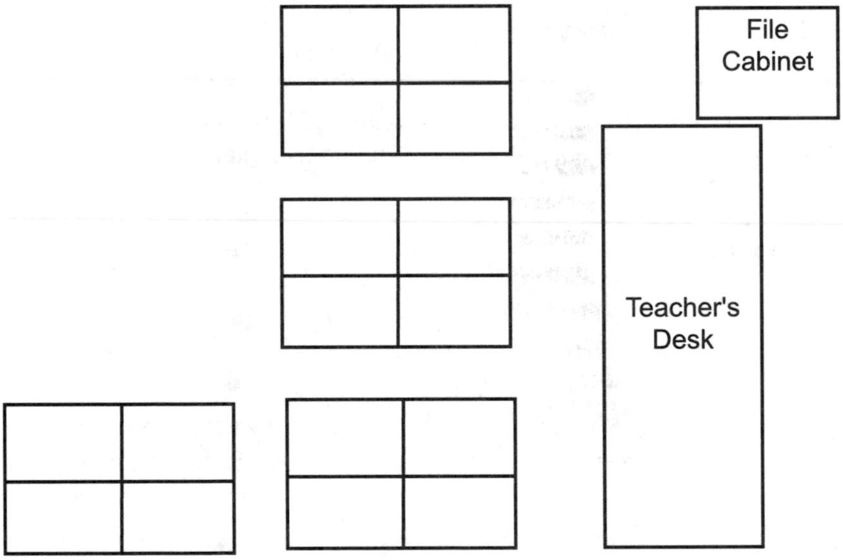

The following are three examples of data that can be recorded easily on a seating chart:

1. Student–teacher question patterns.

2. Reinforcement and feedback.

3. Classroom movement patterns

Using the seating chart to track question patterns can provide data as to whether the teacher focuses only on a few students on one side of the room, or track classroom movement patterns to determine whether the teacher lectures from the front of the room only, or the types and frequency of feedback and reinforcement given to students.

Use Technology to Assist with Tracking Classroom Observation Data

Advances in technology have provided new ways to collect data during classroom observations. Supervisors can enter data on a handheld device, import the data to a laptop, and print the data collected during a classroom observation. Follow-up notes can be communicated prior to the postobservation conference using e-mail.

With the prevalence of the laptop computer and built-in and external recording devices, supervisors can use the laptop to not only take notes during observations, but also to videotape teaching. When tools are combined with the features offered by computer database and spreadsheet applications, a rich rendition of teaching can be portrayed. Synchronous clinical observation tools offer the opportunity to capture the series of events that involve teachers and students. These events or "sets of communication" (Gagné, Briggs, & Wager, 1992) occur on the canvas of time. Supervisors can make observations much more valuable when observations are connected to accurate references of time. Computer time clocks have the ability to automate the collection of data by time and thereby improve observation precision and usability of data for review in the postobservation conference. Data can be collected synchronously through video with the events categorized by time using a database application and then using Filemaker Pro and Quicktime Pro to connect anecdotal, numerical, and video data to the internal clock of a laptop computer. Video is collected from an attached web camera that records into Quicktime Pro. Filemaker Pro generates timestamps for each observation entry (referred to as a record). Automating timing and video functions allows the supervisor to focus on those aspects of the classroom that are under investigation.

Anecdotal observation is a versatile technique that is made more powerful when it is connected with time-coding and video. The Synchronous Anecdotal Observation Instrument allows the supervisor to enter text about events related to the focus agreed on during the preobservation conference. This text can be analyzed based on connected computer and video timings (Figure 5.10 on the next page).

Figure 5.10 Synchronous Anecdotal Observation Instrument[3]

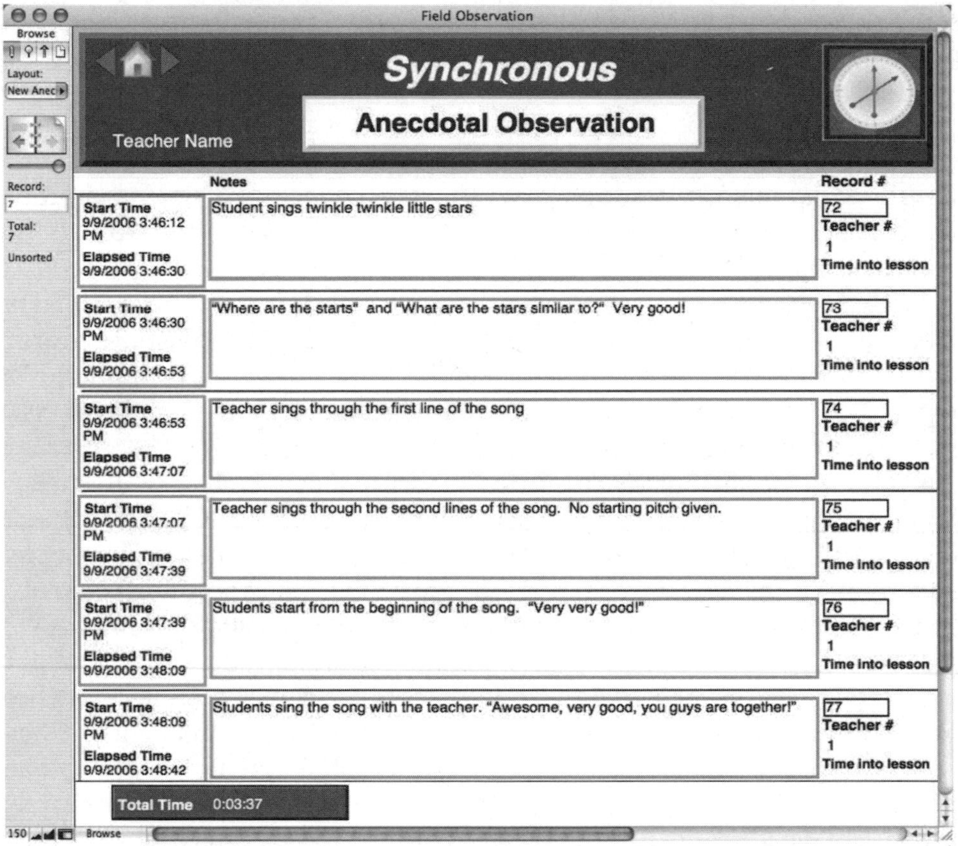

Revisiting the video allows the teacher and supervisor to replay specific events when more contextual data are desired. The Synchronous Anecdotal Observation Instrument can be used to analyze the rate/speed of teacher speech, question wait time, teacher movement, activity pacing, and comparisons of time spent in different types of teacher and student activities.

When numerical classroom data are paired with time codes, the frequencies of classroom events can be analyzed and later graphed by Microsoft Excel. Teachers frequently request an observation focus related to classroom management practices. Synchronous observation tools can collect data on the number of off-task students at any point in a timed manner. If measurements of off-task behavior are made frequently (at a recommended rate of 1 obser-

---

3 Developed by Kevin Johnson, University of Georgia. Used with permission.

vation per 20 seconds), the supervisor can generate a descriptive report of off-task behavior.

For example, a supervisor and a first-year choral teacher could use the synchronous off-task tool to identify problems and strengths in classroom management. The supervisor would first need to determine the definition of off-task behaviors and plan for the classroom observation. Using a laptop computer, the supervisor records activity descriptions, counts of off-task students, and lets the computer provide time-stamp codes.

The supervisor could present the collected data using a table, line chart as illustrated in Figure 5.11.

Figure 5.11. Analysis of Calculated Percent of Students On-Task[4]

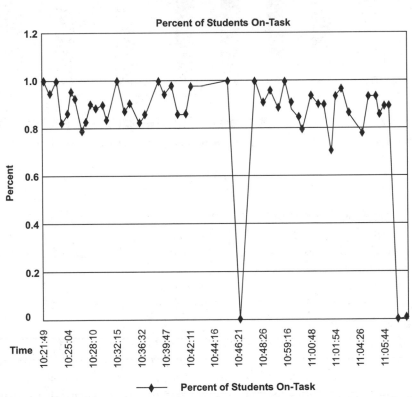

Data could also be presented using a histogram (Figure 5.12 on next page).

---

4   Developed by Kevin Johnson, University of Georgia. Used with permission.

Figure 5.12. Portrayal of Computer-Generated Data Using a Histogram[5]

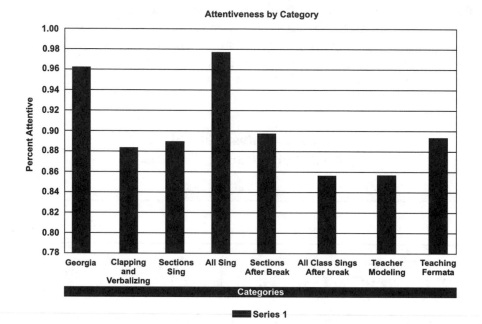

The supervisor would be able to present an overview of the timings, descriptions, numbers of off-task students, and percentage of on-task students. The line chart could identify trends of off-task behavior over time. To identify the relationship between off-task behaviors and groups of time (classroom activities), the supervisor could calculate averages of off-task behavior for each activity. A histogram could then be constructed using Microsoft Excel to illustrate differences in student activities.

During the postobservation conference, the teacher and supervisor could use the histogram chart (Figure 5.12) to generate discussion about student off-task behavior. The teacher would be able to identify that students were most on-task when they were singing in the classroom, and least engaged when the teacher was modeling a vocal technique.

Future advances in technology will help supervisors to capture the events of the classroom more reliably. However, there are a few caveats to consider when using technology to capture the events of the classroom. First,

---

5 Developed by Kevin Johnson, University of Georgia. Used with permission.

the availability of technology might be limited, and the supervisor might need to find funding sources to purchase a laptop, video camera, and other software applications. Second, at first, teachers might not want to be videotaped, so it is best to ask before taping. There also might be union consider ations to consider. In some systems, classroom observers can only observe without taking notes. Third, some systems strictly forbid students from being videotaped without written permission of parents. Fourth, supervisors would need to be trained in the uses of technology and have the opportunity to practice the skills needed to use technology to support classroom observations.

Extended Reflection

There are many advantages to using technology to assist supervisors to capture reliable data when observing teachers. However, there might be concerns about the use of technology, such as videotaping a teacher. Identify the pros and cons about the use of technology to record the events in a classroom. After identifying the pros and cons surrounding the use of technology and classroom observations, develop a position statement related to this topic.

♦ *Activity 1:* In a small group, exchange ideas and report to the large group your ideas and position statements.

♦ *Activity 2:* In a small group, develop a plan for implementing the use of technology to collect stable data. What resources are needed to implement such a plan?

Whichever method of data collection is chosen, it is a good idea to detail major events such as teacher questions and student responses. A few strong examples with complete and accurate information will make more sense for both the teacher and the supervisor than will a long record of unfiltered information.

Tips from the Field

After the preobservation conference, the supervisor should take time to plan for the observation and then the postobservation conference. Each extended classroom observation offers a valuable opportunity; effective supervisors learn to make the most of it. At this point, attention to details will pave the way. The tips listed in Figure 5.13, on the next page, can assist the supervisor before, during, and after the classroom observation.

Figure 5.13. Tips from the Field

Before the observation

Make 15 to 20 copies of the seating chart. Several techniques for observing student and teacher behaviors make use of the seating chart.

Advantages:

♦ A lot of information fits on a single chart.

♦ The supervisor can record individual student behavior while observing the teacher and the class as a whole.

♦ To track the observation in five-minute increments, turn to a new chart every five minutes. (It is easy to get five minutes' worth of data on a single seating chart.)

Examples of data that can be recorded easily on a seating chart:

♦ Student/teacher question patterns

♦ Reinforcement and feedback

♦ Classroom movement

During the observation

• Start small—focus on observing one or two items, and take notes that relate directly to the focus identified during the preobservation conference.

• Arrange to arrive a few minutes before class begins to have materials ready (laptop plugged in, video recorder set up).

After the observation

• Set aside time immediately afterwards to organize notes and thoughts.

• Send a note to thank the teacher for sharing the classroom experience.

• Secure resource materials (if applicable) related to the focus. Materials could include professional journal articles, videos, or professional development descriptions.

Overview and Application of Observation Tools and Methods

A tool is useful only if the worker knows how to use it. Mastery comes with practice over time. This section details 13 tools that can help supervisors, peer coaches, and teachers as they track data from classroom observations. To illustrate their application, the description includes

♦ Background;

♦ The context of the classroom observation introducing the teacher;

♦ An observation focus;

♦ The appropriate tool for the observation;

♦ Directions and approaches for using the tool;

♦ Data collected from the observation;

♦ Suggested postobservation strategies and a discussion of the strategies; and

♦ Where appropriate, alternate data collection techniques to extend data collection.

These tools and methods offer a point of departure; feel free to revise these forms or develop your own to reflect the context of your classroom observations. In short, exercise your imagination to expand your toolbox.

Tool 1: Observation Guide Using Bloom's Taxonomy

Background

Teachers spend much time talking with students—lecturing, giving directions, and asking and answering questions. To ensure understanding and application of knowledge, teachers commonly engage students in question-and-answer sessions (also referred to as Q & A). Questions can prompt responses ranging from simple recall of information to abstract processes of applying, synthesizing, and evaluating information. Bloom (1956) and his colleagues developed a continuum for categorizing questions and responses. Bloom's Taxonomy from lowest to highest order includes

◆ *Knowledge:* recalling specific facts

◆ *Comprehension:* describing in one's own words

- *Application:* applying information to produce some result
- *Analysis:* subdividing something to show how it is put together
- *Synthesis:* creating a unique, original product
- *Evaluation:* making value decisions about issues

Bloom's Taxonomy frames the analysis of both written and oral questions. Figure 5.14, on the next page, provides an overview of Bloom's Taxonomy of questioning. Note that the continuum represents lower-order to higher-order thinking.

Figure 5.14. Bloom's Taxonomy

Bloom's Taxonomy and Definition	Sample Verb Stems	Students' Responses Indicate Skills Such As
Lowest Order *Knowledge/Recall:* Students are asked to remember information.	Summarize, describe, interpret	◆ Remembering. ◆ Memorizing. ◆ Recognizing. ◆ Identifying. ◆ Recalling.
Comprehension: Students demonstrate that they have sufficient understanding to organize and arrange material.	Classify, discuss, explain, identify, indicate, locate, report, restate, review, translate	◆ Interpreting. ◆ Translating from one medium to another. ◆ Describing in one's own words. ◆ Organizing and selecting facts and ideas.
Application: Students apply previously learned information to reach an answer to a different but similar problem.	Apply, choose, demonstrate, dramatize, employ, illustrate, interpret, operate, practice, schedule, sketch, solve	◆ Solving problems. ◆ Applying information to produce an end product.
Analysis: Students critically examine events and perform certain operations such as separating whole to part or part to whole.	Analyze, calculate, categorize, compare, contrast, criticize, differentiate, discriminate, examine, question	◆ Subdividing. ◆ Finding, identifying, and separating a whole into parts.
Synthesis: Students produce an original work, make predictions, and/or solve problems.	Arrange, create, assemble, compose, construct, design, develop, formulate, manage, organize, plan, prepare, propose	◆ Creating an original product.
Highest Order *Evaluation:* Students answer a question that does not have an absolute answer; provide an educated guess about the solution to a problem; or render a judgment or opinion with backup support.	Appraise, argue, assess, attach, defend, judge, rate, support, value, evaluate	◆ Making a decision. ◆ Prioritizing information. ◆ Drawing a conclusion.

Applying the Tool in Practice

The Context of the Classroom Observation Ms. Anita Rodriguez, a third-grade teacher, is seeking feedback on the types of questions she asks while teaching fractions and decimals. Although Anita is a veteran teacher (15 years at the same school), until this year she taught first grade. During the preobservation conference, Anita expressed concern that her questions might be too "elementary."

Observation Focus Anita Rodriguez and her supervisor, principal Donald Taylor, agree that the classroom observation focus will center on the level of thinking skills elicited by the questions that Ms. Rodriguez asks of her students.

Observation Tool Mr. Taylor explains to Ms. Rodriguez that he will use a data collection method called *Selective Verbatim*. Using the form (Figure 5.15 on the next page), he will record only the questions Ms. Rodriguez asks.

Directions and Approaches for Using the Tool Write the sentence in the left-hand column. Put a check in the box that best describes the cognitive level of the question. (This may be part of the postobservation conference.)

Figure 5.15. Bloom's Taxonomy—Levels of Questions

Teacher: <u>Anita Rodriguez</u>   Date of Observation: <u>September 18, 2006</u>
Observer: <u>Donald Taylor</u>
Class: <u>4th Grade</u>   Period of the Day: <u>Morning Block</u>
Time of Observation: Start: <u>10:10</u>   End: <u>10:30</u>
Total Time Spent in Observation: <u>20 Minutes</u>
Number of Students Present: <u>17</u>   Grade Level: <u>4th Grade</u>
Topic of the Lesson: <u>Decimals</u>
Date of Postobservation Conference: <u>September 19, 2006</u>

		Levels of Thinking					
Time	Questions, Activities	Knowledge	Comprehension	Application	Analysis	Synthesis	Evaluation
10:10	How many have heard the word decimal?	√					
	What do you think decimals mean?	√					
	How do you know?	√					
	Have you ever seen a decimal?	√					
	What do you think that means?	√					
	Why the decimal? Why that period?	√					
10:15	Decimal points do what?	√					
	What makes the cents, not the dollar?	√					
	Why is 99 not a dollar?		√				
10:25	How would you write $200?	√					
	What does 00 mean?	√					
	Is that where Desmond saw a decimal point?	√					
	What instrument...temperature?	√					
	How many kinds of therm? Name 2.	√					
10:30	What is she looking for?	√					
	What is a normal temperature?	√					
	Have you seen your temperature written?	√					
	Why do you think you need to use a decimal point?		√				

Suggested Postobservation Conference Strategies   To promote engagement in the postobservation conference, Mr. Taylor brought the form to the conference with only the verbatim questions listed. Mr. Taylor encouraged Ms. Rodriguez to

- Identify the level of thinking for each question noted and then to place a check mark in the grid (e.g., knowledge, comprehension, application, synthesis, evaluation);
- Tally the number of questions at each level; and
- Rework a few of the lower-order questions into higher-order questions.

Throughout the last step, Mr. Taylor asked probing questions: "What did you eventually want students to be able to do with the information being taught?" "How did the examples presented along with the questions help students understand the materials?" "Are there any clusters of questions that could have been extended beyond the knowledge level?"

Mr. Taylor relied on the data to lead the discussion. He let Ms. Rodriguez analyze the data, reflect on what the data meant for student learning, and rework questions that she had asked. Viewed within the framework of Bloom's Taxonomy, these questions enabled Ms. Rodriguez to reconstruct her instruction in terms of her focus—levels of questions.

During the last 20 minutes of the postobservation conference, Mr. Taylor and Ms. Rodriguez targeted a few strategies to try before the next classroom observation. Of the ideas discussed, Ms. Rodriguez chose the following two:

1. Have a colleague videotape a lesson that includes a question-and-answer segment. Watching the video, record the questions she asked. Analyze the cognitive level of student responses and identify any patterns in what she asked of her students.

2. Use a professional release day to observe a teaching colleague at another school in the district.

Tips

- During the observation, write the question and then in the postobservation conference have the teacher identify the level of thinking for each question noted.
- An alternate strategy is to ask the teacher to rework a lower-order question into a higher-order question. Go back and forth.

Alternate Approach to Using This Tool

Another way to portray data using a more wide-angle lens related to teacher questions and the level of questions is presented in Figure 5.16.

Figure 5.16. Bloom's Taxonomy Levels

Teacher: <u>Anita Rodriguez</u>   Date of Observation: <u>September 18, 2006</u>
Observer: <u>Donald Taylor</u>
Class: <u>4th Grade</u>   Period of the Day: <u>Morning Block</u>
Time of Observation: Start: <u>10:10</u>   End: <u>10:30</u>
Total Time Spent in Observation: <u>20 Minutes</u>
Number of Students Present: <u>17</u>   Grade Level: <u>4th Grade</u>
Topic of the Lesson: <u>Decimals</u>
Date of Postobservation Conference: <u>September 19, 2006</u>

Time	Teacher Questions	Taxonomy Level
8:10	How many have heard the word decimal?	
	What do you think decimals mean?	
	How do you know?	
	Have you ever seen a decimal?	
	What do you think that means?	
	Why the decimal? Why that period?	
10:15	Decimal points do what?	
	What makes the cents, not the dollar?	
	Why is 99 not a dollar?	
10:25	How would you write $200?	
	What does 00 mean?	
	Is that where Desmond saw a decimal point?	
	What instrument...temperature?	
	How many kinds of therm? Name 2.	
10:30	What is she looking for?	
	What is a normal temperature?	
	Have you seen your temperature written?	
	Why do you think you need to use a decimal point?	

Tool 2: Focus on Wait Time

Background

This data collection tool helps teachers examine how long they wait before calling on students to answer their questions. A staple in teaching is the lecture and discussion in which student response carries the rate and pace of the experience. Teachers, noticing cues from students, make adjustments in the pace and pitch of the classroom discussion. At the heart of lecture, discussion, and group processing of knowledge, is the asking of questions. How the teacher responds to questions is important for two reasons: the quality of response is related to wait time and the quality of the answer is related to wait time. Stahl (1994) related that when students are given three seconds or more of undisturbed "wait-time," there are certain positive outcomes, such as the following:

- The length and correctness of their responses increase.
- The number of their "I don't know" and no answer responses decreases.
- The number of volunteered, appropriate answers by larger numbers of students greatly increases.
- The scores of students on academic achievement tests tend to increase.
- When teachers wait patiently in silence for three seconds or more at appropriate places, positive changes in their own teacher behaviors also occur.
- Teachers' questioning strategies tend to be more varied and flexible.
- Teachers decrease the quantity and increase the quality and variety of their questions.
- Teachers ask additional questions that require more complex information processing and higher-level thinking on the part of students. (pp. 3–5)

From the research of Stahl and others (e.g., Rowe, 1986), wait time is think time, and three seconds is reported as the ideal amount of time to wait for a student response.

Applying the Tool in Practice

The Context of the Classroom Observation Mr. Haidong Chen, a ninth-grade English teacher, is seeking feedback on his use of wait time. During the preobservation conference, Mr. Chen told his assistant principal, Ms.

Francesca Duncan, that he feels his students are "just not with him" following the flow of book discussions.

Observation Focus   Mr. Chen and Ms. Duncan agree that the classroom observation will focus on wait time.

Observation Tool Ms. Duncan explains to Mr. Chen that she will use a narrow-lens tool (Figure 5.17) to observe how long Mr. Chen waits after asking a question before he calls on a student for a response. This tool can assist the teacher to focus on the amount of wait time between the question and the response while also examining the complexity of questions. This type of data can help the teacher and observer examine student engagement, understanding of concepts, and the pace of questions asked.

Directions and Approaches for Using the Tool   Write just the stem of each question the teacher asks. Using a watch with a second hand, measure the elapsed time from the end of the question to the call for a response. Once the teacher completes articulating the question, track the wait time afforded before calling on a student to answer the question.

Figure 5.17. Wait Time

Teacher: _Haidong Chen_   Date of Observation: <u>April 18, 2006</u>
Observer: <u>Francesca Duncan</u>
Class: <u>English I</u> Period of the Day: <u>Period 1</u>
Time of Observation: Start: <u>8:05</u> End: <u>8:20</u>
Total Time Spent in Observation: <u>15 Minutes</u>
Number of Students Present: <u>24</u>   Grade Level: <u>Grade 9</u>
Topic of the Lesson: <u>S. E. Hinton's *Rumble Fish*</u>
Date of Postobservation Conference: <u>April 19, 2006</u>

Teacher Question	Wait Time (in seconds)
… in what year?…James?	2
When you think of the lessons the characters learned by the end of the book, who do you think grew up the most?	3
How does the Siamese Fighting Fish come to be symbolic of the characters in this book?	5
Leslie, are there any other symbols?	4
Do these other symbols relate to the importance of the Siamese Fighting Fish?	2
Why do you suppose S. E. Hinton chose Siamese Fighting Fish rather than another type of domestic fish?	6

Tip

♦ Have the teacher examine the types of questions and examine the amount of wait time afforded to students to answer the questions.

Alternate Application of This Tool

Another way to track wait time is to landscape data by also including the taxonomy level of the questions related to wait time (Figure 5.18). This type of data can enhance analysis and reflection by examining both the type of questions (using Bloom's Taxonomy) and the amount of wait time.

Figure 5.18. Wait Time and Question Taxonomy Level

Teacher: _Haidong Chen_   Date of Observation: _April 18, 2006_
Observer: _Francesca Duncan_
Class: _English I_ Period of the Day: _Period 1_
Time of Observation: Start: _8:05_ End: _8:20_
Total Time Spent in Observation: _15 Minutes_
Number of Students Present: _24_   Grade Level: _Grade 9_
Topic of the Lesson: _S. E. Hinton's Rumble Fish_
Date of Postobservation Conference: _April 19, 2006_

Teacher Question	Wait Time (in seconds)	Question Domain
...in what year?...James?	2	Knowledge
When you think of the lessons the characters learned by the end of the book, who do you think grew up the most?	3	Synthesis, Evaluation
How does the Siamese Fighting Fish come to be symbolic of the characters in this book?	5	Evaluation
Is there any deeper meaning to letting the fish out of their tanks at the end of the story?	3	Evaluation

Tips

♦ Suggest the teacher analyze wait time in terms of the type of question asked.

♦ Leave the Question Domain column blank and let the teacher fill in the level of taxonomy.

- If there is an overreliance on lower-level domains, role play with the teacher, rephrasing the questions and moving toward higher-order domains.

Suggested Postobservation Conference Strategies   Ms. Duncan prepared for the postobservation conference by thinking about the wait time in relation to the type of questions Mr. Chen asked. During the postobservation conference, Ms. Duncan

- Invited Mr. Chen to review his questions and the amount of wait time he allowed.

- Suggested that Mr. Chen analyze wait time in terms of the type of question asked, using Bloom's Taxonomy. (Ms. Duncan had added an extra column to the observation form.)

- Encouraged Mr. Chen to determine if there were any other patterns to questions—more or less wait time during question groupings (e.g., Evaluation vs. Knowledge).

Tool 3: Focus on Cause-and-Effect Data

Background

This tool gives the teacher information about the influence of the teacher's actions on student responses. This tool can be useful in observing a teacher's classroom management, questioning strategies, direction giving, and other teacher behaviors that ask for a student response.

Applying the Tool in Practice

The Context of the Classroom Observation   James Ackman, second-year accounting teacher at Altoon High School, is curious about why he often feels his students are "not following the program" during class periods, especially when he is trying to get students working on software applications at the computer stations. James shares with the Business Department chair, Dr. Juanita Powell, that at times he feels as if he is losing control of the learning environment.

Observation Focus   James Ackman and Dr. Juanita Powell agree that the classroom observation lens should be a narrow one. They decide on an interrelated focus: what James says or does and what students do in response.

Observation Tool   Dr. Powell explains that she will use a narrow lens to focus on what James says and does and its effect on what students say and do.

Directions and Approaches for Using the Tool   Divide a blank sheet of paper into two columns. Record teacher actions or words in the left-hand column. Record student response to these actions or words in the right-hand column (Figure 5.19).

Figure 5.19. Cause-and-Effect

Teacher: <u>James Ackman</u>   Date of Observation: <u>November 7, 2006</u>
Observer: <u>Juanita Powell</u>
Class: <u>Accounting I</u> Period of the Day: <u>6th Period</u>
Time of Observation: Start: <u>1:15</u> End: <u>1:40</u>
Total Time Spent in Observation: <u>30 Minutes</u>
Number of Students Present: <u>26</u> Grade Level: <u>Mixed (Juniors & Seniors)</u>
Topic of the Lesson: <u>Using Accounting Software</u>
Date of Postobservation Conference: <u>November 8, 2006</u>

Teacher	Student Response and/or Activity
Bell (1:15)	Milling around room
Takes roll Makes announcements Collects homework	Quietly talking
Turns on overhead and says: "Take out your notebooks and open your book to page 140; we'll go to the computer stations in a minute."	Students pull out materials. Red shirt slapping boy next to him (Blue shirt)
1:18 "Folks, heads up to the overhead and focus on the chapter objectives." "Go to the computer stations" and "wait for the software application to pop on the screen." Begins stating the objectives for the chapter. Walks back to his desk and reminds students to "hurry and quietly." Reminds students to review the learning objectives as they are moving to the back of the room.	Shuffling to get their books out and open to page 140. Start to move to the computer stations; Rick trips a student who yells, "Hey…" Seven students do not have books.
1:25: "Read from pages 140 to 145." Teacher sitting at desk getting software to boot up for a demonstration	Students without books: 2 are talking with each other 2 are sleeping 3 are reading from nearby student's books

1:31: "Who would like to offer a summary while I see what the problem is with the server?" Asks Steve to give the summary.	4 students are still reading; 3 students (who did not have book) are talking with their neighbors; 4 students raise their hands.
In a loud and booming voice, "Stop the talking, now."	There is quiet and students focus attention to the front of the room.
1:33: "OK, the program should be loaded." Click on the program and start entering data into the spreadsheet following the numbers in your book, page 140."	Students quickly start entering data; 2 students raise their hands.
1:34: "There appears to be an error in the text, enter the number 56 in the third row, second cell."	
1:35: Teacher moving from computer station to computer station, answering questions and checking work.	Rick smacks Tony and Tony pushes Rick out of his seat.
1:37: Walks over to Rick and Tony "follow me"	Students jeering—Mary (next to Rick walks to the front of the room
Pushes the call button and tells students to get back to their work—"calm down, get back to your work...fighting will not be tolerated—period"	Students quiet down and return to their work entering data.

Tip

+ Focus on concrete actions, directions, or words of the teacher and the effect these have on student response or behavior.

Suggested Postobservation Conference Strategies Leaving the room, Dr. Powell passes the assistant principal who is responding to the call for assistance. Dr. Powell is tempted to report to the assistant principal what she just observed, but she decides to wait until after the postobservation conference with James. Dr. Powell decides to

+ Ask James how he thought the lesson went.
+ Ask James about his classroom procedures: What procedures and consequences are in place for students who do not come to class with their books? Does he have any extra books he can lend? What is his first line of defense when a student is off-task?
+ Encourage James to revisit his classroom procedures.

- Arrange for a follow-up observation during the same class period in two weeks.
- Encourage James to consult the assistant principal about how to handle situations that escalate beyond what the teacher should deal with during a class period.

A Case Study

The assistant principal, Joel Moody, asks Dr. Juanita Powell to write a detailed account of what occurred in Mr. Ackman's classroom. Moody then asks for detailed summaries of all classroom observations of Mr. Ackman.

- What issues are at stake here?

- How should Dr. Powell proceed with the request and her work with Mr. Ackman?

Tool 4: Focus on Variety of Instructional Methods

Background

Regardless of subject area, grade level, or the teacher's experience, a single class period should include a variety of instructional methods. Research has cast new light about the way children learn, and no longer can we assume that any one instructional strategy reaches all learners all of the time. Effective teachers not only use a variety of instructional strategies, they also differentiate strategies. To differentiate, teachers provide alternate approaches to the methods used to present content and the ways in which students show mastery of learning objectives. Given the myriad ability levels of students and the recognition that no two learners learn at the same rate or way, differentiated instruction shows great promise as a way of thinking about teaching and learning. In a classroom where instruction is differentiated, students are offered a variety of ways to learn. According to Tomlinson (1999), differentiated instruction flourishes when

- Teachers begin where the students are.
- Teachers engage students in instruction through different learning modalities.
- A student competes more against himself or herself than others.
- Teachers provide specific ways for each individual to learn.
- Teachers use classroom time flexibly.

- Teachers are diagnosticians, prescribing the best possible instruction for each student. (p. 2)

The attention span of the average seventh-grade student is estimated to be approximately 10 minutes; that of a ninth-grade student, 12 minutes. Supervisors are encouraged to read books that detail the developmental levels of the students served at their site.

Applying the Tool in Practice

The Context of the Classroom Observation Karla Jones and her ninth-grade students are in the middle of a unit on World War II in her World History class. Mrs. Jones wants feedback on the variety of instructional strategies she uses during a class period. Karla also shares that she often loses track of time when dealing with discipline issues.

Observation Focus Mrs. Jones and her supervisor, principal Rita McCan, agree that the essential first step is to get baseline data on what instructional strategies Mrs. Jones uses during a typical class period. They further agree that other information could be useful: the length of each strategy, student engagement, and transitions from one activity to another. Recognizing that Mrs. Jones has 10 years of experience teaching at this level, Mrs. McCan believes that Mrs. Jones is capable of handling a variety of information; however, they both ask, "How much is too much?"

Observation Tool Mrs. McCan explains to Mrs. Jones that she will use a narrow-lens tool to focus on the number of instructional strategies used, the length of each, and the activities students engage in during each. (Note that an observer can collect a great deal of data even through a narrow lens.)

Directions and Approaches for Using the Tool For each instructional strategy used, indicate the time and what the teacher and the students are doing (Figure 5.20 on the next page).

Figure 5.20. Variety of Instructional Methods

Teacher: <u>Karla Jones</u>   Date of Observation: <u>October 10, 2006</u>
Observer: <u>Rita McCan</u>
Class: <u>World History</u>   Period of the Day: <u>Second Block</u>
Time of Observation: Start: <u>1:30</u> End: <u>2:30</u>
Total Time Spent in Observation: <u>60 Minutes</u>
Number of Students Present: <u>19</u>   Grade Level: <u>9th Grade</u>
Topic of the Lesson: <u>Word War II—Causes, Events, and Outcomes</u>
Date of Postobservation Conference: <u>October 11, 2006 (before school)</u>

Time	Instructional Method	Teacher Behavior	Student Activities
1:30–1:42	☐ Video on Patton	☐ Monitoring the students	☐ Watching video
1:42–1:55	☐ Lecture about one aspect of the video	☐ Drew map on overhead	☐ Listening and asking questions ☐ Two students working on research papers at computers
1:56	☐ Video continues	☐ Teacher monitors	☐ Students watch video
2:05–2:12	☐ Video is paused and "Battle of the Bulge" is discussed	☐ Shows map of Europe and gives history	☐ Students listen and ask questions
2:13–2:17	☐ Video resumes	☐ Monitoring the students	☐ Watching video
2:18–2:25	☐ Questioning	☐ Asks review questions	☐ Students answer and give comments ☐ Three students in the back row have their heads down during the movie while teacher is leading the question-and-answer session. ☐ Max and Sheila are exchanging notes.

2:25–2:30	☐ Guided reading activity	☐ Hands out guided reading papers and gives directions ☐ Helps individuals	☐ Listen to directions and do guided reading. They use textbooks to follow along and answer the guided reading prompts.

Suggested Postobservation Conference Strategies   Later the same day, Mrs. McCan visited Mrs. Jones for a few minutes and asked her to review the completed instrument so she could analyze the data on her own. The next day, Mrs. McCan and Mrs. Jones met before school to discuss the classroom observation. Mrs. McCan began the conversation with the question, "What patterns do you see?" During the postobservation conference, Mrs. Jones reviewed the various instructional strategies used, the amount of time spent on each, what students were doing during each, and what learning objectives were being met. Upon reflection, Mrs. Jones decided that she would experiment in the future by not breaking into the video so much, and that she would not start her students with a guided reading with only five minutes left until the bell (2:30).

Tool 5: Examining Teacher–Student Discussion with a Focus on How Student Comments are Incorporated into the Lesson

Background

Instruction of any kind can improve when the teacher incorporates student responses into the lesson. Incorporating student responses as part of a lecture increases student engagement, promotes student ownership in the activities of the class, and keeps students focused on learning objectives. Student responses also cue the teacher to what students know and what areas need to be retaught. Nothing keeps a class moving forward more than a lively discussion in which student responses are incorporated into the lesson. Teachers who incorporate student responses into lessons extend learning and are able to check more readily for understanding. Student responses also serve to assess student learning, giving cues to the connections students are making with content, their ability to apply what they are learning, and what areas need to be reinforced or retaught. When a teacher incorporates student comments, such behavior signals a student-centered classroom in which student questions often serve to extend concepts that are being studied.

Applying the Tool in Practice

The Context of the Classroom Observation   Max Johnson, an English teacher, and his peer coach, Julie Thompson, have undertaken an action research project to examine what they do with student responses during classroom discussions.

Observation Focus   Max and Julie agree that the classroom observation will focus on what Max does to incorporate student responses in his classroom discussions. This technique can also help a teacher gain insight about mastery of prior materials taught.

Observation Tool Julie will use a sheet of paper with three columns to record the time of the comment, the student's comments, and what Max does with student comments (Figure 5.21, next page).

Directions and Approaches for Using the Tool   Notate what the teacher says (focusing on questions), the student response to the question, and then what the teacher does with the student response.

Figure 5.21. Incorporating Student Comments and Ideas into Discussion

Teacher: <u>Max Johnson</u> Date of Observation: <u>September 26, 2006</u>
Observer: <u>Julie Thompson</u>
Class: <u>English 1</u>Period of the Day: <u>Second Period</u>
Time of Observation: Start: <u>8:50</u> End: <u>9:30</u>
Total Time Spent in Observation: <u>50 Minutes</u>
Number of Students Present: <u>23</u>   Grade Level: <u>9</u>
Topic of the Lesson: <u>Rumble Fish</u>
Date of Postobservation Conference: <u>September 28, 2006 (release period)</u>

Time Teacher Question/Comment	Student Comment	What the Teacher Does with the Student Comments
8:55	SR1: Siamese rumble fish	Can you expand on this? (Max asks)
8:56	SR2: The gangs are made up of people who can't get along with one another.	Cite an example of this from the text?
9:01		Relate this to the end of the book.
9:06	SR3: See page 47.	Does this parallel the death of the character?
9:10	SR4: At the end, the Siamese fighting fish are let go.	

Suggested Postobservation Conference Strategies   Have the teacher track the type of responses students give and what the teacher does to incorporate student responses into the discussion. Track what strategies the teacher uses while incorporating comments. Questions to ask of the teacher include the following:

- Have students expanded on each other's ideas?
- Did students look up information in the book to support answers?
- Did students write their ideas in notebooks?

Tool 6: Selective Verbatim—Teacher Verbal and Student Physical or Verbal Behaviors

Background

This tool selectively records the exact words of the teacher, the students, or both. This tool can provide useful information about how the teacher asks questions, gives directions, praises or corrects students, and the like.

Applying the Tool in Practice

The Context of the Classroom Observation Sam Jilnick, a middle school English teacher, is having difficulties with his sixth-grade group of "slow" students. He believes that he is constantly issuing verbal corrections. Sam asks the lead teacher, Marty Burton, to observe him working with this group of students and to track the types and frequency of his verbal corrections.

Observation Focus Marty Burton will use the narrow tool of selective verbatim to capture the verbal corrections that Sam makes to his students and then record the students' reactions to the corrective statements.

Observation Tool A sheet of paper with two columns, headed *Teacher Verbal* and *Student Physical or Verbal Response*.

Directions and Approaches for Using the Tool Record the teacher's words in the left-hand column and student responses (verbal or physical) to these words in the right-hand column (Figure 5.22, next page).

Figure 5.22. Selective Verbatim— Verbal and Physical Response

Teacher: <u>Sam Jilnick</u>   Date of Observation: <u>December 12, 2006</u>
Observer: <u>Marty Burton</u>
Class: <u>English</u>   Period of the Day: <u>7th Period</u>
Time of Observation: Start: <u>2:15</u> End: <u>2:45</u>
Total Time Spent in Observation: <u>30 Minutes</u>
Number of Students Present: <u>21</u>   Grade Level: <u>Grade 6</u>
Topic of the Lesson: <u>Verbs</u>
Date of Postobservation Conference: <u>December 14, 2006 (prep period)</u>

	Teacher Verbal	and	Student Physical or Verbal Response
1	Look at the Word of the Day (breed) on the board and write a sentence using the word.	1	Just one sentence or two?
2	One sentence, like we do every day.	2	We didn't do a word yesterday.
3	OK, then like the one we did a few days ago.	3	
4	Tom, read your sentence.	4	I'm not done...I came in late.
5	Randy, let's hear your sentence.	5	My pen is out of ink...I can say the sentence I would have written.
6	Randy, this is the third time this week you have not come to class prepared to work.	6	Yeah, yeah, yeah. I only have pencils.
7	That's right...you can only use a pen to write class notes.	7	I don't like pens...you can't erase the marks.
8	Pens are what you must use....What don't you understand about this?	8	Why can't I use a pencil?...Mrs. Scott lets us use pencils....So do all my teachers, but you.
9	That's right, young man, stand out in the hall for the next 15 minutes. Go to the office...now.	9	Jerk...

(Figure continues on next page.)

10	Pull out your books and let's start looking at "ing" words on page 103.	10	Students pull out books…
11	Writes the following sentence on the board: The man walking his dog was struggling to control his pet. Directs students to write the sentence in their notebooks. Reminds Fred to bring a pen to class.	11	Students start writing the sentence in notebook; Fred asks Shirley for a pen.

Suggested Postobservation Conference Strategies Marty Burton leaves the classroom very concerned about the combative verbal exchanges she has just heard. She knows that the intensity of the encounter left the student and Sam at an impasse. As the lead teacher, Marty takes responsibility for providing teachers the support they need. During the postobservation conference, Marty

- Asks Sam Jilnick to pinpoint where this confrontation really started.

- Does a role-playing exercise. She plays Sam, and Sam plays the student. As Sam, she gives the student a pen and says, "I'll come back to you in a few minutes," then asks another student to share his work.

- Asks Sam to discuss how he can defuse negative verbal exchanges.

- Asks Sam what consequences he has used with this student in the past, what kind of relationship he has with this student, and whether he has spoken with the parents, guidance counselor, or other teachers about the student.

- Suggests that Sam read some materials she will provide on more proactive ways of dealing with student outbursts.

Tool 7: Wide Angle: No Focus

Background

Some teachers might want to get a general idea of how things are going in the classroom; others might not be able to decide on a focus. The wide-angle lens enables the supervisor to report generally what is occurring in the classroom.

Applying the Tool in Practice

The Context of the Classroom Observation Bob Cooper, in his seventh year of teaching second grade at St. Anthony's Elementary School, is curious about his third-period block. Bob is experimenting with incorporating games into his lesson design, and he wants some feedback, in a general sense, on how things are going. Sandy Adams, the principal, will observe his classroom while Bob incorporates games within the lesson.

Observation Focus   None.

Observation Tool Running notes with a time line of activities.

Directions and Approaches for Using the Tool   Write out events of the classroom as they occur (Figure 5.23 on the next page).

Figure 5.23. Wide-Angle Observation Tool— Running Notes with a Time Line

Teacher: <u>Bob Cooper</u>   Date of Observation: <u>January 9, 2007</u>
Observer: <u>Sandy Adams</u>
Class: <u>2nd Grade</u>   Period of the Day: <u>Mid-morning</u>
Time of Observation: Start: <u>10:00</u>   End: <u>11:00</u>
Total Time Spent in Observation: <u>60 Minutes</u>
Number of Students Present: <u>16</u> Grade Level: <u>Grade 2</u>
Topic of the Lesson: <u>Fractions</u>
Date of Postobservation Conference: <u>January 11, 2007 (after school)</u>

Lecture (10 Minutes)	10:00	Lesson begins with discussion back and forth between teacher/students
	10:05	Lecture/discussion about fractions (how to reduce)
	10:10	Instructions for game/game begins
Game (20 Minutes)	10:15	Game continues exploring fractions
	10:20	Game continues comparing fractions using cards
	10:25	Game continues
	10:30	Game ends; math book and reporting sheet-work begins
	10:35	Reviewing learning from lesson connecting with previous learning
	10:40	Work with problems in math book lecture— explaining reducing a fraction
Group Work (20 Minutes)	10:45	Work in book working independently on assignment, in math book(teacher helping individual students)
	10:50	Continuing to work on assignment independent work
	10:55	Students working independently and in small groups on assignment
	11:00	Teacher calls group back together lesson ends —class goes to assembly

Suggested Postobservation Conference Strategies   Sandy plans to ask Bob to examine what students were doing during the game and then to go over how he used time throughout the period for students to work on independent work (workbook assignment). To encourage reflection, Sandy develops the following series of open-ended questions:

♦ What do you suppose students learned through the game?

♦ What will you do to follow up tomorrow?

♦ How can you assess the value of the game as part of instruction?

♦ Do you plan to use other games?

Tool 8: Focus on Calling Patterns and Patterns of Interaction

Background

Teachers often wonder about their calling patterns. They want to know whom they are calling on and how often, whether they call on everyone, and whether they favor any one group of students or an area of the classroom.

Applying the Tool in Practice

The Context of the Classroom Observation   Susan Petrulis, a middle school social studies teacher, wonders whether she plays favorites. Susan is concerned because a parent complained that she was ignoring her daughter and a few other students who were recently suspended for smoking. More importantly, however, Susan just wants to know whether she is providing many opportunities for students to answer. Susan asked Francie Parker, the assistant principal, to observe her, focusing on her calling patterns.

Observation Focus   Calling and interaction patterns during a class period.

Observation Tool Seating chart with legend of codes for calling and interaction patterns.

Directions and Approaches for Using the Tool   Identify with the teacher the most common calling patterns (entire class responding, individual response, individual assistance, and so on). Develop a code for each. During the observation, track calling patterns on seating chart (Figure 5.24 on the next page).

Figure 5.24. Tracking Calling Patterns

Teacher: Susan Petrulis   Date of Observation: October 25, 2006
Observer: Francie Parker
Class: Social Studies   Period of the Day: 4th Period
Time of Observation: Start: 11:00   End: 11:55
Total Time Spent in Observation: 55 Minutes
Number of Students Present: 17   Grade Level: 7th Grade
Topic of the Lesson: Vietnam War
Date of Postobservation Conference: October 25, 2006 (after school)

Legend: ECR—Entire Class Responding
           R—Response
           IH—Individual Help
           Q—Question
           C—Comment

Front of Room

	A	B	C	D
1.	**CHARLES** 11:30-R	**JAMES** 11:33-R 11:37-R 11:53-R	**MARY** (sitting in back) 11:30-R 11:46-Reading 11:47 R/R	**SAM** 11:04-R 11:12-Q 11:26-IH 11:51-R
2.	**CHRISTINE** 11:20-Q to teacher 11:31-R (w/re-peat)	**TONY** 11:03-R 11:07-C (we're good!) 11:08-R 11:30-C 11:39-R 11:49-huh? To Randy 11:49-Reading 11:52-R	**ANDREA** 11:13-C made by teacher 11:23-IH 11:52-R	**RANDY** 11:03-R 11:48-Reading 11:51-R
3.	**MICHAEL** 11:04-R 11:52-R	**TIFFANY** 11:03-R 11:29-C 11:30-R 11:31-R/R 11:45-Q	**JEAN** 11:11-C/R 11:26-IH 11:33-R 11:43-C 11:53-R	**SANDY** 11:11-Q (moving) 11:51-R

4.	PATRICK Suspended	JEFF	KRISTY 11:06-Q 11:23-IH 11:28-R 11:32-R 11:33-R 11:47-R 11:50-Reading 11:52-R 11:53-R 11:53-R	AMBER 11:09-C 11:39-Q 11:48-Q
5.	ANDREW 11:04-R 11:47-Reading 11:51-R 11:53-R	TYSON 11:13-C made by teacher 11:29-C C 11:32-R 11:36-R 11:43-Q 11:44-Q 11:51-R		KATE Absent

Suggested Postobservation Conference Strategies   The data record-ed on the chart enables the teacher to review her own calling patterns (fre-quency, gender, and so forth).

Suggested Postobservation Conference Strategies   Lead the teacher through examining the calling patterns as portrayed in Figure 5.25, on the next page.

Alternate Approach to Collecting Data Related to Calling Patterns

Figure 5.25. Tracking Calling Patterns—Seating Chart

Teacher: <u>Susan Petrulis</u>   Date of Observation: <u>October 25, 2006</u>
Observer: <u>Francie Parker</u>
Class: <u>Social Studies</u>   Period of the Day: <u>4th Period</u>
Time of Observation: Start: <u>11:00</u>   End: <u>11:55</u>
Total Time Spent in Observation: <u>55 Minutes</u>
Number of Students Present: <u>17</u>   Grade Level: <u>7th Grade</u>
Topic of the Lesson: <u>Vietnam War</u>
Date of Postobservation Conference: <u>October 25, 2006 (after school)</u>

Alternate Data Collection Approach to Track Calling Patterns focusing broadly on distribution of calling patterns across boys and girls.[6]

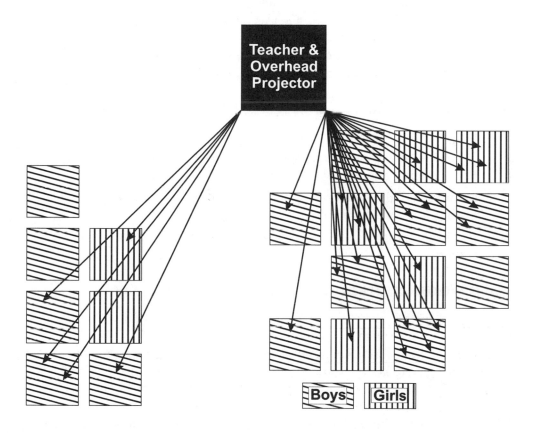

---

6 This tool was developed by Meredith A. Byrd, Clayton County Public Schools (Jonesboro, GA).

The patterns as depicted in the following analysis will lead to follow-up questions. Teaching is full of blind spots, such as avoiding certain areas of the classroom, overcalling on certain students such as students who are easily distracted, and, in some cases, calling on more boys than girls or girls than boys. The key is to help the teacher "see" the patterns that emerge in the data.

Analysis
- 20 students in the classroom
  - 7 female and 13 male
    - 9 directed to females
  - All 7 females were interacted with
    - 9 students interacted with one time
    - 5 students interacted with two times
    - 1 student interacted with three times
    - 1 student interacted with four times
  - 19.2% of teacher interaction was directed to the right side of the classroom which consisted of 7 students
  - 80.8% of teacher interaction was directed towards the left side of the classroom which consisted of 13 students

Tips

- Record events in 5-minute intervals
- Record enough information so that the teacher can make sense of the overall events of the classroom.
- Include verbal statements as necessary to focus conversation during follow-up with the teacher.
- Avoid making value judgments while chronicling what is observed.

Tool 9: Focus on Tracking Transition Patterns

Background

The transition is, in a sense, an instructional method. Smooth transitions conserve time, help keep students focused on learning objectives, and lessen opportunities for classroom disruptions. Through advanced planning, transitions are enhanced when materials are ready to lessen the loss of time in between activities or when moving from one method of instruction to another. Transitions are seamless, with students assuming some responsibility for efficient operation. Transitions are a more seamless instructional technique when teachers

- Establish and reinforce routines aligned with the needs of learners.
- Cue students to a transition so they are ready to transition to the next activity.
- Have materials (handouts, materials, equipment) readily available before the transition begins.
- Provide clear directions as part of the transition.

Applying the Tool in Practice

The Context of the Classroom Observation Transitioning from one activity to another is an important part of instruction, especially for longer class periods (regardless of the grade or subject matter). Cheryl Hofer is in her fifth year of teaching 4th grade social studies at Lincoln Elementary School. Cheryl is concerned that she is "losing time" during classroom activities so she has asked her principal, Dr. June Kaufman, to focus on transitions during the upcoming observation.

Observation Focus Transition strategies

Directions and Approaches for Using the Tool Observation Technique The supervisor tracks what techniques the teacher uses in between instructional segments or in other words, how the teacher gets students from point A to point B. Record broadly the instructional activity and then the transition (cues, clarity of directions) used to move students from one activity to another, focusing on student responses based on the transition strategy (Figure 5.26 on pages 140–142).

Figure 5.26. Tracking Transition Patterns

Teacher: <u>Mrs. Cheryl Hofer</u>   Date of Observation: <u>January 18, 2006</u>
Observer: <u>Dr. June Kaufman</u>
Class: <u>4th Grade Social Studies</u>   Period of the Day: <u>Morning</u>
Time of Observation: Start: <u>10:10</u>   End: <u>11:05</u>
Total Time Spent in Observation: <u>55 Minutes</u>
Number of Students Present: <u>18</u>   Grade Level: <u>4th Grade</u>
Topic of the Lesson: <u>Map Activity—Geography</u>
Date of Postobservation Conference: <u>January 19, 2006</u>

Instruction/Activity	Transition	Student Response
10:10–10:14 Getting students into cooperative groups	Gives directions for small cooperative group.	Students meander, finding their group members; 4 students ask clarifying questions during movement
	Stops movement to give clarifying instructions	
	Hands out worksheets, maps, and other supplies	Two students were called out to the office
	Teacher directs team captains to pick up direction sheet for their groups	
	Materials are packaged on teacher's desk; packets have a number on them corresponding to the group (e.g., 1, 2, 3)	
10:15–10:24 Students are working in groups. Teacher is walking from group to group redirecting students, answering questions		
10:20 Teacher reminds students that they have "4 minutes left" to complete task		

(Figure continues on next page.)

Instruction/Activity	Transition	Student Response
10:24 Teacher calls time and starts getting students back into large group	Flicks lights on and off, asks Group 1 to send their rep to the front of the room to give a summary	Students are moving desks
10:28	Teacher moving overhead to the desk and directing attention to the large-group activity	Group 1 rep starts the summary using an overhead transparency
10:33		Group 2 rep begins the summary
10:35		Group 3 rep begins the summary
10:38		Group 4 rep begins the summary
10:41		Group 5 rep begins the summary
10:45 Directs students to put away their books, return map resource materials used in the small-group work, and pull out their laptops for the next activity		Students follow the teacher's cues and are getting organized (putting materials away, pulling out laptops, etc.)
10:48 Teacher: "Hurry and get with the program"		

(Figure continues on next page.)

Instruction/Activity	Transition	Student Response
10:52 Directs students to turn on their laptops and find The Atlas of North America website	Students are waiting for their computers to boot up; Teacher gives directions on what to do once at the site	Students are talking among each other as they wait for their laptops to load and get to the website
	Teacher taps on blackboard to get student attention; resumes with directions (Go to How America Uses Water and review the site to ready for tomorrow's lesson)	5 students are helping others find the URL; 6 students are on the site reviewing materials; 4 students are talking; 2 students return from the office; 2 students are visiting other sites
10:57: Teacher passes out a worksheet (map of U.S. dams) and asks students to put in their folders	Students pull out folders	
11:00: Teacher directs attention to a different web site, The Earth Explorer Asks students to brainstorm the reasons for building a dam		About half of the students are talking among themselves and about half are focused on their laptop screens
11:03: Asks students to come up independently with a list of reasons for building dams		Student questions: By ourselves or in groups? Will you collect the lists? Isn't lunch about to start?
11:05 Teacher redirects students to focus on her: "moment, moment, moment"		Students stop all activity and focus on teacher

Suggested Postobservation Conference Strategies   Encourage the teacher to examine the transitions and how students respond throughout the transition periods. Suggest that the teacher examine the minutes involved in the transition, the directions or cues, and how students respond to these directions and cues.

Tool 10: Tracking the Beginning and Ending (Closure) of Class

Background

Effective teachers engage in bell-to-bell instruction. The first few minutes and the last few minutes are known to be two critically important points of time. Research shows that time wasted with beginning and ending class can never really be recouped; once time is lost, it is gone. Effective teachers establish daily routines for beginning and ending class. Grade level dictates the types of routines established. Although there are vast differences between an elementary, middle, and high school classroom, they all share a commonality: the need for routines to begin and end instruction.

Beginning Class Routines

Teachers who have routines for the beginning of a class period use the time immediately before the tardy bell for getting students ready and organized for learning. Strategies to maximize time on-task and to reduce "empty air time" before formal instruction begins include

- Taking attendance as students are entering the room.
- Having a sponge activity for students to start working on as they are getting ready for class to start. Sponge activities, purposefully short but related to the overall lesson and course content, "soak up" those extra few minutes at the beginning or ending of class that if not used would be wasted. Sponge activities can include a math problem to be solved, a sentence to diagram, a vocabulary word to include in a sentence, a short quiz.
- Posting a daily agenda detailing the lesson objectives and what materials to get ready before the bell rings.
- Distributing class materials and collecting homework.

All of these activities help prepare students so that the moment the bell begins, instruction or other activities related to the lesson can begin.

Ending Class Routines

Effective teachers use the time immediately before the ending of a class period to recapitulate lessons learned and to help bring closure to the class activities. They relate what needs to be done to prepare for the next day so that once the bell rings, students can be dismissed. Different cues give students time to put away supplies and equipment and get ready to leave the class in an orderly manner.

Applying the Tool in Practice

The Context of the Classroom Observation Although Ms. Amy Kleiber has been an English teacher for 15 years, she is experiencing difficulty with her afternoon English I class. She just cannot get control of the class or the routines at the beginning or at the ending of the class period. Dr. Chen, a former English teacher and now assistant principal, has done a few informal classroom observations in which he has observed some of the difficulties in this classroom. Ms. Kleiber and Dr. Chen both agree she could use some assistance. In their formal preobservation conference, they agree that Dr. Chen should observe the first and last 15 minutes of her first hour block period.

Observation Focus Either the activities within the first 15 minutes of class beginning or the 15 minutes before the ending of the class.

Observation Tool Narrow focus, using anecdotal notes to examine the routines used to begin or to come to closure of the class.

Directions and Approaches for Using the Tool Chronicle the activities and procedures the teacher uses to begin or to end class instruction. Note the amount of time it takes the teacher to either open or close class, paying particular attention to the routines, student familiarity with routines, and the cues the teacher uses to signal students (Figure 5.27, pages 145–146).

Figure 5.27. Tracking Beginning of Period Activities

Teacher: <u>Amy Kleibar</u>   Date of Observation: <u>September 12, 2006</u>
Observer: <u>Dr. Sou Chen</u>
Class: <u>English I</u>   Period of the Day: <u>Period 1 (first block)</u>
Time of Observation: Start: <u>8:05</u> End: <u>8:20</u>
Total Time Spent in Observation: <u>15 Minutes</u>
Number of Students Present: <u>23</u>   Grade Level: <u>9th</u>
Topic of the Lesson: <u>Essay Writing (NA due to focus on beginning of class</u>
            <u>routines)</u>
Date of Postobservation Conference: <u>September 13, 2006</u>

	Beginning of the Period	Student Behavior
8:05	Attendance taken as students enter the room. Teacher in the doorway stopping students as they enter, reminding students to take off coats and hats.	Students entering the room and stopping by T's desk to pick up graded papers; students comparing grades as they walk to their desks. (Clusters of students clog the doorway and area around T's desk.)
8:07	Bell Rings T closes door and picks up papers left on desk—calls students up to the front of the room to pick up papers.	Students sitting at desk while T gives students their papers; student in row 3 trips a student; 2 students in row 5 push around books while walking up the aisles.
8:08	Announcements from the activities office; opens the door for late students; stops at the computer station to log tardy students.	Students sitting at desk: 9 students turned around talking to other students during announcements; 5 students are digging materials out from their book bags; 3 students lined up at the pencil sharpener.
8:11	Teacher cues students to review due dates for next essay—points to the board and tells students, "get these dates in notebooks."	Students start opening notebooks; three are trying to borrow paper (no notebooks).
8:12	Teacher cues students, "Review my comments on your papers. Revisions are due tomorrow—rewrite only the parts of the essay circled in green."	Students start thumbing through essays. One student asks what to do if there are no "green circles." Lots of laughter.

Time	Teacher	Students
8:13	Teacher cue: "It's a bit noisy in here today. Let's begin by reviewing the elements of an introductory paragraph, but first pull out Writing Tip Sheet 3 from your writing folders.	Students begin looking in book bags for writing folders. Several begin to move closer to one another.
8:14	Teacher offers copies of Writing Tip 3 to students who do not have this sheet…gives out sheet to 13 students.	A student asks, "Are we going to finish our group activity from yesterday?"
8:14	Teacher: First, we're going to review the elements of an introductory paragraph…review silently for a moment the key elements of an introductory paragraph…	Students start to read the Tip Sheet.
8:15	Teacher walks around the room as students read Writing Tip Sheet.	Students are quietly reading sheet.
8:18	Teacher turns on overhead. Overhead has a sample introductory paragraph written by the student who had "no green circles" on his paper. Teacher cues students to the paragraph and asks them to (a) read the paragraph, (b) compare the elements of an introductory paragraph to the sample on the overhead, and (c) write a few thoughts about the sample paragraph related to the elements found on Tip Sheet 3.	Students focus on the paragraph, quietly reading it. Many students are writing notes in notebook; a few students are talking with their neighbors. Talk is quiet.
8:19–8:20	Teacher is walking around the room monitoring	

Now, the focus shifts to end of classroom activities (Figure 5.28, pages 147–148).

(Text continues on page 149.)

Figure 5.28. Tracking Ending of Class Patterns

Teacher: <u>Amy Kleibar</u>   Date of Observation: <u>September 12, 2006</u>
Observer: <u>Dr. Sou Chen</u>
Class: <u>English I</u>   Period of the Day: <u>Period 1 (first block)</u>
Time of Observation: Start: <u>8:05</u> End: <u>8:20</u>
Total Time Spent in Observation: <u>15 Minutes</u>
Number of Students Present: <u>23</u>   Grade Level: <u>9th</u>
Topic of the Lesson: <u>Essay Writing (NA due to focus on ending of class routines)</u>
Date of Postobservation Conference: <u>September 13, 2006</u>

	Ending of the Period	Student Behavior
8:45	Teacher is moving from group to group, speaking with students, examining work.	Students are in small groups discussing essays.
8:48	Teacher cues students to move desks back in place for large group processing.	Students start to break out of groups by moving desks back in rows; minimal noise. A student from each group is putting books (thesaurus, dictionary, etc.) back on teacher's desk.
8:49	Teacher is in front of the room readying for instruction; makes a few statements: (1) Please bring notebooks tomorrow, and I'll add more information about the essay. (2) Also, rewrites on the areas circled in green are due tomorrow. Just rewrite the sections circled in green.	Student desks are in a row and students are listening to the teacher, quietly.
8:50	Let's recap the importance of the advanced organizer in the introductory paragraph and how this organizer serves as a transition to subsequent paragraphs.	Students sit quietly for about 10 seconds; hands start going up.
8:50	Jamie.	The organizer is the road map and helps the writer point to the major points that get discussed in the essay; in a way it's a writer's compass.

8:51	That's an interesting metaphor—a compass. Is there any other value to a compass?	Fred responds, the organizer is for the reader, too. The compass helps the traveler know what direction he is in…going.
8:52	Excellent parallel. Let's look at a sample from an essay. Teacher flips the overhead on and focuses students to the advanced organizer sentence that is in all BOLD on the screen. Look at this advanced organizer. Comment on its importance and value. Lauren, what do you think?	Lauren responds: This organizer has three items in it. The symbols in the book (1) help to illustrate the deeper meaning, (2) provide an understanding of the what motivated the main character, and (3) foreshadow the ending of the book.
8:54	Superb! Now what does the writer need to do next.	Several hands go up.
8:55	Jackson, what do you think?	Take time to write another sentence or two; the organizer acts as a segue to the next paragraphs. Student asks a question: Does the advanced organizer have to always have three points?
8:56	Actually, the number of points is not important because…	Student responds: …it depends on what the essay is trying to get across.
8:56	That's correct. And we'll be reviewing several more introductory paragraphs tomorrow. Let's recap from the day. Teacher highlights the Tips for Writing Introductory Paragraphs, the uses and misuses of advanced organizer and the purpose of the advanced organizer	Students are listening and taking notes. Three students are starting to pack up their materials. Teacher cues disapproval by standing by the desk of one student; the others stop packing up their materials.
9:00	Bell rings and teacher thanks the class for working hard and wishes them well for the rest of the day	Students pack up their bags and start leaving the room.

Tips

- ◆ Record data in one- and two-minute increments.
- ◆ Record major events with detail. A few strong examples with complete and accurate information will make more sense than trying to record extraneous information.
- ◆ Leave a space, such as a large column in the margin, to be used during the postobservation conference to make notes (e.g., teacher analysis, questions, concerns, or ideas).
- ◆ It might be useful to observe a teacher having trouble with beginning or ending of class routines across two or three successive days to get a more expanded data set. This expanded data might shed more light on patterns found within the routines.

Tool 11: Observing Cooperative Group Learning

Background

Cooperative learning is an instructional model in which students complete work as a collaborative learning team in small groups. The work of a cooperative learning group is structured so that each group member contributes to the completion of the learning activity. Cooperative learning group work is sometimes "chaotic," with students talking with one another, perhaps even across groups, comparing answers, quizzing one another, or securing materials from bookshelves. In cooperative learning, students assume a variety of active roles, including for example, Reader/Explainer, Checker, and Recorder (Johnson & Johnson, 1994). Within the structure of the cooperative group, the teacher should encourage students to rotate roles to give them opportunities to serve as the Reader/Explainer, Checker, and Recorder.

The directions the teacher provides, the monitoring the teacher does within and across groups, and the eye to time on task are essential for cooperative learning to be successful. In cooperative learning, the teacher assumes responsibility for monitoring students' learning and intervening within the groups.

Applying the Tool in Practice

The Context of the Classroom Observation Ms. Lipinski has been teaching for nine years, the past three years in a high school, after a six-year stint as a middle school teacher. Ms. Lipinski is aware of the differences in the learning needs of these two groups of students, but she wants to ensure that she is using cooperative learning groups in a way that maximizes student engagement and time on-task; she also wants to ensure that she is monitoring student time on-task while students are in small cooperative groups.

Observation Focus   Student interaction, teacher assistance, and monitoring and assessing learning activities.

Observation Tool Because the cooperative learning model is dependent on small-group work, a narrow-lens approach will be used to track both the work of students as well as how a teacher attends to the work of students in small groups. Ms. Lipinski wants Ms. Overman to focus on the work her students do while in groups, and on the monitoring strategies she uses to ensure students are on-task.

Directions and Approaches for Using the Tool   Once students are in groups, record the interactions of students and the strategies the teacher uses to monitor the work of students within groups (Figure 5.29 on the next page). Through monitoring the group activities, Ms. Overman will be able to determine individual student involvement (Johnson & Johnson, 1994), and she can assist Ms. Lipisnki in assessing the work of students, individually or in groups, by collecting data on what students are doing and how students are interacting with one another in cooperative learning groups.

Figure 5.29. Tracking Cooperative Learning Groups

Teacher: Theresa Lipinski Date of Observation: December 3, 2006
Observer: Carol Overman
Class: English 1   Period of the Day: 7th Period
Time of Observation: Start: 1:50 End: 2:10
Total Time Spent in Observation: 20 Minutes
Number of Students Present: 23   Grade Level: Freshman (Honors)
Topic of the Lesson: *Romeo and Juliet*
Date of the Postobservation Conference: December 5, 2006

Group	Number in Group	Student Interaction	Teacher Monitoring Strategies
1	4	Discussing the use of foreshadowing; one student recording comments; one student finding supporting citations from the text; two students talking with one another	Teacher with group 4
2	3	2 students reading book, scanning for citations—no talking; 1 student sketching a crest for the Montague family	Teacher physically with group 4 but "eye scanning" group 5 (see notes)
3	4	One student asking questions; one student writing responses; one student doodling in notebook (Capulet crest); one student reading book	Teacher moves to group 5; teacher speaking with group members; full attention to group 5
4	4	Students reading text and alternately speaking with one another; one student starts to draw the family crest for the Capulets	Teacher just moved to group 5
5	4	2 students talking loudly; 1 student looking in book bag; 1 student talking to a student in group 6	Teacher "making eye contact" from position in with group 4; teacher breaks in with an announcement (8 minutes left for group work)

6	4	2 students sharing a book; 1 student trying to borrow colored pencils for the crest (Capulet); 1 student reading teacher handout	Teacher now walking around the room, moving from group 1 to group 2; teacher announces 4 minutes left; asks for a volunteer group to share artistic rendition of the family/royal crest; teacher moves to the front of the room to set up the overhead projector and CD player; teacher moves back to group 5; asks for examples of foreshadowing; calls time by asking the question: "How does Shakespeare use foreshadowing from scene 2 forward? Students start to move desks around to break out of groups

Tips

♦ Track teacher movement from group to group

♦ Record teacher verbal cues

Depending on when the observer enters the room, a variation to data collection includes using anecdotal notes across the categories that Johnson and Johnson (1994) identified as essential to framing cooperative learning. The following data collection tool (Figure 5.30, pages 153–154) can help the principal script anecdotal notes while observing in a classroom where cooperative learning is being used.

Alternate Approach to Collecting Data

Figure 5.30. Tracking Cooperative Learning Group Work

Teacher: <u>Janie Adams</u>   Date of Observation: <u>December 3, 2006</u>
Observer: <u>Dr. Brenda Arlin</u>
Class: <u>U.S. History</u> Period of the Day: <u>2nd Period</u>
Time of Observation: Start: <u>9:05</u> End: <u>9:25</u>
Total Time Spent in Observation: <u>20 Minutes</u>
Number of Students Present: <u>26</u>   Grade Level: <u>Juniors</u>
Topic of the Lesson: <u>Examining How a Bill is Passed</u>
Date of Postobservation Conference: <u>December 5, 2006</u>

Focus on Cooperative Learning	Presence or Absence	Notes
Objectives for the cooperative learning group	X	◆ Objective for the activity was written on the whiteboard ◆ Teacher referred to the objective as students asked questions ◆ Teacher returned to the objective during closure of group activity
Clarity of directions	X	◆ Before breaking students into groups, teacher gave directions ◆ Teacher distributed directions for each group once students moved into their groups
Movement into groups	X	◆ 6 minutes for students to move into groups ◆ Materials were bundled for each group in advance of movement
Monitoring and intervening strategies	X	◆ Teacher turned lights on and off to get attention ◆ Teacher broke into group time 3 times with clarifying directions ◆ Teacher visited each group 4 times
Evaluation Strategies		
Interaction with students	X	◆ Asked questions and gave feedback to groups while monitoring ◆ Clarified directions ◆ Became a member of each group

(Figure continues on next page.)

Follow-up instruc- tion—large-group processing	X	◆ After 23 minutes, teacher called end to group work ◆ Students moved desks and chairs back in order ◆ Group reporter gave report ◆ Teacher asked and answered questions

Tool 12: Technology Implementation and Integration

Background

Technology in the form of computers and peripheral components has been in place in our schools since the 1970s. Used appropriately, technology has changed the way many teachers have modified their teaching. Technology can bring the outside world into a classroom. Technology can be used to differentiate instruction, particularly in small-group or individualized instruction. Used in classroom activities, technology can be used to globally explore our universe, provide instructional support through games, reviews, simulations, and tutorials—all to extend learning opportunities by enhancing critical thinking and problem-solving skills.

Because there is very little written in the field of instructional supervision related to classroom observations and the work supervisors do to support teachers, the layout of the tools in this section looks different from the tools presented so far in this chapter.

The questions in Figure 5.31[7] (next page) are suggestions of what a preobservation conference could include when preparing for an observation to assess how a teacher incorporates the use of technology into the curriculum and instruction. Although the indicators are in question form, they are intended to be open ended so as to generate discussions.

---

7 The *Technology Integration Preobservation Conference Form* was developed by Ann G. Haughey as part of her coursework in Supervision Theory and her Problem of Practice while working toward her Specialist in Education degree at the University of Georgia. Ann G. Haughey is the technology coordinator for Wilkes County Schools (Washington, GA).

Figure 5.31. Technology Integration Preobservation Conference Form

Questions	Yes	No	Comments
Do you use technology applications such as word processing or spreadsheets for general productivity uses?			
Do you use e-mail to communicate with other faculty members, students, and parents?			
Do you use presentation tools such as PowerPoint in your classes?			
Do you use other types of technology tools or peripherals with your students (e.g., digital cameras, scanners, iPods)?			
Do you use an electronic grade book (Integrade Pro) to calculate and store student grades?			
Do you encourage students to use technology to gather and interpret data, research, write papers, etc?			
Do you promote the use of electronic portfolios and other types of authentic assessments with students?			
Do you use tools such as multimedia projectors, SmartBoards, or ActivBoards during your lesson?			
Do you feel that you have received enough professional learning in the area of technology?			
Do you use the Internet to search for instructional ideas, teaching tips, or lesson plans?			
Do you use online games, Web quests, or other online educational resources with students?			
Classroom Observation Focus:			

Applying the Tool in Practice

The Context of the Classroom Observation Art Roberson, a social studies teacher at Hudson Middle School, has been teaching 7th grade for 15 years. Art is aware of the benefits of integrating technology as a learning tool. He has attended professional development sessions, and he took an intensive week-long course, Using Technology in the Middle Level Social Studies Classroom, during the summer. Art shared with his principal, Dr. Cindy Fields, that his students are better informed than he is when it comes to using computers. Art has set as a long-term professional development goal that he will actively use technology to enhance his teaching, supplement curricular materials, and track what he and his students learn along the way.

Observation Focus During the preobservation conference, Mr. Art Roberson and Dr. Cindy Fields think through Art's lesson. Art believes he can lead his students to learning about this time in history and that the use of technology can enhance the learning experience. They decide that because Art has just completed an introductory lesson on immigration and Ellis Island, it would be a good time for Dr. Fields to observe his classroom to see how things are going with his integration of technology relative to the curriculum and how he and his students use technology during the period. Dr. Fields will use mixed methods—a checklist and running notes. Art and Dr. Fields agree that she will focus on how the integration of technology enhances the curriculum and adds depth and breadth to how his students learn from various sources on the Web.

Observation Tool Data will be collected using a mixed-method approach. Dr. Fields will use the *Classroom Observation Guide to Track Technology Integration*[8] (Figure 5.32, next page) and she will take scripted notes throughout the observation.

Directions and Approaches for Using the Tool Script notes as events in the classroom unfold. Check off items in the *Classroom Observation Guide to Track Technology Integration* (Figure 5.32 on pages 157–160) related to the focus agreed on during the preobservation conference. In this instance, Dr. Fields tracks and notates how Mr. Roberson uses technology, specifically to enhance the curriculum and as a learning tool to extend learning for students.

(Text continues on page 160.)

---

8 The *Classroom Observation Guide to Track Technology Integration* was developed by Ann G. Haughey who is the technology coordinator for Wilkes County Schools (Washington, GA). Used with permission.

Figure 5.32. Classroom Observation Guide to Track Technology Integration

Teacher's Name: _Art Roberson_ Observation Date: _September 6, 2006_
Observer: _Cindy Fields_
Class: _Social Studies_   Period of the Day: _Morning Block_
Time of Observation: Start: _10:10_   End: _11:10_
Total Time Spent in Observation: _60 Minutes_
Number of Students Present: _17_   Grade Level: _7th_
Topic of Lesson: _Immigrants and Ellis Island_
Date of Postobservation Conference: _September 7, 2006_

Indicators for Technology Integration

Rate each of the following using this rating scale:

1   _Little_ evidence of technology use.

2   _Some_ evidence that technology is used in limited amounts and with simple tasks—more productivity oriented.

3   Evidence that teacher _uses_ technology and provides assistance to students with spreadsheets, word processing, demonstrations.

4   Teacher is _comfortable_ with technology use. A _variety_ of technology is used daily, and technology is an integral part of classroom instruction.

☐ Teacher does not use any technology

Teacher uses technology as a productivity tool

| 3/4 | Uses technology for classroom attendance

Uses attendance software (i.e., Class XP) effectively

Uses technology to maintain and document grades

Uses grading software/spreadsheets (i.e., Integrade Pro) effectively

| 3/4 | Uses technology to design worksheets, labs, quizzes, and tests

Evidence of instructional computer-generated assignments

Responds appropriately and in a timely manner using e-mail

No evidence of using e-mail while supervising students

| 4 | Uses the Internet to search for lesson plans and classroom activities

(Figure continues on next page.)

Teacher allows student use of computers

| 3 | Students use computers for drill and practice activities |

       Use of stand-alone computer software

       Use of networkable programs such as Accelerated Reader and Accelerated Math

       Use of instructional Web-based software such as Riverdeep

| 4 | Students use computers for instructional purposes |

       Use of computers for performance assessments—e.g., PowerPoint, Excel, etc.

       Use of computers for Web-based research

       Using computers to gather data

       Using a combination of software and Web-based research to analyze data and draw conclusions

       Taking data and conclusions and presenting it using some type of multimedia presentation

| 3 | **Teacher uses presentation software such as PowerPoint during instruction** |

| 4 | **Teacher uses projection tools during instruction** |

       Uses overhead projector

       Uses multimedia projector

       Uses multimedia projector with VCR

       Uses multimedia projector with SmartBoard or ActivBoard

| 4 | **Teacher incorporates the use of other devices during instruction** |

       Digital camera

       Scanner

       iPod

       Graphing calculators

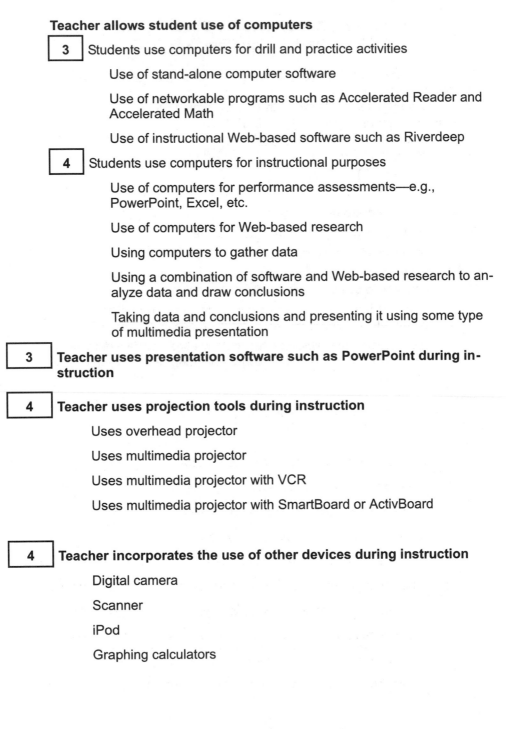

(Figure continues on next page.)

| 4 | Teacher incorporates a variety of simple technology within the lesson and student work is indicative of seamless transitions between traditional instruction and technology integration |

How was the teacher using technology in the classroom? (Give specifics)

10:10- 10:20	Mr. Roberson spent approximately ten minutes recapping information from the prior day: What occurred once immigrants arrived at Ellis Island (docking, medical exams), the large numbers of immigrants that arrived at Ellis Island between 1892 and 1924 (about 22 million), etc.
10:21	Pulls up a PowerPoint presentation that has several Web addresses for students to mark in their browsers, and he directs student pairs to go to the computers in the back of the room. Students already know their "pairs" and proceed to the back of the room. Computers are already "booted up." Directs students to type the URL http://teacher.scholastic.com/activities/immigration/tour/index.htm and then to wait for further directions. Roberson is walking the walk to ensure students have the URL plugged in and are on the virtual tour of Ellis Island home page.
10:23	Directs pairs to begin the tour with the audio off and to click on each tour page (approximately 7 "click points"). At the end of the tour, students are asked to click onto the immigration home page URL. Students are directed to read and review Yesterday and Today.
	Students are reading and reviewing these pages
10:33	Mr. Roberson asks students to return to their seats. Explains the next project: In pairs, "come up with three questions you have about the Ellis Island experience, and write these questions on a sheet of paper."
10:43	Calls time. Asks a person from each pair to share their questions. Mr. Roberson is at the front of the room, typing in the questions of each group. Develops a "master list" of questions.
10:54	Asks pairs to go to the computers and begin a Google search to try to find answers to their questions. Students return to their computers with notebooks and begin searching the Web for resources to answer their questions.
10:56	Breaks in and asks students to save the link sites where they found answers to their questions and to be prepared to print off a page or two from each site.
11:00	Observation ends.

(Figure continues on next page.)

Were students engaged during the technology portions of the lesson? If yes, describe.

Students were quiet and focused, very little fringe talking. Teacher monitored the work of pairs, visiting each pair on average of two times. Students were "glued" to the monitors searching for sites and for information to answer their questions.

Any other comments or suggestions?

Here are some questions to help guide our discussion:

1. In the end, what will students do with the answers to their questions? Will they share the information with one another? If so, will students use technology, such as developing a PowerPoint presentation? Share Web sources?

2. What is the next step in this lesson?

Teacher's Signature: _____

Date: _____

Suggested Postobservation Conference Strategies

♦ Focus more on the scripted notes seeking clarification on how technology and its integration is supporting the curriculum and extending student learning.

♦ Focus attention on next steps of how what was experienced by students will be extended to other learning opportunities in upcoming class sessions.

Tip

♦ Take detailed scripted notes and use the scripted notes to extend discussion.

Tool 13: Classroom Traffic

Background

The classroom is often marked with the movement of teachers and their physical proximity with students. Movement could include movement during a lecture, while checking on student progress during independent work or work in cooperative groups, and during demonstrations. Because of content, some classes require more movement for teachers and students. Think of the fast-paced nature of instruction in the gym, a consumer science course (sewing or foods lab), a band or choral room, and even the "traditional classroom" where demonstrations occur. Teachers seek feedback regarding their own movement and often time the movement of their students. Teachers often wonder if there are any "blind" spots, or areas of the classroom in which students are not being attended to during the instructional period. Tracking classroom traffic gives teachers insight on their movements during class.

Applying the Tool in Practice

The Context of the Classroom Observation Shirley West has been teaching algebra for three years, and she is concerned about her movement in the class while she is working independently with students. Two days prior to the classroom observation, Shirley gave basic examples of how to graph and write equations for hyperbolas, and she is going to have students practice these skills independently while she moves through the room lending assistance and checking on mastery of skills. She has this "nagging" concern that she is not getting to all students and providing enough feedback.

Observation Focus Teacher movement around the room and contact with students.

Observation Tool A seating chart.

Directions and Approaches for Using the Tool Using a seating chart (Figure 5.33 on next page), track with lines, the movement of the teacher. Notate times along the lines so that not only the movement of the teacher can be tracked but also the length of time the teacher works with each student.

Figure 5.33. Classroom Traffic—Seating Chart

Teacher: <u>Shirley West</u>   Date of Observation: <u>April 26, 2006</u>
Observer: <u>Paula Aguilar</u>
Class: <u>Algebra II</u>   Period of the Day: <u>1st Hour</u>
Time of Observation: Start: <u>7:45</u> End: <u>8:25</u>
Total Time Spent in Observation: <u>40 Minutes</u>
Number of Students Present: <u>18</u>   Grade Level: <u>Mixed 10th and 11th</u>
Topic of the Lesson: <u>Hyperbolas—How to graph and write equations of</u>
   <u>hyperbolas that consist of two vaguely parabola-</u>
   <u>shaped pieces that open either up and down</u>
Date of Postobservation Conference: <u>April 27, 2006</u>

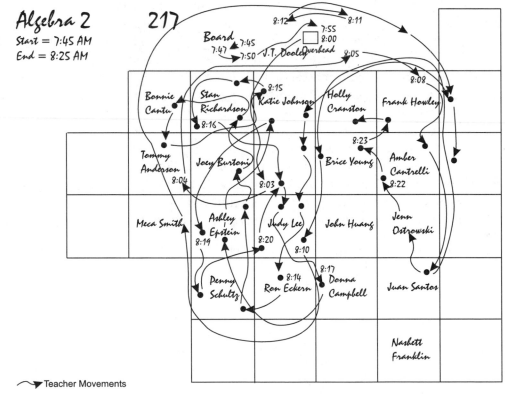

Teacher Movements
● Checking Student Work

Suggested Postobservation Strategies   With the seating chart as a backdrop for the postobservation conference, lead the teacher into "seeing" the patterns of movement. Probing questions could include the following:

+ Which students did you spend a majority of the time observing?
+ Were there students who did not need assistance?

From the data in Figure 5.33 (previous page), it is obvious that Ms. West started class at the front of the classroom and then began rotations around room. Her goal was to check understanding and mastery of the subject matter and to motivate students by checking on the completeness of their homework assignment.

Ms. West talked to almost every student, but there were a few with whom she had little contact. Much attention was given to the middle of the class.

Tips

+ Use more than one seating chart for an extended classroom observation, notating the start and end time at the top of the seating chart.
+ Record anecdotal notes in the margins or on another sheet of paper.

Summary

The classroom observation requires preparation—conducting a preobservation conference, selecting a data collection technique, and then readying for the postobservation conference. Given the fast pace of events in a typical classroom, mastering the techniques of classroom observation takes time. The choice of instrument or technique (wide-angle or narrow-angle) depends on factors such as the focus, the teacher's experience level, and the supervisor's experience level. In any case, the goal is to collect data that will make sense for the teacher during the postobservation conference.

Suggested Activities

From Theory to Practice

With the teaching colleague who has agreed to work with you, conduct a classroom observation using a data collection tool presented in this chapter.

Group Processing

In a small group, debrief about the experience of conducting an extended classroom observation. Identify any difficulties you encountered in scheduling the classroom observation, choosing a technique, collecting data, or other steps of the process.

Reflection

Identify the most challenging aspect of conducting an extended classroom observation, and explore several ways to meet that challenge.

References

Acheson, K. A., & Gall, M. D. (1997). *Techniques in the clinical supervision of teachers: Preservice and inservice applications* (4th ed.). New York: Longman.

Bloom, B. S. (Ed.) (1956). *Taxonomy of educational objectives: The classification of educational goals.* New York: Longman.

Gagné, R. M., Briggs, L. J., & Wager, W. W. (1992). *Principles of instructional design* (4th ed.). Fort Worth, TX: Harcourt Brace.

Johnson, D. W., & Johnson, R. T. (1994). Learning together. In S. Sharan (Ed.), *Handbook of cooperative learning methods* (pp. 51–65). Westport, CT: Greenwood Press.

McGreal, T. (1983). *Effective teacher evaluation.* Alexandria, VA: Association for Curriculum and Supervision.

Rowe, M. B. (1986). Wait time: Slowing down may be a way of speeding up. *Journal of Teacher Education, 37*(1), 43–50.

Stahl, R. J. (1994). *Using "think-time" and "wait-time" skillfully in the classroom.* Bloomington, IN: ERIC Clearinghouse for Social Studies/Social Science Education. Retrieved February 25, 2005, from http://atozteacherstuff.com/pages/1884.shtml

Tomlinson, C. A. (1999). *The differentiated classroom: Responding to the needs of all learners.* Alexandria, VA: Association for Supervision and Curriculum Development.

6

The Postobservation Conference

In This Chapter...

♦ The purposes of the postobservation conference

♦ Lesson reconstruction, constructivism, and the zone of proximal development

♦ Preparing for the postobservation conference

♦ Supervisory approaches and the postobservation conference

♦ Feedback, trust, and the Johari Window revisited

♦ After the postobservation conference, then what?

Introducing the Postobservation Conference

The primary intent of formative instructional supervision is to provide ongoing developmental opportunities for teachers to explore their teaching and student learning. The postobservation conference is the final stage in a cycle of clinical supervision, but the word final is deceptive, as the postobservation conference is a learning opportunity that spurs further growth. The postobservation conference is grounded in the reality of the teacher's world—the classroom, where learning occurs for both students and teachers. At its core, the postobservation conference presents a forum where teacher and supervisor talk about the events of the classroom observation.

Like children, adults are active learners. Teachers learn by examining data that reflects their classroom practices. If appropriately and accurately presented in the postobservation conference, these data can help teachers see and hear their practices and the effect of these practices on student learning. Adults need to be able to construct meaning by reconstructing the events of the classroom; the data collected in the classroom observation provide the building blocks for teachers to assemble and reassemble knowledge with the assistance of the supervisor or a peer.

The supervisor's communication skills and the trust between the teacher and supervisor can enhance the presentation of data and may motivate teachers to examine their practices more closely during future cycles of supervision.

The Purposes of the Postobservation Conference

The postobservation conference provides opportunities for teachers to talk about, inquire into, and reflect on their practices with the assistance of the supervisor (or, in the case of peer coaching, a teaching colleague). The purposes and intents of the postobservation conference are for the teacher and supervisor collaboratively to

- Review and analyze the data collected in terms of the focus they established in the preobservation conference;
- Develop a working plan for ongoing growth and development, predicated on what is observed in the classroom and what is discussed in the postobservation conference; and
- Ready the teacher to set a focus in the next preobservation conference.

In the postobservation conference, the teacher does not listen passively as the supervisor reads from notes; rather, the teacher reconstructs the events of the classroom with the supervisor or peer as facilitator.

Lesson Reconstruction, Constructivism, and the Zone of Proximal Development

Lesson Reconstruction

Bellon and Bellon (1982) promoted a postobservation conference technique called *lesson reconstruction*, in which the teacher reconstructs the events of the lesson based solely on the data derived from the classroom observation. Lesson reconstruction puts learning from the data at center stage, with teachers engaged as active learners. Lesson reconstruction is constructivist, in that "learners construct meaning from what they experience; thus, learning is an active meaning-making process" (Glatthorn, 1990, p. 6).

Constructivism

As active learners, teachers need to construct their own meanings based on what they do and experience. During the postobservation conference, supervisors can support the construction of knowledge by fostering critical inquiry and reflection on practice so that knowledge and insights about teaching can be

- ◆ Physically constructed by learners who are involved in their environment;
- ◆ Symbolically constructed by learners who are making their own representations of action;
- ◆ Socially constructed by learners who convey their meaning making to others; and
- ◆ Theoretically constructed by learners who try to explain things they do not understand. (Gagnon & Collay, 2001)

The Zone of Proximal Development

Another concept that enriches the supervisor's approach to the postobservation conference is the zone of proximal development (Vygotsky, 1978). Vygotsky asserts that the learner individually constructs knowledge with the assistance of another person who can help the learner rise to higher levels of knowledge or practice. Working in the zone of proximal development, the learner keeps stretching to construct new knowledge slightly above his current level of knowing. Figure 6.1, depicts the zone of proximal development as described by Vygotsky.

Figure 6.1. The Zone of Proximal Development

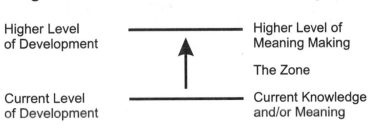

The key tenet of constructivist theory as it relates to supervision "is that people learn by actively constructing knowledge, weighing new information against their previous understanding, thinking about and working through discrepancies (on their own and with others), and coming to a new understanding" (O'Neil, 1998 p. 51).

A Case Study

Al Murphy set as an instructional goal incorporation of technology in his biology lessons. As a starting point, he attended a workshop on using noninvasive dissection software. A veteran biology teacher with 12 years of experience, Al feels confident in the lab overseeing and instructing students on dissection techniques; however, learning how to use software as an instructional tool is a new challenge. Jana Ruiz, a recent graduate with a master's degree in biology, is proficient with the software programs simulating animal dissection.

Al and Jana work together as peer coaches; Al is also Jana's assigned mentor for her first year of teaching. Al asked Jana to observe him teaching a lesson on dissection with the science department's new software. During the observation, Al struggles with using the software. Al's computer skills are more than adequate, but he is not confident or sure of what to do next; he told Jana that he just "can't get over the learning curve" with using the program during simulations.

- ◆ What can Jana do during the postobservation conference to help Al move through the zone of proximal development?

- ◆ How can a veteran teacher learn from a beginning teacher?

- ◆ What evidence suggests that Al and Jana are engaging in reciprocal learning?

Lyons and Pinnell (2001) offer eight generalized principles for organizing and implementing constructivist-based learning for adults. These principles (Figure 6.2, next page) can illustrate what effective supervisors do in the postobservation conference to encourage growth and development.

Figure 6.2. Organizing and Developing a Constructivist-Based Learning Environment for Adults

Principles of Constructivist-Based Learning Activities for Adults

- Principle 1: Encourage active participation.

- Principle 2: Organize small-group discussion around common concerns.

- Principle 3: Introduce new concepts in context.

- Principle 4: Create a safe environment.

- Principle 5: Develop participants' conceptual knowledge through conversations around shared experience.

- Principle 6: Provide opportunities for participants to use what they know to construct knowledge.

- Principle 7: Look for shifts in teachers' understanding over time.

- Principle 8: Provide additional experiences for participants who have not yet developed [the] needed conceptual understanding[s].

Source: Lyons & Pinnell, 2001, pp. 4–6.

The principles of constructivism, when applied to the postobservation conference, can help teachers make better sense of observation data so that "the focus is puzzling, inquiring, and problem solving" (Sergiovanni & Starratt, 1998, pp. 266–267).

Preparing for the Postobservation Conference

Meeting the professional needs of teachers as adult learners is a time-consuming endeavor for the instructional supervisor. Heavily involved in noninstructional tasks, supervisors often are distanced from classroom environments. The longer that supervisors hold positions that separate them from regular contact with students and teachers, the more noticeable this distance becomes to teachers.

Effective postobservation conferences

◆ Occur within 48 hours of the observation;

◆ Are held in the classroom where the observation occurred; and

◆ Invite ongoing dialogue between the teacher and supervisor.

Time is important: If too much time elapses between the observation and the conference, the classroom data lose meaning and teachers lose motivation to work with them. *Place is significant:* Holding the conference in the principal's office puts the principal in a position of authority, whereas the classroom offers the context of the learning environment to enrich the discussion. *Atmosphere is essential:* The postobservation conference opens the door to future dialogue and growth.

Effective supervisors take time to prepare for the postobservation conference. In the original models of clinical supervision, both Cogan (1973) and Goldhammer (1969) included a planning stage in which the supervisor assembled and interpreted data before meeting with the teacher. This planning time gives the supervisor the opportunity to organize the raw data gathered during the observation. Teaching is fast-paced, and the supervisor is recording observations at an equally fast pace, not always with perfect clarity. In its final form, the data must be clear and understandable to both the teacher and the supervisor. To lay the groundwork for a successful postobservation conference, the supervisor tackles several tasks:

Revisit the Focus (Purpose) of the Classroom Observation Reviewing the data, the supervisor looks for direct or striking examples of classroom practices that relate specifically to the focus. One approach is to identify events that contributed to achieving an objective or prevented the teacher from achieving an objective.

Resist the Temptation to Infuse Personal Values and Beliefs
Effective supervisors avoid preconceived judgments. Supervision is ongoing and formative. Acheson and Gall (1997) believed it was the supervisor's job to hold up the "mirror of practice" for the teacher. The biases or values of the supervisor cloud the mirror and get in the way of teachers as they work to make sense of their practice.

A Case Study

Jackie, a veteran Spanish teacher and now assistant principal, is "appalled" at what she saw in Ms. Evans' classroom. Ms. Evans was teaching a Spanish class how to tell time, and she was using a radio clock—with a digital readout. Jackie always used a clock with hour and minute hands, so students could more readily learn the phrases for "quarter till four," "half past three," and so on.

Jackie writes in her notes, "Ms. Evans needs help learning how to teach the right way." Pulling from her files the lesson plan she used in past years, she puts it in Ms. Evans' mailbox. She sits down to compose a series of suggestions for Ms. Evans.

Discuss the implications of Jackie's actions. How will they affect the discussion in the postobservation conference?

Determine Whether Observation Notes Need to Be Rewritten
Rewriting does not mean adding new data or the supervisor's own ideas. More often, it means filtering out extraneous data. In their eagerness to do a good job at collecting data, new supervisors will record every word or incident—even those unrelated to the observation focus. These extras can obscure the notes related directly to the focus and, depending on the experience level of the teacher, can lead to information overload.

Develop a Strategy for Presenting the Data Collected During the Observation Providing the teacher with objective feedback means not only displaying the data clearly, but also continually returning to the data for clarification, explanation, or extension during the postobservation conference. The observer's role is to facilitate the teacher's self-analysis and reflection, based on the data. The conference plan should keep the teacher reflecting and analyzing the events of the classroom.

Frame an Opening to Get the Teacher Thinking and Talking about Teaching Effective invitations to dialogue, also called icebreakers, are open-ended statements related to some aspect of teaching. Figure 6.3 (on the next page) presents examples of icebreakers for the postobservation conference.

Figure 6.3. Sample Postobservation
Icebreaker Statements

Icebreaker Statements	Conversation Stoppers
Think back to [some aspect of the lesson or the class] and tell me about it.	Prove to me that the students were prepared for independent practice.
The approach you chose to break students into small groups helped students learn how to cooperate. Tell me how you were able to get students to this level of cooperation.	No matter what you say, I just can't believe that the students will be ready to work in cooperative groups.
Tell me more about [some aspect of the class, student response, an instructional method, predictions about how students will perform on an assessment].	I'd like for you to turn in the results of your next quiz. I saw too many students struggling with their work during independent practice. Don't you think that more guided practice would have been more appropriate?
When you looked at Johnny, he knew immediately to stop talking.	Don't get too confident about Johnny, he'll talk while you are working with other students.
After the small group activity began, you used the down time to help students who had been absent the day before	Just analyze my notes and then get back to me if you have any questions about my assessment of your teaching.
How did you know that the student would try to…	Stop babying these kids; trust me, I know them better than you do.

Embrace the Spontaneity of the Discussion Although effective postobservation conferences are planned around the focus, spontaneous interaction makes clear that the supervisor is willing to listen and able to acknowledge the teacher's point of view regarding the self-assessment of strengths and weaknesses.

Supervisory Approaches and the Postobservation Conference

To conduct a positive postobservation conference, the supervisor must have a facilitative style—open to hearing what the teacher has to say. The teacher's point of view must permeate the discussion. Talking about teaching is a cooperative endeavor. It is the supervisor's responsibility to engage the teacher in reviewing, analyzing, and reflecting on data. The postobservation conference is the forum for supervisors to help teachers make meaning of their practices. Through effort, patience, and willingness to be of assistance, supervisors can help teachers move up a notch in their development. The goal is for supervisors to understand the learning needs of their teachers and for supervisors and teachers to chart the next steps in the learning process.

To establish a cooperative learning experience for the teacher, the supervisor's style and approach to communication must promote teacher talk. Figure 6.4 (on the next page) identifies supervisory approaches for promoting teacher talk, inquiry, and reflection.

Extended Reflection

Ms. Roberts observed Mr. Fiedler during first hour on Monday morning. Mr. Fiedler anxiously awaited hearing from Ms. Roberts. By Thursday afternoon, he had heard nothing. On Friday during his prep period, Mr. Fiedler went to Ms. Robert's office. When he knocked on her door, Ms. Roberts signaled him to enter. When Mr. Fielder asked how the observation went, Ms. Roberts explains that she will get back to him next week.

Mr. Fielder leaves the office feeling a bit uneasy about the response that Ms. Roberts gave to him. Mr. Fielder goes to the faculty lounge to get a soft drink. What do you suppose he will share with his colleagues about his classroom observation? His visit to Ms. Roberts' office?

Do you think Ms. Roberts will be able to regain a sense of credibility with Mr. Fielder?

Figure 6.4. Supervisory Approaches for Promoting Teacher Talk, Inquiry, and Reflection

Supervisory Approach	Example
Remain objective by providing the teacher with observational data that is value-free and nonjudgmental.	Here are the events that led to the small group…
Listen more—talk less—in order to hear (understand) what the teacher is trying to communicate.	Examining the following notes, tell me what responses you anticipated from students after you asked for…
Acknowledge, paraphrase, and ask probing/clarifying questions that encourage the teacher to talk more. Open-ended questions help the teacher make discoveries, identify recurring patterns, and reflect on possible alternatives or extensions to instructional practices.	From your point of view, what made this lesson successful?
Encourage the teacher to expand on statements that share beliefs about teaching, learning, and students.	When the student in the red shirt, said: "This is stupid," what made it possible for you to continue with the activity?
State what went well and ask reflective questions to focus on what needs improvement from the teacher's point of view.	The small group activity really worked well. How do you think the transition back to large group could have been different?
Avoid giving directive types of advice —even if asked. Instead, engage the teacher in role-playing reprises of events you observed, then invite extended thinking. Role playing and simulations that reflect the teacher's practices are more realistic. (This is one reason the postobservation conference should take place in the teacher's classroom; this extends the realism needed to make credible decisions for future improvement.)	Let me pretend I am a student in your fourth hour class. How would you help me?

(Figure continues on next page.)

Refuse to engage in talk not related to what you directly observed or to the improvement of instruction.	That thought is important. After the postobservation conference, I'll share your idea with the dean of students.
Offer to return for further observations in order to keep the momentum going for the teacher.	When would be a good time for me to come back to see the students apply the formula?
Provide ongoing support for the decisions the teacher makes in the postobservation conference by investigating with the teacher follow-up learning or enrichment activities.	The district is offering an after-school workshop on higher order thinking. Perhaps you'd like to go…Mrs. Simpson signed up for the workshop. I'll call in a reservation for you.
Be aware of nonverbal behavior that can send mixed messages.	Looking at the clock, facial expressions, body language such as folded arms.

Feedback, Trust, and the Johari Window Revisited

Feedback

Kallick (1997) believes that "learners are in a state of continuously working to improve, grow, and learn" (p. 216), and one strategy to promote learning is to receive feedback on performance. For best results, the supervisor uses the data collected in the observation to frame feedback. Feedback, in a sense, is "the breakfast of champions" because teachers need and want to know how they are doing and what they can do to improve or modify an approach.

Feedback can be constructive or destructive. Consider these two statements:

> *Statement 1* "Mrs. Ritter, you really need to take the workshop. All the questions you asked were lower-level ones. Students were obviously bored with your inability to ask for more than recall of information."

> *Statement 2* "Mrs. Ritter, your insight about your questions asking students for recall reminds me of how I used to ask opening questions. I benefited from the county workshop Questioning Strategies That Promote Higher-Order Thinking. This session is on the schedule for next month; would you be interested in attending? We have the funds and with advance notice, I can lock in a sub for you."

Statement 1 is destructive; it is too blunt, and it puts down the teacher with a personal attack. Statement 2 communicates the same message—the teacher needs assistance with questioning strategies more proactively.

Proactive feedback provides objective insight based on data without criticizing the teacher or finding fault. It encourages risk-taking and promotes changes in practice. By contrast, destructive feedback attacks aspects that are beyond control (such as the sound of the teacher's voice) and belittles teachers by compiling data that point only to weaknesses. Figure 6.5 lists effective feedback characteristics.

Figure 6.5. Characteristics of Effective Feedback

Effective feedback in the postobservation conference:

- Supports the teacher in examining both the positive and the not-so-positive aspects of practice.
- Promotes footholds for follow-up.
- Nurtures a sense of worth and positive self-esteem.
- Facilitates self-assessment and self-discovery.
- Focuses on a few key areas.
- Describes accurately what was observed.
- Is authentic and free of meaningless or patronizing platitudes.
- Clarifies and expands ideas for both the teacher and the observer.
- Deals with the concrete examples observed (actions, behaviors, words of the teacher or students).
- Promotes goal setting and the development of strategies.
- Avoids
  - making assumptions about teachers;
  - overloading the teacher with detail after detail after detail;
  - evaluating the teacher's overall credibility as a teacher;
  - asserting or making inferences about the teacher; and
  - judging and labeling a practice as good or bad.
- Guides the teacher to think beyond the lesson observed.
- Accepts and incorporates the points the teacher makes as part of the feedback process.

In an attempt to be helpful, some supervisors fall into the trap of overwhelming the teacher with too much information. Beginning supervisors, in particular, may seek to establish their credibility by offering a laundry list of observations based on their view of the lesson. But supervision is not about the supervisor; supervision is about the teacher and the learning opportunity that data and feedback from an observation can provide.

The tenor of the feedback in the postobservation conference sets the tone for future interaction between the supervisor and teacher. However, even carefully framed feedback may not be well received. The way a teacher receives feedback depends on variables such as the degree of trust between the supervisor and teacher, the experience level of the teacher, the patterns of communication at the school, and the conditions surrounding the classroom observation.

Trust

Supervisors who are new to the setting or who are implementing new supervisory practices need to establish their credibility. New supervisors do not have a personal history; as unknown commodities, they must first establish a foundation for their supervisory relationships with teachers. Built over time and established by the supervisor's words and deeds, trust is the cornerstone of the supervisory relationship.

Poor communication can compromise trust. Supervisors are wise to be aware of the trust-blocking responses outlined by Pascarelli and Ponticell (1994), presented in Figure 6.6 on the next page. What is said and how it is said can enhance or impede future interactions between a teacher and supervisor. Effective communication underpins the collaboration of supervisor and teacher in the pre- and postobservation conferences.

Figure 6.6. Trust-Blocking Responses

♦ **Evaluating** Phrases such as the following tend to evoke defensiveness: "You should…," "Your responsibility here is…," "You are wrong about…"

♦ **Advice-giving** Advice is best given if requested; responses such as "Why don't you just…," "You would be better off…," or "Your best action is…" can go in one ear and out the other if unsolicited.

♦ **Topping** "That's nothing, you should have seen…," "Well, in my class…," When that happened to me…," "You think you have it bad, well…" are phrases of one-upmanship. They shift attention from the person who wants to be listened to and leaves him/her feeling unimportant.

♦ **Diagnosing** Phrases that tell others what they feel ("What you need is…," "The reason you feel that way is…," "You really don't mean that…," "Your problem is…") can be a two-edged sword, leaving the person feeling pressured (if the speaker is wrong) or feeling exposed or caught (if the speaker is right).

♦ **Warning** "You had better…," "If you don't…," "You have to…," or "You must…" can produce resentment, resistance, or rebellion if the recipient feels the finger of blame pointed in his/her direction.

♦ **Lecturing** "Don't you realize…," "Here is where you are wrong…," "The facts simply prove…," or "Yes, but…," can make the person feel inferior or defensive. Full, descriptive data and problem-solving questioning allow the individual to make logical decisions for him or herself.

♦ **Devaluating** "It's not so bad…," "Don't worry…," "You'll get over it…," or "Oh, you really don't feel that way…" take away or deny the feelings of the speaker. Conveying nonacceptance of the speaker's feelings creates a lack of trust, feelings of inferiority or fault, and fear of risk-taking.

Source: Pascarelli & Ponticell, 1994.

The Johari Window Revisited

The principles of the Johari Window (Luft & Ingham, 1955) are introduced in Chapter 4 in relation to communication during the preobservation conference. (See Figure 4.4, page 78, for a portrayal of the Johari Window.) To recap: The four panes of the Johari Window are the open pane (aspects known to the self and to others), the hidden pane (known to the self, unknown to others), the blind pane (unknown to the self, known to others), and the unknown pane (unknown to the self and to others).

During the postobservation conference, the supervisor leads the teacher in exploring aspects of his teaching or other classroom behaviors. The flavor and intensity of this learning opportunity will vary depending on the teacher's awareness of these aspects at the start. Exploration in the open pane is relatively straightforward; exploration of aspects the teacher has kept in the hidden pane requires a deeper foundation of trust. Through objective feedback, the supervisor can help the teacher open the blind pane and become aware of behaviors as others see them. Through listening and support, the supervisor can help the teacher explore the unknown pane, learning about possible areas of weakness—but also resources and strengths—that neither has recognized until now. Consider the following case study.

A Case Study

Mary Westhover, a first-year physics teacher at Patriot High School, is struggling to keep students focused and on track. Mary has tried a variety of tactics, from mild scolding to yelling, and from speaking individually to students after class to phoning the parents of the major offenders. Mary asks Martin Corals, the assistant principal, to observe her during this class.

In the preobservation conference, Mary and Martin agree that the focus for the observation will be the interactions between Mary and her students. During the classroom observation, Martin tracks the way Mary uses cues to get students back on-task. The data clearly indicate that Mary's words are appropriate, but that she continually smiles while she is correcting student misbehavior. Student responses show that the students are confused because her words and demeanor don't match. Students are receiving mixed messages.

Martin's task is to coach Mary to explore both a blind and an unknown pane of her Johari Window. Given the explanation of the Johari Window in Chapter 4 and the feedback techniques discussed in this chapter, outline a strategy for revealing the information that lies behind Mary's blind pane.

After the Postobservation Conference, Then What?

The end is the beginning. The postobservation conference can serve to link supervision to professional development and evaluation. In Chapter 1, Figure 1.7 (page 14) portrays a visual for linking supervision, professional development, and evaluation. By completing a full cycle of clinical supervision, both the teacher and the supervisor are aware of areas to focus through professional development that could include such activities as

♦ Attending workshops, seminars, and conferences;

♦ Observing another teacher in the building or district;

♦ Enrolling in a graduate course;

♦ Engaging in action research with a common grade or subject area teacher;

♦ Reading a book or a series of articles related to a topic of interest; and

♦ Developing or refining a portfolio.

The possibilities for professional development are endless, and professional development should relate directly to helping teachers capitalize on the information learned from the processes of supervision—the preobservation conference, data collected in an extended classroom observation, and the insights gained from examining, reflecting, and inquiring on these data in the postobservation conference.

Many school systems assist teachers through the development of a plan. A professional growth plan would include goals, areas for the teacher to explore, and ways in which the teacher can explore these areas. At the end of the postobservation conference, the teacher and supervisor map activities included in Figure 6.7.

Figure 6.7. Professional Growth Plan

Date: <u>November 12, 2006</u>   Teacher: <u>Anne Hawkins</u>
Grade/Level: <u> 9 </u>   <u>Freshman English</u>

1.   Highlights from the postobservation conference:

2.   Area(s) to target:

3.   Short-term goal:

4.   Resources needed:

5.   Follow-up:

6. Date to begin the next cycle of supervision:

Figure 6.7 should be adapted for the context in which supervision occurs and the format used—clinical, peer coaching. The point is that effective supervision does not end once the postobservation conference has concluded; effective supervisors seek ways to keep the momentum for learning from one cycle of supervision to the next.

Summary

The postobservation conference holds great promise as a supervisory tool. During this time, teachers have the opportunity to analyze and make sense of data that bring into focus some aspect of their teaching. Lesson reconstruction as advocated by Bellon and Bellon (1982) engages the teacher in reconstructing the events of the classroom using data to analyze effectiveness. The supervisor's objective feedback positions the teacher to make informed judgments about practice and to develop further plans for growth and change.

Suggested Activities

From Theory to Practice

Conduct the postobservation conference with the colleague you observed. Videotape the conference.

Group Processing

In a small group, debrief about the events of the postobservation conference. Identify the hurdles encountered not only during the postobservation conference, but also in completing the full cycle of clinical supervision: the preobservation conference, the extended classroom observation, and the postobservation conference.

Reflection

Discuss the insights you have gained about the process of conducting full cycles of clinical supervision. What areas might you need to improve upon before assuming a position that will require conducting classroom observations?

References

Acheson, K. A., & Gall, M.D. (1997). *Techniques in the clinical supervision of teachers: Preservice and inservice applications* (4th ed.). New York: Longman.

Bellon, J., & Bellon, E. C. (1982). *Classroom supervision and instructional improvement: A synergetic process* (2nd ed.). Dubuque, IA: Kendall/Hunt.

Cogan, M. (1973). *Clinical supervision.* Boston: Houghton Mifflin.

Gagnon, G. W., & Collay, M. (2001). *Constructivist learning design.* Retrieved May 27, 2001, from http://www.prainbow.com/cld/cldp.html

Glatthorn, A. A. (1990). *Supervising leadership: Introduction to instructional supervision.* New York: HarperCollins Publishers.

Goldhammer, R. (1969). *Clinical supervision: Special methods for the supervision of teachers.* New York: Holt, Rinehart and Winston.

Kallick, B. (1997). Measuring from in the middle of learning. In A. L. Costa & R. M. Liebmann (Eds.), *Supporting the spirit of learning: When process is content* (pp. 203–219). Thousand Oaks, CA: Corwin Press.

Luft, J., & Ingham, H. (1955). *The Johari window: A graphic model for interpersonal awareness.* Proceedings of the Western Training Laboratory in Group Development. Los Angeles: University of California Western Training Lab.

Lyons, A. A., & Pinnell, G. S. (2001). *Systems for change in literacy education: A guide to professional development.* Portsmouth, NH: Heinemann.

O'Neil, J. (1998). Constructivism-wanted: Deep understanding. In J. O'Neil and S. Willis (Eds.), *Transforming classroom practice* (pp. 49–70). Alexandria, VA: Association for Supervision and Curriculum Development.

Pascarelli, J. T., & Ponticell, J. A. (1994). *Trust-blocking responses. Training materials developed for co-teaching.* Chicago.

Sergiovanni. T. J., & Starratt, R. J. (1998). *Supervision: A redefinition* (6th ed.). New York: McGraw-Hill.

Vygotsky, L. (1978). *Mind in society: The development of higher psychological processes.* Boston: Harvard University Press.

7

Career Stages, Adult Learning, and Supervision

In This Chapter...

♦ The nexus between adult and student learning

♦ Career stages

♦ Goal setting, tracking faculty goals, and attributes of goals

♦ Principles of adult learning

♦ Supervision that embraces the adult learner across career stages

Introducing Career Stages, Adult Learning, and Supervision

A primary intent of supervision is to promote teacher growth and development. Supervisors face the challenge of considering and meeting the various learning needs of all the adults in a school community. Adult learners have unique learning needs, and according to Jalongo (1991), "the key to understanding adult development is to recognize that, under anything approximating normal conditions, human beings will tend to seek growth" (p. 52). Without learning opportunities that take into account the varying needs of adults, teachers will stagnate to the point that they become "educational sales clerks" and teaching becomes a "humdrum job" (Schaefer, 1967, cited in Kleine-Kracht, 1993, p. 2).

In theory, research advances in such fields as professional development, group development, learning communities, and constructivism—all broadly related to social learning theory—have fueled increasing support to examine more closely the ways in which adults learn. However, in practice, the reality of "life in schools" for adults will remain grim unless supervisors seek opportunities for adults to grow and to learn from the work they accomplish.

> Tragically, schools are all too full of "corpses" who faithfully, persistently, heroically each day place oxygen masks on youngsters' faces, while they themselves are anoxic. A school is no different than a 757; if we want youngsters to put on the oxygen mask of learning, we adults must do it first, and right alongside them. (Barth, 2001, p. 25)

Barth's message is clear—adults must set the example of continuous learning for students and more profoundly for their peers. To foster adult learning and professional growth, the supervisor must identify unique needs based on career stage, prior education, and the past experiences that teachers bring to the school.

The Nexus Between Adult and Student Learning

Although research on the connection between learning opportunities for adults and student achievement has yielded sketchy results, a common thread seems to emerge in the findings that identify how teacher development supports student learning. Figure 7.1 (next page) identifies two national perspectives on the link between teacher and student growth. Both these reports call for fundamental change in the ways teachers work with one another and, by implication, in the ways supervisors work with teachers.

Extended Reflection

Consider this statement: The more teachers learn, the better students learn.

- ♦ From your perspective, is this statement true?

- ♦ Provide support for your insight.

Figure 7.1. National Perspectives on Learning Opportunities for Adults

The National Commission on Teaching and America's Future recommends that learning be

- Connected to teacher's work with their students;
- Linked to concrete tasks of teaching;
- Organized around problem solving;
- Informed by research; and
- Sustained over time by ongoing conversations and coaching.

Source: National Commission on Teaching and America's Future, 1996, p. 43.

The National Foundation for Improving Education believes schools need to promote activities that

- Have the goal of improving student learning at the heart of every school endeavor;
- Help teachers and other school staff meet future needs of students who learn in different ways and who come from diverse cultural, linguistic, and socioeconomic backgrounds;
- Provide adequate time for inquiry, reflection, and mentoring and is an important part of the normal working day of all public educators;
- Are rigorous, sustained, and adequate to the long-term change of practice;
- Are directed toward teachers' intellectual development and leadership;
- Foster a deepening of subject-matter knowledge, a greater understanding of learning, and a greater appreciation of students' needs;
- Are designed and directed by teachers, incorporates the best principles of adult learning, and involve shared decisions designed to improve the school;
- Balance individual priorities with school and district needs and advance the profession as a whole;
- Make best use of new technologies; [and],
- Are site based and supportive of a clearly articulated vision for students.

Source: National Foundation for Improving Education, 1996, pp. 6–7.

Career Stages

Picture yourself as a new supervisor meeting "your" entire faculty at a start-of-the-year meeting. Whom would you see? What would their needs be? Typically, you would see a faculty diverse in experience, age, and race—a group that includes first-year teachers (traditionally and alternatively certified), midcareer teachers, and veteran teachers. Beyond these obvious characteristics lie similar but distinctly different adult learning needs, different learning styles (auditory, visual, and so on), and different motivation levels.

Although application can be only approximate, career stage and developmental stage theories can guide interested school personnel to implement appropriate supervisory practices. Before exploring career stages and the principles of adult learning, consider a perspective offered by Merriam, Caffarella, and Baumgartner (2007):

> But just as there is no single theory that explains human learning in general, no single theory of adult learning has emerged.... Rather, there are a number of theories, models, and frameworks, each of which attempts to capture some aspect of adult learning. (p. 103)

Identifying the characteristics of a school's faculty is not simple. The process of thinking about adult learning starts with getting to know your people as adult learners, eager to refine the practices that shape their classroom practices.

Know Your People

Figure 7.2 (next page) can assist in broadly profiling a school's faculty by gathering statistical information about its members. This statistical profile can help the supervisor reflect on the adult learning needs of the faculty. A faculty sign-in sheet offers a tool to help track and tally information.

Figure 7.2. Assessing the Characteristics of a Faculty

1. Number of teachers _____   Male _____   Female _____
2. For each teacher, indicate the number of years in teaching and then total the number of years of experience. _____

   Then, calculate the average years of faculty experience. _____
3. Number of teachers whose experience falls years in the ranges:

   a. 1 to 3 years _____   b. 4 to 7 years _____
   c. 8 to 11 years _____   d. 12 to 15 years _____
   e. 16 to 19 years _____   f. 20+ years _____
4. Number of first-year teachers _____
5. Number of teachers who will retire at the end of the year _____
6. Wild cards:

   First-year teachers with experience _____

   Alternatively certified teachers _____

   Teachers returning to work after an extended leave _____

   Other _____
7. What overall patterns do you notice?

The patterns a supervisor discovers about a faculty can provide a basis for understanding the overall learning needs of teachers. The information gleaned from such a profile is very broad; in a sense, it relates to all but to none. The supervisor needs to dig deeper to uncover more about each teacher. Expanding on the information collected in Figure 7.2 yields a profile of the faculty (or a group of teachers, such as a department or a grade level). Figure 7.3 is an example of information that describes the general characteristics of specific teachers.

Figure 7.3. Faculty Profile

Teacher	Years of Experience	Highest Degree	Specialized Training
Baker	7	B.S.	Cooperative learning applied to math.
Davis	15	M.A. + 15 Spanish & French	Spent three months in Spain.
Franklin	2 (15 years prior experience as a chemist)	Ph.D. (alternatively certified) Chemistry	Unknown

This profile highlights experience and education; however, such a profile provides little insight about the developmental and professional career stages of teachers. Adult learning needs change over time as a result of experiences, professional development activities, and personal life events. If teachers trust and respect their supervisor, they will communicate what they need to learn in a way that makes sense.

Career Stage Theories and the Career Stage Continuum

Supervisors help teachers become fully functioning professionals by recognizing their developmental needs and by affording learning opportunities that meet these needs. A first step is to assess teachers' needs by examining career stages and the generalized principles that characterize adult learning within a particular stage.

Fuller (1969) very broadly identified three stages of teacher's concerns: preteaching phase = nonconcern; early teaching phase = concern with self; and late teaching phase = concern with pupils (Hall, George, & Rutherford, 1998). Figure 7.4 highlights more specifically the stages of concern as developed by Fuller.

Figure 7.4. Fuller's Stages of Concern

Stage of Concern	Motivation	Description
Survival	External	Seeks approval and affirmation from peers and administrators. Time spent primarily on coping with the immediacy of complex and unfamiliar situations and making decisions.
Task Stage	External	Focuses on tasks that need to be implemented.
Impact Stage	Internal	Focuses on meeting the needs of learners; self-growth and development are attended to through learning new skills and refining existing practices based on cues from students.

Source: Fuller, 1969.

Burden's (1982) research revealed that teachers go through three distinct stages: survival stage (first year of teaching), adjustment stage (years two through four), and mature stage (years five and beyond). He asserted that "administrators or supervisors should provide different types of supervisory assistance and vary their supervisory strategies when working with teachers at different developmental levels" (p. 4).

Burke, Christensen, and Fessler (1984) expanded the career cycle model to include eight stages. Huberman (1993), relying on concepts of developmental psychology, indicated that teachers travel through several stages:

- ♦ Survival and discovery (feelings of fear and enthusiasm);
- ♦ Stabilization;
- ♦ Emancipation and diversification (or possible stagnation);
- ♦ Reassessment;
- ♦ Serenity and relational distance;
- ♦ Conservatism and complaints; and
- ♦ Disengagement.

Huberman (1993) cautions that not all teachers move through all these stages, that movement is unpredictable, and that not all teachers move through these stages at the same rate or intensity. Figure 7.5 (next page) depicts dominant ideas about teacher stage and career development. Supervisors are encouraged to think about their teachers while reviewing this table. A list of faculty members (as illustrated in Figure 7.3, page 187) might offer a starting point for analyzing teacher stages and the developmental needs of faculty members. The exercise might yield insight on providing supervisory opportunities that match the needs of teachers.

Extended Reflection

Think about a teacher who is in a period of disengagement. What would be the signs or markers of a teacher who is in a period of disengagement?

Figure 7.5. Career Stages and
Developmental Needs of Teachers

Stage	Name	Years in Field (approximate)	Developmental Theory and Needs
1	Preservice	0	Training and preparation for a profession.
2	Induction	1–2	Survival stage (Burden, 1982; Feiman & Floden, 1980): Seeks safety and desires to learn the day-to-day operations of the school and the complexities of facing new situations in the classroom
3	Competency	3–5	Confidence in work mounts as does understanding. Building of the multifaceted role of teaching.
4	Enthusiasm	5–8	Actively seeks out professional development and other opportunities for professional growth; high job satisfaction (Burke, Christensen, & Fessler, 1984, p. 15).
5	Career frustration	Varies	Teacher burnout (Burke, Christensen, & Fessler, 1984, p. 15).
6	Stability	Varies	Complacency sets in; innovation is low.
7	Career wind-down	Varies	Coasts through on past laurels; status lets the teacher get by without exerting much effort.
8	Career exit	Varies	End of a teaching career.

Source: Adapted from Burden (1982); Burke, Christensen, & Fessler (1984); Christensen, Burke, Fessler, & Hagstrom (1983); Feiman & Floden (1980); Huberman, 1993; Katz, 1972; Newman, Dornburg, Dubois, & Kranz (1980).

One caveat: Identifying the stages of teacher development is tricky business, because there are no absolutes. The supervisor who is familiar with general attributes of adult development and career stage theories will make a more informed assessment. A teacher's practice, beliefs, and knowledge will change as a result of experiences gained on the job, formal coursework taken in graduate schools, participation in site and district-wide professional development opportunities, and personal lifetime events. Burden (1982) found in his research that changes occur over time in teachers'

- Job skills, knowledge, and behaviors—in areas such as teaching methods, discipline strategies, and curriculum planning;
- Attitudes and outlooks—in areas such as images of teaching, professional confidence and maturity, willingness to try new teaching methods, and concerns; and
- Job events—in areas such as changes in grade level, school, or district; involvement in additional professional responsibilities; and age of entry and retirement. (pp. 1–2)

Newman, Burden, and Applegate (1980) developed a method to take the guesswork out of this process—ask teachers themselves to identify where they are. They suggested that supervisors have teachers identify their own current stage of development and its markers. Figure 7.6 highlights this process more fully. After introducing the idea at a faculty meeting, the supervisor could meet with each teacher individually to discuss markers and needs for meeting goals.

Figure 7.6. Assessing Teacher Career Stages

Process

1. Have teachers draw a horizontal line across the blank page. This represents the time line of their teaching careers.

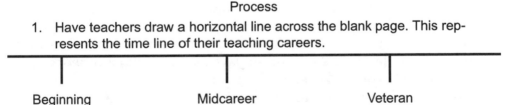

2. Say, "Careers may be marked by different stages, experiences, changes. If you were to divide your teaching career into several parts, what would mark your divisions? Mark them down on the line. Jot down the special characteristics of each part" (p. 8).

3. After teachers have identified where they are in their careers, the supervisor needs to provide a forum for sharing this "private" information.

Source: Newman, Burden, & Applegate, 1980

Maslow's Hierarchy of Needs

Maslow's (1954) hierarchy of needs might inform a supervisor's effort to provide learning opportunities based on the needs of the learner. A critical component of effective learning is that teachers become more satisfied, gain self-confidence, and derive value from work and working with others. Competence at lower levels of development lays the foundation for working toward higher levels of growth and learning.

Motivation theory and career stage theory support the assumption that teachers who focus on survival as they learn the day-to-day tasks of teaching cannot be expected to fulfill their potential for intellectual achievement, aesthetic appreciation, and self-actualization. The supervisor who knows how individual teachers perceive their own unmet needs can respond appropriately to specific, rather than global, needs. Figure 7.7 (Hlavaty, 2001), on the next page, correlates Maslow's hierarchy of needs to broadly accepted teacher career stages.

Figure 7.7. A Comparison of Maslow's Hierarchy of Needs and Teacher Career Stages

Maslow's Stage	Teaching Stage
Self-actualization	Realizes that teaching is not just a job—teaching is a profession.
↑	↑
Aesthetic appreciation	Enjoys teaching. Seeks additional knowledge for self-satisfaction.
↑	↑
Intellectual achievement	Learns things that are applicable. Shares successful strategies with others.
↑	↑
Self-esteem	Is recognized by coworkers for efforts. Feels appreciated by students and parents.
↑	↑
Belonging and love needs	Getting to know coworkers. Feels comfortable about asking questions.
↑	↑
Emotional and physical safety	Classroom routine established. Keeping up with workload.
↑	↑
Basic survival	Beginning career. Getting through each day.

Regardless of the stage of career development, all teachers have needs. Their needs and potential for growth can be met only when the overall principles of adult learning and development are considered. The following principles can serve as points of departure in working with teachers.

A Case Study

Irene Turner, principal of Bakersfield North High School, hired 15 teachers this past year. One of the new teachers is Stan Redmond, who graduated from a prestigious MBA program and worked as an accountant for 20 years before changing careers. Stan always wanted to be a teacher, and he attended an alternative certification program during summers. As a first-year teacher, Stan grapples with the realities of teaching.

 ◆ What types of supervision and support should Irene give Stan?

 ◆ How might Stan's needs differ from those of the other first-year teachers?

Goal Setting, Tracking Faculty Goals, and Attributes of Goals

The process of determining placement along the continuum of career stages and development (Figure 7.6, page 191) and individual teacher needs would be incomplete without follow-up activities. Goal setting is a natural follow-up activity. The goals identified by the teacher—influenced by life experiences, prior knowledge, and present needs—can frame a more tailored, differentiated and developmentally appropriate supervisory plan. Working together, teacher and supervisor can determine what types of supervision—clinical, peer coaching, action research, portfolio—will help the teacher achieve those goals.

Short- and Long-Term Goal Setting

Goal setting, a critical component of professional growth, contributes to supervision and professional development as well. Individual goal-setting conferences promote a professional relationship between teacher and supervisor. Held at the start of the year, they help teachers target areas to pursue through professional development, supervision, independent study, or formal coursework. For the supervisor, such conferences inform planning for professional development activities and provide a baseline for assessing overall performance and growth at year's end. The process is enhanced if the format for setting goals includes those that center on

 ◆ Instruction;

 ◆ Classroom procedures;

- Student achievement (e.g., how teachers are going to measure the impact of their instruction on gains in student learning); and

- Professional development (e.g., starting a master's degree or attending a cooperative learning seminar).

Figure 7.8 depicts a sample goal-setting form.

Figure 7.8. Sample Goal-Setting Form

Name _____   Grade Level _____
Department _____   Courses Taught _____

Please take time to reflect on your professional learning priorities for the year and develop one or two goals for each area. We'll meet in the next week or two to discuss your goals. My role is to learn what's important to you and to discover ways in which I can be of assistance to you in meeting your goals. I look forward to meeting with you.

Instructional Goal(s):

Classroom Procedure Goal(s):

Student Achievement Goal(s):

Professional Development Goal(s):

Date _____

Fieldwork

- Ask a group of teachers to develop goals for the year using Figure 7.8.

- Then go to Figure 7.9 (page) and track the goals developed by these teachers.

- With each teacher, develop a plan for achieving and monitoring goals for the year.

Encouraging teachers to identify both short- and long-term goals can help them stay focused on their development and help the supervisor provide the necessary support. Effective goal setting requires follow-through. Individual goal setting can also boost organizational development. The supervisor who tracks instructional goals can begin to profile the needs and aspirations of teachers across grade levels and subject areas. For example, if the sophomore English teachers are interested in exploring the topic of reader response, then the supervisor can concentrate on providing professional development opportunities relevant to that need.

A Case Study

Becky Morton, Dave Stevens, and Anna Cruz are sixth-grade team members at Franklin Middle School. At the beginning of the year, Joan English, the principal, asked teachers to develop goals for the year and to chronicle their goals on the form (Figure 7.8, page 195). As a group, Becky, Dave, and Anna decide to work on the goal of incorporating portfolio assessments across the team. Full of enthusiasm, they submit their forms to Ms. English and request a team meeting with her to review their goals for the year.

Motivated by district policies that require the site administrator to develop, monitor, and evaluate individual goals, Ms. English denies this request. She asks each teacher to submit forms that reflect "individual, not team, goals."

- ◆ Develop an alternate way for Ms. English to handle this situation.

- ◆ Include a plan for incorporating individual goals with team goals.

- ◆ List the steps Ms. English needs to take to clear the way for her teachers to work with one another.

Also include a strategy for Ms. English to communicate with district administrators.

Tracking Faculty Goals

Goal setting enables the supervisor to coordinate cost-effective measures to support teachers' efforts with resources such as journals, books, videos, and local experts (from within the building and outside). To track individual learning needs efficiently, the supervisor can use a spreadsheet or database program to sort faculty by grade level, by subject area, and by interest. Figure 7.9, on the next page, provides a sample spreadsheet printout for tracking goals.

Figure 7.9. Tracking Faculty Goals

Teacher and Subject Area	Instructional Goal(s)	Classroom Procedure Goal(s)	Student Achievement Goal(s)	Professional Development Goal(s)
Adducci (English)	♦ closure on cooperative learning activities	♦ getting students into groups	♦ eliminate "D" grades by providing tutoring	♦ apply to a master's degree program
Barker (Spanish)	♦ learn how to incorporate technology (Internet) in lessons	♦ getting students back on task while in cooperative learning groups	♦ how to grade student work while in cooperative learning groups	♦ attend a seminar or workshop in using technology ♦ read more about technology
Crandal (History)	♦ employ more higher-ordered questioning techniques ♦ work on incorporating student responses in question and answer sessions	♦ how to get class started without confrontational measures.	♦ work on developing a fair make-up policy for missing homework assignments (for students who do not do their homework)	♦ learn more about the history fair sponsored by the local university

Personal goal setting can also enhance another organizational function: charting the course of the school itself. An effective school has a plan for the present and the future. Ideally, the school's goals converge with those of its teachers. A caution is offered here: Personal and organizational goals cannot be forced into alignment. When the school's goals are imposed on teachers, supervision or formalized professional development initiatives deteriorate to a one size-fits-all phenomenon that stifles learning and growth.

Open dialogue and involvement in institutional and personal goal setting can add purpose to both. The supervisor can act as a sounding board by openly listening and letting teachers review individual learning goals that propel their professional development. Very few (if any) parameters should be imposed on individual goal setting. The supervisor, through questioning, can lead teachers as they define their goals and determine the path to achieve them.

Attributes of Goals

To assist supervisors as they lead faculty through the goal setting process, the attributes of goals as described by Lunenburg (1995) have been adapted to match the processes as they relate to supervision and professional development. Goals are

- ♦ **Specific:** Goals are specific when they are clearly stated and understood. Specific goals are less likely to be ignored if each teacher is involved in generating his/her own professional development goals.

- ♦ **Measurable:** Measurable goals are precise. Although there are no absolutes in meeting goals, articulated goals can be measured over time. Through classroom observations and the discussions that follow, the supervisor and teacher are able to discuss progress toward achieving goals. Moreover, professional development activities tied to supervision can enhance their relevance to goals.

- ♦ **Achievable:** Goals are achievable if they are realistic. Effective principals encourage teachers to set goals that will make them stretch rather than allow them to coast. Growth occurs as a result of achievable goals. The effort needed to reach a goal can inspire greater effort; unrealistic goals are self-defeating.

- ♦ **Relevant:** Goals are relevant if they are viewed as important to the individual and to the organization. Superficial goals are often forgotten because they have no meaning to the individual or to the organization.

- ♦ **Trackable:** Goals need to be trackable to check progress. Goals should not be so numerous or complex that they confuse rather than direct the actions of those involved in accomplishing them.

- ♦ **Ongoing:** Because professional development is an ongoing process, not all goals will be completed by the end of the year. Some goals are achieved over a longer period of time; others can be reached more quickly.

To extend the credibility of setting individual goals, the supervisor can build in a mechanism for teachers to evaluate their progress. Some supervisors might prefer to hold a midyear meeting with each teacher. Others might prefer to ask teachers to identify markers of meeting their goals and track progress on their own. In any case, the supervisor and the teacher should come together at the end of the year to assess growth and learning.

Progress toward goals need not stop at year's end. Often teachers take the summer to reflect on their year, attend workshops, reconfigure curriculum materials, and refine their instructional approaches. Therefore, the beginning of the school year is an opportune time for teachers to set goals, which in turn can frame the supervisor's work with teachers throughout the year.

Principles of Adult Learning

Brookfield's (1995) view of the adult learner provides an optimistic outlook for the supervisor to embrace while preparing to work with teachers.

> Viewing teachers as adult learners means that we focus on how they learn to make critically reflective judgments in the midst of action, and how they change subsequent actions to take account of these insights. (p. 222)

If applied, the following six principles for working with adult learners will guide the supervisor in setting the stage for adults to succeed in the classroom and to deepen their knowledge of the teaching craft.

Make Learning Authentic for the Adult Learner

Adults want authentic learning experiences with immediate application in their real worlds of teaching. Langer and Applebee's (1986) research in the area of reading and writing instruction offers a construct for making learning authentic for adults. Authentic learning embraces ownership, appropriateness, structure, collaboration, internalization, reflection, and motivation.

Ownership   When teachers own their learning pursuits, they are more intrinsically motivated to face the thorny issues of teaching and self-learning.

Appropriateness   The maxim no two learners are the same also applies to adult learners. The one-size-fits-all learning approach gives way to differentiated approaches, based on teachers' levels of experience (number of years in the school, experience with subject and grade level), career stages, and developmental levels (e.g., a first-year teacher at a new site who has nine years experience elsewhere).

Structure   Mechanisms are in place to support teacher choices about learning: peer coaches, mentors, portfolio development, and action research.

Collaboration Opportunities exist for teachers to talk about their learning and for learning to occur in the company of others. For adults, this means that the talk about learning goes beyond casual exchanges in the hallways or at the photocopier. Teachers need to be involved in "animated conversations about important intellectual issues" (Prawat, 1992, p. 13).

Internalization   For teachers to extend their classroom practices, they need to practice and experiment with new methods, receive supportive feedback, and then refine practices gained through the insights that result.

Reflection Without reflection, supervision is ritualistic. Reflection supports teachers to "learn by actively constructing knowledge, weighing new information against their previous understandings, thinking about working through discrepancies (on their own and with others), and coming to new understanding" (O'Neil, 1998, p. 51).

Motivation Adults often seek new knowledge in response to a need. Cross (1981) indicates that adults are motivated by the need to

- Achieve practical goals;
- Achieve personal satisfaction and other inner-directed goals;
- Gain new knowledge; and
- Socialize with others.

Know What Motivates the Adult Learner

The changes that mark various stages of life can either motivate or demotivate the adult learner. Adult learning is not static; what motivated an adult in previous years might not do so now. Prior learning experiences affect adults and their current beliefs, self-confidence, levels of self-esteem, and overall drive to succeed at learning. Thompson (1996) points to three very broad assumptions about motivation:

1. Motivation involves the behavior of *individuals*, and this has important implications for principals trying to motivate others. *Principals create conditions* in the workplace that enhance the ability of other individuals to motivate themselves.

2. Individual motivation is driven by something, whether it is goals, needs, or desires, and principals who wish to be successful in creating conditions for motivation must be cognizant of the particular goals, needs, and desires which drive staff members to behave in certain ways.

3. Motivation entails not only initiating, but also maintaining and directing behavior. Therefore, the principal's creating conditions to enhance the motivation of others is not a "one-shot" effort. (pp. 4–5, emphasis in the original)

Empower Transformational Learning

The primary objective of transformational learning is "to help learners learn what they want to learn and at the same time acquire more developmentally advanced meaning perspective" (Mezirow, 1991, p. 199). Supervisors challenge the status quo by empowering teachers to

- Make critical judgments;
- Ask critical questions of their practice; and
- Revise methods based on active inquiry over time.

Support Active Construction of Knowledge

The principles of constructivism outlined in Chapter 6 offer insights about adult learning. Figure 7.10 highlights the intersections between the constructivist paradigm and the principles of adult learning.

Figure 7.10. Intersections Between Constructivism and Principles of Adult Learning

Intersections	Constructivism	Principles of Adult Learning
Experience	Although knowledge is personal, knowledge includes "the social interaction with other cognizing subjects" (von Glasersfeld, 1989, p. 126).	Adults learn best in the company of others (Knowles, 1973).
Learning	Learning is "an active process; developmental, internally driven, influenced by the learner's intellectual development; self-referencing ..." (Jenkins, 1996, pp. 141–142).	Adults seek knowledge that applies to their current life situation; they want to know how this new information will help them in their development (Dalellew & Martinez, 1988, p. 28).
Transformation	Learning progresses from the external to the internal and from the social (interpersonal) to the individual (intrapersonal) (Brinner, 2001).	Adult learning is more self-directed. The impetus for learning is to share information, to generate one's own need for learning (Dalellew & Martinez, 1988, p. 28).

Establish a Climate Conducive to Adult Learning

An environment of open discussion fosters adult learning. McCall (1997) states, "Underlying all others is a basic assumption that adult learning is best achieved in dialogue" (p. 32). Wheatley (1992), cited in Lambert (1995), believes that "individuals generate information in their interactions with each other, information then becomes a feedback spiral enriching and creating additional information" (p. 32).

A relationship of mutual trust and respect between teachers and their supervisors enhances the likelihood of professional and personal growth. Adult learners are more motivated to take risks if they feel support from their supervisors and colleagues, and they are more likely to try new skills if there is no threat of retribution should they falter.

Create an Organizational Structure for Participative Planning

An environment of dialogue and trust sets the stage for adult learning, but the effective supervisor also takes active and concrete steps to foster the rich spiral of adult interaction and professional growth. The following *Tips for Supervisors* (Figure 7.11, next page), developed by Fischer (cited in McNamara, 1999), can serve as a guide.

Fieldwork

An excellent source on adult learning is the book, *Learning in Adulthood: A Comprehensive Guide* by Merriam, Caffarella, and Baumgartner (2007, John Wiley & Sons). Read "Part Two: Adult Learning Theory and Models." Develop a comprehensive list of the principles of adult learning and then apply these principles to the practices of instructional supervision.

Principles of Adult Learning	Supervisory Practices That Support Adult Learning

---

Figure 7.11. Tips for Instructional Supervisors

- Help the learner identify the starting point for a learning project and discern relevant [ways] of examination and reporting.
- Encourage adult learners to view knowledge and truth as contextual...and [believe] that they can act on their world individually or collectively to transform it.
- Create a partnership with the learner by negotiating a learning contract for goals, strategies, and evaluation criteria.
- Be a manager of the learning experience rather than an information provider.
- Teach inquiry skills, decision making, personal development, and self-evaluation of work.
- Help learners develop positive attitudes and feelings of independence relative to learning.
- Recognize learners' personality types and learning styles.
- Use techniques such as field experience and problem solving that take advantage of adults' rich experience base.
- Encourage critical thinking skills by incorporating...such activities as seminars.
- Create an atmosphere of openness and trust to promote better performance.
- Behave ethically, which includes not recommending a self-directed learning approach if it is not congruent with the learners' needs.
- Obtain the necessary tools to assess learners' current performance and to evaluate their expected performance.
- Provide opportunities for self-directed learners to reflect on what they're learning.
- Promote learning networks, study circles, and learning exchanges (self-managed teams of self-directed learners).
- Provide staff training on self-directed learning and broaden the opportunities for its implementation.

Source: Fischer (cited in McNamara, 1999)

Supervision That Embraces the Adult Learner Across Career Stages

The sequence of learning activities must enable adults to build on prior experiences. Adults need time to practice new skills and to receive friendly feedback from supportive colleagues. Learning in the company of others is powerful, and "teachers learn from one another while planning instruction, developing support materials, watching one another work with students, and thinking together about the impact of their behavior on their students' learning" (Showers & Joyce, 1996, p. 14). Glickman, Gordon, and Ross-Gordon (1995) state that regardless of the career stage of teachers,

- Effective supervision responds to the principles of adult learning;
- Effective supervision responds to and fosters teachers' stage development;
- Effective supervision recognizes and supports different phases within teachers' life cycles;
- Effective supervision helps teachers to understand, navigate, and learn from life transition events;
- Effective supervision recognizes and accommodates teachers' various roles; and
- Effective administration and supervision foster teacher motivation. (pp. 77–78)

Supervision for novice and veteran teachers is very different, but in each of these stages, teachers need supervision that promotes growth and development.

Supervision for Beginning Teachers

One of the few constants in American schools is the apprehensive excitement of a teacher entering the classroom for the first time. Equipped with a knowledge base of subject matter, teaching strategies, and planning skills, novice teachers embark on an odyssey of emotions including exhilaration, frustration, uncertainty, confusion, and isolation. Veenman (1984) referred to this phenomenon as reality shock. Gaede (1978) wrote that this shock is "symptomatic of the abrupt change in the environment experienced by the beginner in moving from the systematic support typical of student teaching to nearly total isolation and independence during that critical first year" (p. 408).

Whatever their background, life experiences, or preparation (traditional or alternative certification), beginning teachers lack experience and expertise in making decisions within the context of the classroom. They often labor to understand the complexities of their students and the cultural influences that make each student unique.

A Case Study

Lori Buenos, a first-year teacher, is struggling to keep her head above water. One concern is that even after midyear, students are uncooperative during daily discussions, e.g., talking while students are answering questions. Lori continues to plan for instruction by developing a daily script of questions to guide her students through book discussions.

Lori decides to stop the open discussions until her students "get with the program." Lori tells her mentor, Robert Jones, that she is ready to discontinue open-ended discussions altogether and have students write reflectively at the end of each class lecture. This was a difficult decision for Lori to make, but after three months of reflecting on the situation, she feels that she has no other options.

As a mentor, Robert believes that Lori's strategy might not resolve the obstacles that she is facing. What course of action would help this first-year teacher?

With limited experience and professional expertise, beginning teachers often solve their problems in a fragmented style, not really knowing or understanding exactly what issues they are addressing and more importantly, even why. This confusion produces a "scaffolding effect" (Zepeda & Ponticell, 1996). Essentially, problems at one level spiral into other areas not related to one another. For example, an instructional issue leads immediately to a classroom management disruption, which, when referred to the supervisor, escalates into a political issue over a homework policy that is not in tune with community norms.

Beginning and veteran teachers have different supervisory needs; effective supervisors recognize the developmental ranges of their teachers and professional staff. Beginning teachers benefit from supervision that is more concrete and directed toward specific needs, rather than more indirect methods. Beginning teachers need supervisory experiences that

- Introduce them to the supervisory process employed by the building and district;
- Engage them in overall goal setting; and
- Include supervisory processes such as preobservation conferences, observations, and postobservation conferences that begin early and continue throughout the year. (Zepeda & Ponticell, 1995)

Supervisors can learn important lessons from the robust research base on first-year teachers by striving to

- Break patterns of isolation (Lortie, 1975; Rosenholtz, 1989);
- Assist with the transition from the role of student to that of professional educator (Huling-Austin, 1988);
- Encourage dialogue, critique, and identification of additional support so that beginning teachers do not feel "neglected by overburdened school supervisory personnel" (Grant & Zeichner, 1981, p. 100);
- Increase the talk of teaching among teachers;
- Attend to the refinement of instructional delivery and assessment of student learning by focusing on "transferring the theories learned in preservice training to appropriate teaching practices" (Fox & Singletary, 1986, p. 14);
- Provide opportunities to take risks (Holland & Weise, 1999); and
- Link professional development, induction, and mentoring activities with a differentiated supervisory program that takes into account the needs of teachers at this vulnerable stage in their careers.

Supervision for Veteran Teachers

In a qualitative study of 12 recently retired teachers, Green and Manke (1994) identified the following intrinsic rewards that motivated veteran teachers:

- Working with children;
- Intellectual rewards of teaching, including autonomy, creativity, variety, solving difficult problems;
- Rewards of belonging to a community;
- Relationships with students; and
- Relationships with other teachers. (pp. 104–107)

Veteran teachers need to derive satisfaction from their work; for them, expertise is a strong motivator. Mature adult learners see themselves as having responsibility for their learning, and they have a generative need to share their expertise.

Experienced teachers prefer collaborative supervision that enables them to direct their own learning. Brundage (1996) reports that veteran teachers in her study wanted the opportunity to talk about professional issues with other teachers who had just as much or even more experience. Bureau's (1993) research on veteran teachers reports that experienced teachers also desired supportive and developmental supervision. Investigating the qualities of supervisory processes that facilitate change in a veteran teacher's beliefs, this research confirms that supportive supervision nurtures

- Mutual trust, collegiality and the freedom to take risks;
- Understanding that leaves ownership of the direction of change with the teacher;
- A climate in which a teacher can express her comfort and discomfort with changes in her teaching, classroom, and beliefs, as well as her intuitive feelings about accepting or rejecting change;
- Engagement of both teacher and supervisor in co-learning and co-reflection; and, listening to a teacher's reflective language for evidence of reflection on and changes in beliefs. (Bureau, 1993, p. 54)

Although most experienced teachers have the skills to perform perfunctory tasks and teach competently, they continue to need new information and knowledge to keep pace with developments in their fields. Veteran teachers need supervisory experiences that

- Acknowledge them as professional career teachers who have experiences to draw upon as they reflect upon their practice;
- Enable them to develop their own plans for learning and experimentation;
- Signal to them that risk-taking is part of the learning process;
- Enable professional sense-making; and
- Encourage self-assessment and reflection. (Zepeda & Ponticell, 1995)

A Case Study

After profiling the faculty at Taylor High School, Ed Jackson realizes that there are seven veteran teachers with over 20 years of experience—all at Taylor. Although Ed knows that these seven teachers will be retiring in four years, he is concerned about providing learning opportunities that speak to these veterans. Even if a teacher has only four years left, those four years are vital. He does the math: A teacher who teaches 30 students per class period, five periods a day, will teach some 600 students in four years. Those last four years could and should be as invigorating as the beginning years.

The faculty profile also shows that for the past few years, Taylor High School has hired approximately 11 new teachers each year to replace retiring teachers. Jackson meets with the administrative team, and they develop a mentoring strategy that pairs new teachers with veteran teachers nearing retirement. A defining feature of the strategy is that these teachers will go through professional development as pairs, learning with and from one another.

- ◆ If you wanted to implement a program such as this, what would you need to do to ensure that both the veteran and the beginning teacher could learn from each other?

- ◆ What types of support would teachers need to participate in such a plan?

How could such a plan be implemented in the school where you work?

Summary

The literature on career stages and adult learning shows that adults have unique learning needs; no one model can be applied across all adult populations. The only constant is that professional development and growth must be ongoing and sustained. An understanding of adult learning constructs and career stage theories can help supervisors and teachers develop a long-term program of growth aligned with current and future developmental learning needs.

Prospective and practicing supervisors might do well to revisit Glickman's (1981) notion about adult learning: "The supervisor must work with teachers in the same developmental manner that teachers are expected to work with their students. Sameness and uniformity of approach are out. Individuality with social responsibility is in" (p. 62). For adult learning to thrive, the supervisor must consider the needs of the learners who make up the community and engage adult learners in activities that are career-stage-specific and steeped in the principles of adult learning.

Suggested Activities

From Theory to Practice

Faced with a shortage of teachers, some school systems hire alternatively certified teachers. The differences between alternatively certified and traditionally certified teachers have been reported in the literature. According to the National Center for Educational Information (2005), self-reported data from individuals entering teaching through alternate routes to certification show the following:

- 70 percent are older than 30 years of age, 38 percent are male and 30 percent are nonwhite.
- 46 percent are teaching in a large city.
- Nearly half were working in a noneducation occupation the year prior to entering an alternative route program.
- 32 percent of entrants into teaching via alternate routes are nonwhite compared to 11 percent of the current teaching force.

Locate an alternatively certified teacher in the system where you work and speak to this person about his learning needs. List what the teacher revealed about his learning needs. Based on career stage theory and the principles of adult learning, how would you provide for the professional needs of the alternatively certified teacher you interviewed?

Group Processing

In a small group, discuss the professional needs of midcareer teachers as defined in this chapter. What special considerations affect the supervision of midcareer teachers? Report findings to the class.

Reflection

Discuss the most difficult aspects of differentiating supervision and professional development for adults.

References

Barth, R. S. (2001). *Learning by heart*. San Francisco, CA: Jossey-Bass.

Brinner, M. (2001). *What is constructivism?* Retrieved June 2, 2001, from http://carbon.cudenver.edu/~mryder/itc_data/constructivism.html

Brookfield, S. D. (1995). *Becoming a critically reflective teacher*. San Francisco, CA: Jossey-Bass.

Brundage, S. (1996). What kind of supervision do veteran teachers need? *Journal of Curriculum and Supervision, 12*(1), 90–94.

Burden, P. (1982, February). *Developmental supervision: Reducing teacher stress at different career stages*. Paper presented at the Association of Teacher Educators National Conference, Phoenix, AZ.

Bureau, W. (1993, April). *Seeing supervision differently: The processes of facilitating change in a veteran teacher's beliefs*. Paper presented at the annual meeting of the American Educational Research Association, Atlanta, GA.

Burke, P. J., Christensen, J. C., & Fessler, R. (1984). *Teacher career stages: Implications for staff development.* Bloomington, IN: Phi Delta Kappa Educational Foundation Whole No. 214.

Christensen, J., Burke, P. J., Fessler, R., & Hagstrom, D. (1983). *Stages of teachers' careers: Implications for professional development.* Washington, DC: National Institute of Education. (ERIC Document Reproduction Service No. ED227054)

Cross, K. P. (1981). *Adults as learners: Increasing participation and facilitating learning.* San Francisco, CA: Jossey-Bass.

Dalellew, T., & Martinez, Y. (1988). Andragogy and development: A search for the meaning of staff development. *Journal of Staff Development, 9*(3), 28–31.

Feiman, S., & Floden, R. (1980). *What's all this talk about teacher development?* East Lansing, MI: The Institute for Research on Teaching. (ERIC Document Reproduction Service No. ED189088)

Fox, S. M., & Singletary, T. J. (1986). Deductions about supportive induction. *Journal of Teacher Education, 37*(1), 12–15.

Fuller, F. (1969). Concerns of teachers: A developmental conceptualization. *American Educational Research Journal, 6*(2), 207–266.

Gaede, O. F. (1978). Reality shock: A problem among first-year teachers. *The Clearing House, 51,* 404–409.

Glickman, C. D. (1981). *Developmental supervision: Alternative approaches for helping teachers to improve instruction.* Alexandria, VA: Association for Supervision and Curriculum Development.

Glickman, C. D., Gordon, S. P., & Ross-Gordon, J. M. (1995). *Supervision of instruction: A developmental approach* (3rd ed.). Boston: Allyn and Bacon.

Grant, C. A., & Zeichner, K. M. (1981). Inservice support for first-year teachers: The state of the scene. *Journal of Research and Development in Education, 14*(2), 97–129.

Green, N., & Manke, M. P. (1994). Good women and old stereotypes: Retired teachers talk about teaching. In P. B. Joseph and G. E. Burnaford (Eds.), *Images of schoolteachers in twentieth-century America: Paragons, polarities, complexities* (pp. 96–115). New York: St. Martin's Press.

Hall, G. E., George, A. A., & Rutherford, W. A. (1998). *Measuring stages of concern about the innovation: A manual for use of the SoC questionnaire.* Austin, TX: Southwest Educational Development Laboratory.

Hlavaty, K. (2001). *Differentiated supervision for veteran teachers.* [Unpublished comprehensive exam]. Athens, GA: University of Georgia.

Holland, P. E., & Weise, K. R. (1999). Helping novice teachers. In L. W. Hughes (Ed.), *The principal as leader* (2nd ed.) (pp. 181–207). Upper Saddle River, NJ: Merrill/Prentice Hall.

Huberman, M. (1993). (Jonathan Neufeld, Trans.) *The lives of teachers.* New York: Teachers College Press. (Original work published 1989.)

Huling-Austin, L. (1988). Factors to consider in alternative certification programs: What can be learned from teacher induction research? In J. Sikula (Ed.), *Action in teacher education. Tenth year anniversary issue* (pp. 169–176). Reston, VA: Association of Teacher Educators.

Jalongo, M. R. (1991). *Creating learning communities: The role of the teacher in the 21st century.* Bloomington, IN: National Education Service.

Jenkins, J. M. (1996). *Transforming high schools: A constructivist agenda*. Lancaster, PA: Technomic.

Katz, L. (1972). Developmental stages of preschool teachers. *Elementary School Journal, 73*(1), 50–54.

Kleine-Kracht, P. A. (1993). The principal in a learning community. *Journal of School Leadership, 3*(4), 391–399.

Knowles, M. S. (1973). *The adult learner: A neglected species*. Houston, TX: Gulf.

Lambert, L. (1995). Toward a theory of constructivist leadership. In L. Lambert, D. Walker, D. Zimmerman, J. Cooper, M. Lambert, M. Gardner and P. J. Ford-Slack (Eds.), *The constructivist leader* (pp. 28–51). New York: Teachers College Press.

Langer, J. A., & Applebee, A. (1986). Reading and writing instruction: Toward a theory of teaching and learning. *Review of Research in Education, 13*, 171–194.

Lortie, D. C. (1975) *School teacher: A sociological perspective*. Chicago: University of Chicago Press.

Lunenburg, F. C. (1995). *The principalship: Concepts and applications*. Englewood Cliffs, NJ: Merrill.

Maslow, A. H. (1954). *Motivation and personality*. New York: Harper & Row.

McCall, J. (1997). *The principal as steward*. Larchmont, NY: Eye On Education.

McNamara, C. (1999). *Strong value of self-directed learning in the workplace: How supervisors and learners gain leaps in learning*. Retrieved May 29, 2001, from http://www.mapnp.org/library/trng_dev/methods/slf_drct.htm

Merriam, S. B., Caffarella, R. S., & Baumgartner, L. M. (2007). *Learning in adulthood: A comprehensive guide* (3rd ed.). San Francisco: John Wiley & Sons.

Mezirow, J. (1991). *Transformative dimensions of adult learning*. San Francisco, CA: Jossey-Bass.

National Center for Education Information. (2005). *Alternative routes to teacher certification*. Washington, DC: Author. Retrieved January 7, 2007, from http://www.ncei.com/Alt-Teacher-Cert.htm#6

National Commission on Teaching and America's Future. (1996). *What matters most: Teaching for America's future*. New York: Author.

National Foundation for Improving Education. (1996). *Teachers take charge of their learning: Transforming professional development for student success*. West Haven, CT: Author.

Newman, K., Burden, P., & Applegate, J. (1980). *Helping teachers examine their long-range development*. Washington, DC: Association of Teacher Educators. (ERIC Document Reproduction Service No. ED204321)

Newman, K., Dornburg, B., Dubois, D., & Kranz, E. (1980). *Stress to teachers' midcareer transitions: A role for teacher education*. (ERIC Document Reproduction Service No. ED196868)

O'Neil, J. (1998). Constructivism—Wanted: Deep understanding. In J. O'Neil and S. Willis (Eds.), *Transforming classroom practice* (pp. 49–70). Alexandria, VA: Association for Supervision and Curriculum Development.

Prawat, R. S. (1992). From individual differences to learning communities—our changing focus. *Educational Leadership, 49*(7), 9–13.

Rosenholtz, S. J. (1989). Workplace conditions that affect teacher quality and commitment: Implications for teacher induction programs. *The Elementary School Journal, 89*(4), 421–439.

Showers, B., & Joyce, B. (1996). The evolution of peer coaching. *Educational Leadership, 53*(6), 12–16.

Thompson, D. P. (1996). *Motivating others: Creating the conditions.* Larchmont, NY: Eye On Education.

Veenman, S. (1984). Perceived problems of beginning teachers. *Review of Educational Research, 54*(2), 143–178.

von Glasersfeld, E. (1989). Cognition, construction of knowledge, and teaching. *Synthese, 80,* 121–140.

Zepeda, S. J., & Ponticell, J. A. (1996). Classroom climate and first-year teachers. *Kappa Delta Pi Record, 32*(3), 91–93.

Zepeda, S. J., & Ponticell, J. (1995). The supervisory continuum: A developmental approach. *The Practitioner, 22*(1), 1–4.

8

Motivation and Supervisory Leadership: An Overview

In This Chapter...

♦ Motivation theories

♦ Leadership and motivation

♦ Implications for supervisors

Introducing Motivation and Supervisory Leadership

Motivation is essentially described as "the forces acting on or within an organism to initiate and direct behavior" (Petri, 1996, p. 3, emphasis in the original). With growth and development as the goal of instructional supervision, the supervisor needs to see the relationship between leadership style and motivation—What approaches will motivate teachers? Unfortunately, there are no clear models that a supervisor can turn on or off, and there are no simple explanations of why the same leadership style can either motivate or discourage change. Although this chapter offers only a very broad overview of motivation, the theories and models presented here can help prospective supervisors understand what motivates or discourages adults.

Motivation Theories

Maslow's Theory of Human Motivation

Maslow's theory of human motivation (1987) offers the supervisor important insight on two levels. First, the theory sheds light on how and why people respond as they do. Second, Maslow's theory clarifies the meaning and significance that people place on work. Maslow believed that human needs extend from the physiological (lowest) to self-actualization (highest). Figure 8.1 illustrates the range of human needs according to Maslow.

Figure 8.1. Maslow's Hierarchy of Needs

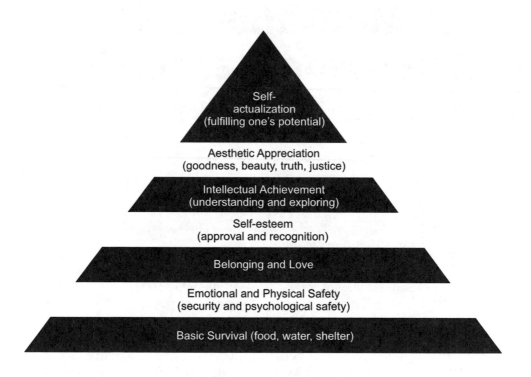

Source: Adapted from Lefrancois, 1982; Maslow (1987); and Woolfolk (2005).

From Maslow's hierarchy of needs, supervisors can conclude that teachers want to feel psychologically safe and secure and have a sense of belonging with others. A supervisor's actions, demeanor, and words can communicate acceptance or rejection of people and their ideas. Teachers want to be productive and to feel useful. They need to know whether they are hitting the mark when they teach, and if they are missing the mark, they want to do better. As teachers mature, they want to assume more leadership within the school, to give back what has been given to them. Motivated teachers are empowered to develop and grow while making a difference in the lives of others. Empowerment is a motivator especially for teachers who in the mid-to-late career stages seek recognition for their expertise and positive contributions over the years.

Extended Reflection

Consult Fuller's Stages of Concern in Figure 7.4 (page 188) and the Career Stages and Developmental Needs of Teachers in Figure 7.5 (page 190).

In small groups of five, go through the exercise found in Figure 7.6 (page 191) in which each member of the group identifies where he/she is relative to career stage. After self-identifying "place" in a career stage, ask each member of the group to predict where he/she is in relation to Maslow's Hierarchy of Needs found in Figure 8.1 (page 214).

As a group, identify

- ◆ Possible external motivators that supervisors need to provide to these teachers;

- ◆ What internally motivates these teachers to achieve;

- ◆ The relationship between external and internal motivators;

- ◆ Possible demotivators for

  - • Beginning teachers;

  - • Midcareer teachers; and

  - • Veteran teachers.

McClelland's Theory of Motivation

McClelland's theory postulates that people are motivated by achievement, power, and affiliation, and motivation can be internally or externally mediated.

Achievement People who are motivated by achievement are competitive, value success, and take pride in accomplishing goals with distinction. They want to do "something better for its own sake, for the intrinsic satisfaction of doing something better" (McClelland, 1987, pp. 227–228). McClelland also believed that people motivated by achievement "do better at moderately challenging tasks, take personal responsibility for their performance, seek performance feedback on how well they are doing, and try new and more efficient ways of doing things" (p. 251). The implications for supervisors are immense.

Extending the Reflection Further

Refer to the preceding Extended Reflection. Now examine achievement as a motivator for beginning, midcareer, and veteran teachers.

What do you believe supervisors can do to foster a sense of achievement for each of these groups of teachers?

Power People who are motivated by power are preoccupied with control and exact precision over people and their activities. Razik and Swanson (1995) identify five types of power that leaders exert (Figure 8.2).

Figure 8.2. Types of Power

1. *Reward power:* Rewards are used to motivate subordinates.
2. *Coercive power:* Punishment is used as a means of motivation.
3. *Legitimate power:* The power-user is viewed as credible and uses this credibility to influence people.
4. *Referent power:* The power-user is respected, and respect creates identification between the power-user and subordinates. This identification motivates people to work with the power-user to achieve goals.
5. *Expert power:* The power-user is perceived as an expert. This perception motivates people because they have confidence in the person with expertise.

Source: Razik & Swanson, 1995.

Supervisors work with teachers at several levels. At one level, supervisors spend time in teachers' classrooms conducting both formal and informal classroom observations. At another level, supervisors collaborate with teachers before and after classroom observations during the pre- and postobservation conferences. At yet a different level, supervisors work with teachers between classroom observations by ensuring that professional development and other learning opportunities align with goals set by teachers.

Uncomplimentary metaphors have emerged in the literature on instructional supervision, portraying supervisors as exerting "power over" teachers (Blase & Blase, 2000). The use of power over teachers discourages and stifles teachers who want to

[e]agerly discuss their practice with supervisors, and extend an open invitation to visit their classrooms. Supervisors, of course, officially may visit any classroom, but they must be accepted psychologically by the teacher during the supervisory visit if the process is to become anything more than ritual. (McBride & Skau, 1995, p. 269)

For supervisors to motivate teachers, they must not be "motivated by a desire to control what teachers do" in their classrooms (Schwan & Spady, 1998).

Extended Reflection

Think of the types of supervision you have experienced.

♦ What types of power did your supervisor use during the experience?

♦ What were your reactions to the uses of power?

Affiliation People who are motivated by collaborative needs value human relations, open communication, and lasting relationships with others. Teachers want to belong and feel a sense of belonging with the adults they work with daily. Supervisors must be available for their teachers; they must promote relationships with teachers and among teachers. Supervisors connect with teachers by providing opportunities for them to collaborate as mentors and peer coaches. Teachers want to form a safety net, giving and receiving support during challenging times. Effective supervisors strive to consult with, collaborate with, and coach teachers and to engage teachers in opportunities to learn from one another.

Herzberg's Theory of Motivation

Frederick Herzberg, a noted psychologist, developed a theory of motivation that delineates the satisfaction workers derive from internal and external rewards. Herzberg classified rewards into two categories: hygiene factors (external factors that might motivate subordinates) and motivators (internal factors that motivate peak performance in subordinates). Hygiene factors include such items as job security, salary and fringe benefits, and the organizational climate and physical conditions of the work environment. Hygiene factors make a critical contribution to the quality of the work environment; however, Herzberg believed that these factors alone could not motivate people to achieve their full potential. Herzberg believed that the internal motivators (achievement, professional and personal growth, added responsibility, and recognition) enabled people to achieve greater personal and organizational results.

Blending Maslow's and Herzberg's Motivation Theories

By examining Herzberg and Maslow's work in relation to motivation, the supervisor is in a better position to nurture an environment that is more responsive to the individual. Figure 8.3 illustrates Herzberg and Maslow's theories.

Figure 8.3. Blending Herzberg's Motivation Model with Maslow's Hierarchy of Needs

	Herzberg's Motivation Model	Maslow's Hierarchy of Needs
	Higher-Order Needs	
Internal Motivators	◆ Job content ◆ Achievement ◆ Recognition ◆ Growth ◆ Advancement	◆ Need for knowledge ◆ Need for understanding ◆ Self-actualization
	Lower-Order Needs	
Hygiene Factors	◆ Pay/salary ◆ Fringe benefits ◆ Type of supervision ◆ Company policies and procedures ◆ Status ◆ Job security ◆ Interpersonal relations	◆ Survival needs ◆ Security needs ◆ Belonging needs ◆ Esteem needs

Source: Adapted from Gage & Berliner (1988); Jennings (1993); and Razik & Swanson (1995).

Making the Connection Between Motivation and Adult Learning

Adult learners need to feel safe and secure in their learning environment—free to try, reflect on, and then use new strategies and methods based on supportive feedback. The supervisor who seeks to motivate teachers would do well to consider that "The primary foundation for encouragement is our caring and acceptance of the [adult] learner" (Wlodkowski, 1985, p. 90). Wlodkowski suggests ways in which personal regard for the learner can be sustained over time (Figure 8.4).

Figure 8.4. Ways to Promote Adult Learning

♦ Give recognition for real effort because any time a person attempts to learn something, that individual is taking a risk, and learning's a courageous act.

♦ Acknowledge the learner's effort—make perseverance a valued trait.

♦ Minimize mistakes while the learner is struggling because sometimes learning is like a battle. The critical edge between advancement and withdrawal or between hope and despair is fragile at best.

♦ Emphasize learning from mistakes.

♦ For each learning task, demonstrate a confident and realistic expectancy that the learner will learn.

♦ Show faith in the adult's capacity as a learner.

♦ Work with the learner at the beginning of difficult tasks.

♦ Reinforce the "process" of learning.

♦ Learning is not a linear progression. There are often wide spaces, deep holes, dead ends, and regressions in learning. Real encouragement signals the task of learning is itself important and emphasizes the intrinsic value of the entire process of learning.

Source: Wlodkowski, 1985, pp. 91–92.

A Case Study

Dr. Cynthia Jones left a postobservation conference with Stacy Elliot, an eighth-grade math teacher who has taught at Cog Hill Middle School for 18 years. Stacy is devastated because Dr. Jones gave her an assignment to complete before the end of the term. Dr. Jones directed Stacy to read the National Council of Teachers of Mathematics (NCTM) Standards for Practice and Turning Points: 2000 and then be prepared to discuss how she can better align her instructional practices based on what she learned from the reading assignment.

Stacy speaks with several colleagues about Jones' request and makes an appointment to see the director of Middle Schools. Before this meeting, Stacy speaks with her union representative.

♦ What went wrong for Dr. Jones?

♦ What options does she have to rectify the problem?

Leadership and Motivation

Leadership is eclectic. No single leadership model is pure; every model has linkages to other models, and subscribing to a particular leadership model or style does not guarantee effective results. The research reports that teachers need and want supervisors who

- Listen;
- Are fair and loyal;
- Have integrity and a strong ethical framework;
- Understand the role of each teacher and recognize that roles change over time; and
- Can be trusted.

Theory X and Y Leaders:
Two Differing Styles of Leadership

Supervisors empower teachers by sharing leadership. They encourage teachers to set the course of their own learning. Effective supervisors are confident in their own abilities and the abilities of the teachers for whom they supervise. McGregor's Theory X and Y leadership model (1961) was based, in large part, on Maslow's hierarchy of needs. Figure 8.5 (next page) highlights McGregor's major premises, which can be applied to supervisory leadership.

Fieldwork

In a setting you are familiar with, identify a supervisor whose practices follow either Theory X or Theory Y. List the everyday practices related to supervision that lead you to this conclusion. See Figure 8.5.

Figure 8.5. McGregor's Leadership Model
Applied to Supervision and Professional Development

Theory X Supervisors

Believe people

♦ are incapable of working autonomously;
♦ want boundaries and directive-oriented supervision; and
♦ desire external directions and reward structures.

Therefore, the organization and supervision

♦ are rigid with inflexible structures;
♦ have detailed rules that make teachers compliant; and
♦ want subordinates to be dependent in order to maintain power relationships.

Result: Hostility, discontent, and aggression.

Theory Y Supervisors

Believe people

♦ are capable of self-direction in analyzing their learning and professional development;
♦ prefer cooperative work relations and a sense of community; and
♦ are creative and strive for excellence because of an intrinsic desire to improve.

Therefore, the organization and supervision

♦ have less emphasis on controls and are a process of continued professional growth;
♦ promote autonomy in subordinates; and
♦ sustain a momentum for the teacher as learner by building a community of learners.

Result: Initiative, creativity, and optimal growth.

Source: McGregor, 1961.

Fusion Leadership

The book *Fusion Leadership: Unlocking the Subtle Forces That Change People and Organizations,* by Richard Daft and Robert Lengel (1998), defines leadership for change using the terms fusion and fission. Figure 8.6(next page) highlights the differences between fusion and fission leaders. Although Daft and Lengel's work is primarily intended for the corporate sector, prospective supervisors might consider how the principles of fusion and fission can be applied to the school setting.

Figure 8.6. Elements of Fusion and Fission Leadership Styles

Organizational Structures

Fission Leadership

♦ splits the whole into parts by creating boundaries—promotes isolation.

♦ maintains "layers of hierarchy" (p. 14).

Fusion Leadership

♦ joins part into a whole by eliminating boundaries—promotes togetherness.

♦ promotes a "common ground and a sense of community based on what people share—vision, norms, and outcomes" (p. 15).

Professional Relationships

Fission Leadership

♦ promotes competition.

♦ promotes "authority and control" (p. 14).

Fusion Leadership

♦ promotes people "joining, coming together, creating connections and partnerships" (p. 15).

♦ promotes "seeing similarities rather than differences" (p.15).

Source: Daft & Lengel, 1998.

Implications for Supervisors

Supervision that makes a difference fosters the internal and external motivation that leads teachers to professional growth. Effective leadership encourages teachers to examine and reflect on their instructional practices, then take up the challenge of strengthening them. Wlodkowski (1985) states, "There appear to be at least six major factors that have a substantial impact on learner motivation—attitude, need, stimulation, affect, competence, and reinforcement" (p. 45). Supervisors who want to motivate teachers take advantage of these factors.

Effective supervisors create the conditions that support motivated teachers. Motivated teachers have higher degrees of persistence and vigor than unmotivated teachers (Petri, 1996). McClelland and Burnham (1997) assert that people who focus on "personal improvement want to do things themselves. They want concrete short-term feedback on their performance so that they can tell how well they are doing" (pp. 63–64). Effective supervisors recognize that teachers need to develop, initiate, and direct their own learning opportunities that go beyond the clinical model of supervision. Teachers need to learn on the job; the National Staff Development Council suggests that at least 25 percent of the workday should be devoted to job-embedded learning.

Effective supervisors seek to individualize learning opportunities. An achievement a veteran teacher might take for granted would bring a sense of real accomplishment for a beginning teacher. However, both can feel the satisfaction of being able to "do something better or more efficiently than it has been done before" (McClelland & Burnham, 1997, p. 63).

Effective supervisors provide opportunities in the zone of proximal development, challenging and motivating teachers to new growth. Without challenges, teachers maintain the status quo. But challenge and growth entail risk; "doing something better often implies doing it differently from before. It may involve finding a different, shorter, or more efficient path to a goal" (McClelland, 1987, p. 249). Teachers who take risks to experiment with innovations in the classroom and extend their own learning need appropriate feedback and a supportive environment.

Effective supervisors have a sense of empathy. They strive to understand how teachers feel about the work they do. Parks (1983), drawing the connection between leadership and motivation, presents five assumptions about professionals and how they relate to work:

1. People want certain things from life. Among these are: (a) to feel good about oneself, (b) to live relatively free from economic worry, (c) to live and work in an environment free from hazards to physical and mental health, (d) to be free to create and exhibit one's creations, and (e) to have opportunities to love and be loved.

2. Most of what people desire from life is achieved through work, either directly or indirectly.

3. How hard one works to complete work tasks and achieve work goals depends, in part, on how that person feels about both.

4. Work tasks must be closely related to the achievement of important goals.

5. The achievement of work goals must be closely related to the fulfillment of personal wants. (pp. 11–12)

Summary

Schools and classrooms are complex, and supervisors working to motivate teachers need to keep many variables in mind such as the teacher's career stage, relative age and experience, and the school environment itself. Supervisors need to determine what workplace conditions motivate or discourage teachers. Supervisors also need to consider how teachers change throughout their professional careers and how learning must vary to foster growth.

Supervisors need to examine their leadership style and its effect on teachers. Though only briefly addressed here, the subject of leadership is far from tangential to instructional supervision; prospective supervisors should be aware of its implications for their work in schools.

Suggested Activities

From Theory to Practice

Ask your principal if you may interview a group of first-year teachers in your building. If permission is granted, meet with these teachers either as a group or individually. Using the following time line, ask what and who has motivated them at these key periods of the first year of teaching.

◆ The first month of school:

◆ From October through December:

◆ From January through March:

What insights did you gather from the experience and examining what these teachers had to say? What are the implications for supervisors and their work with beginning teachers?

Group Processing

In a small group, identify the external and internal motivators for teachers related to professional growth and development. Identify what supervisors can do to provide the conditions to enhance teacher motivation.

Reflection

Consider the following statement by Galileo: *You cannot teach a man anything; you can only help him find it within himself.*

Given Galileo's words, respond to the following: Supervisors can do nothing to enhance a teacher's internal motivation to grow and develop.

References

Blase, J., & Blase, J. (2000). *Empowering teachers: What successful principals do* (2nd ed.). Thousand Oaks, CA: Corwin Press.

Daft, R. L., & Lengel, R. H. (1998). *Fusion leadership: Unlocking the subtle forces that change people and organization.* San Francisco, CA: Berret-Koehler.

Gage, N., & Berliner, D. (1988). *Educational psychology* (4th ed.). Dallas, TX: Houghton Mifflin.

Jennings, D. F. (1993). *Effective supervision: Frontline management for the 90's.* Minneapolis, MN: West Publishing Company.

Lefrancois, G. R. (1982). *Psychology for teaching: A bear always usually sometimes rarely faces the front* (4th ed.). Belmont, CA: Wadsworth.

Maslow, A. H. (1987). *Motivation and personality* (rev. ed.). New York: Harper & Row.

McBride, M., & Skau, K. G. (1995). Trust, empowerment, and reflection: Essentials of supervision. *Journal of Curriculum and Supervision, 10*(3), 262–277.

McClelland, D. C. (1987). *Human motivation.* New York: Cambridge University Press.

McClelland, D. C., & Burnham, D. H. (1997). Power is the great motivator. In S. Kerr (Ed.), *Ultimate rewards: What really motivates people to achieve* (pp. 63–82). Boston, MA: Harvard Business School Publishing.

McGregor, D. M. (1961). The human side of enterprise. In W. G. Bennis, K. D. Benne, and R. Chin (Eds.), *The planning of change* (pp. 422–431). New York: Holt, Rinehart, and Winston.

Parks, D. J. (1983). Leadership in time of austerity. *Educational Leadership, 40*(5), 11–13.

Petri, H. L. (1996). *Motivation: Theory, research, and applications* (4th ed.). Pacific Grove, CA: Brooks/Cole.

Razik, T. A., & Swanson, A. D. (1995). *Fundamental concepts of educational leadership and management.* Englewood Cliffs, NJ: Prentice Hall.

Schwan, C. J., & Spady, W. G. (1998). *Total leaders: Applying the best future-focused change strategies to education.* Arlington, VA: American Association of School Administrators.

Wlodkowski, R. J. (1985). *Enhancing adult motivation to learn.* San Francisco, CA: Jossey-Bass.

Woolfolk, A. E. (2005). *Educational psychology* (9th ed.). Englewood Cliffs, NJ: Prentice Hall.

9

Peer Coaching

In This Chapter...

♦ Defining peer coaching

♦ Types of peer coaching

♦ Processes and components of peer coaching

♦ Conditions for successful peer coaching

♦ Connecting peer coaching to other forms of supervision

Introducing Peer Coaching

Peer coaching provides opportunities for teachers to support and learn from each other and to engage in realistic discussions about teaching and learning—their own and that of their students. Peer coaching derives strength not only from the social nature of the model, but also from its constructivist aspects in which meanings are developed through interacting with others and then from the process of constructing meaning.

Peer coaching—in its purest sense is a model of professional development and instructional supervision—can extend to professional learning opportunities such as action research and portfolio development. Joyce and Showers (1981, 1982) provided the first documented model of peer coaching as a form of professional development. They developed this model as a means for peers to coach each other while implementing in the classroom new strategies learned during in-service (professional development). "Like athletes, teachers will put newly learned skills to use—if they are coached" (Joyce & Showers, 1982, p. 5).

Social learning theory as envisioned by Bandura (1986) included observation and modeling, key aspects of peer coaching. Peer coaching promotes reciprocal learning; the peer who is being observed and the coach who is conducting the observation learn from each other. Modeling is a complex and powerful learning tool that involves three stages: (a) exposure to the responses of others; (b) acquisition of what one sees; and (c) subsequent acceptance of the modeled acts as a guide for one's own behavior (Bandura, 1986).

Like the clinical supervision model, peer coaching includes a preobservation conference, an extended classroom observation, and a postobservation conference. Yet peer coaching can extend the clinical model of supervision. One application of peer coaching is to ensure the transfer of newly learned skills from an in-service (professional development) learning opportunity into practice—that is, to teach new instructional strategies to teachers. In this respect, peer coaching is a multifaceted tool that can be implemented as an instructional strategy, a professional development strategy, and a complement to instructional supervision.

Learning from each other empowers teachers. Peer coaching can foster ongoing and sustained examination of practices, with those closest to instruction—teachers—providing guidance, encouragement, and motivation to continue learning from the events that unfold in the classroom. This chapter outlines the premises of peer coaching as a complement to the overall supervisory program.

Defining Peer Coaching

Originally conceived as a form of professional development, peer coaching consisted of a cycle that included the presentation of theory as well as a demonstration. Teachers were then led through practice, given feedback, and coached accordingly (Figure 9.1 on the next page). The coaching aspects of the model mirror the clinical supervisory model by including extended "in-class training by a supportive partner who helps a teacher correctly apply skills learned in a workshop" (Joyce & Showers, 1982, p. 5).

Figure 9.1 Peer Coaching Cycle

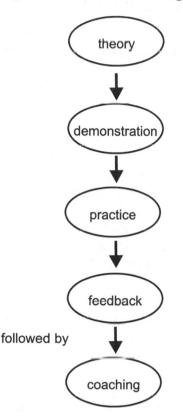

Source: Joyce & Showers, 1995.

The peer coaching model provides a bridge between the topics and skills addressed during large-scale in-service programs (typically delivered by outside experts) and the day-to-day application of newly learned theory. Coaching occurs at two levels: in the classroom with a coach observing a teacher, and in the feedback conference. Because coaching occurs in the classroom, feedback is more realistic, steeped in the context where skills and techniques are applied. Peer coaching is a realistic approach for supporting teachers because, according to Joyce and Showers (1981), coaching "involves a collegial approach to the analysis of teaching for the purpose of integrating mastered skills and strategies into

◆ a curriculum;

◆ a set of instructional goals;

◆ a time span; and

◆ a personal teaching style." (p. 170)

Peer coaching is supervision that teachers do "with one another" instead of something that is done "to them" (Pajak, 1993, p. 223). Coaching conducted among peers needs an environment that encourages collegiality; Ackland (1991) asserts, *"Peer coaching is distinct from evaluation,* and perhaps the most important reason for emphasizing peer is to ensure that peer coaching will not be used to evaluate a teacher's classroom performance" (p. 24, emphasis in the original). Ackland is not stating that supervisors should not coach, but that what is learned about a teacher's practice in coaching sessions should not become a summative assessment of performance. Peer coaching can help to create an environment where teachers can be secure, connected, and empowered to work with one another.

Peer coaching is perhaps one of the earliest forms of job-embedded learning—"learning that occurs as teachers and administrators engage in their daily work activities" (Wood & Killian, 1998, p. 52). When learning is job-embedded, transfer of new skills into practice is more likely. In peer coaching, teachers are able to observe one another at work, share strategies, engage in guided practice as follow-up to professional development, and reinforce learning through feedback, reflection, and ongoing inquiry. In school communities that support and nurture peer coaching, leadership among teachers can be developed and sustained over time.

Types of Peer Coaching

Numerous types of coaching have evolved, most notably through the work of Costa and Garmston (1986, 1994), Garmston (1987), and Joyce and Showers (1981, 1982, 1995).

Technical Coaching, Collegial Coaching, and Challenge Coaching

Garmston (1987) delineates three types of coaching: technical coaching, collegial coaching, and challenge coaching (Figure 9.2, next page).

Figure 9.2. Types of Coaching

Type of Coaching	Description/Definition
Technical Coaching	Technical coaching helps teachers transfer training to classroom practice and gives teachers a shared vocabulary to talk about their craft. The approach assumes that objective feedback given in a nonthreatening and supportive climate can improve teaching performance. Technical coaching generally follows staff development workshops in specific teaching methods. (p. 18)
Collegial Coaching	The model assumes that teachers acquire and deepen career-long habits of self-initiated reflection about their teaching when they have opportunities to develop and practice these skills. The long-range goal is self-coaching for continuous, self-perpetuating improvements in teaching. (p. 20)
Challenge Coaching	Challenge coaching helps teams of teachers resolve persistent problems in instructional design or delivery. The term challenge refers to resolving a problematic state. The model assumes that team problem-solving efforts by those responsible for carrying out instruction can produce insightful, practical improvements. Because trust, collegiality, and norms supporting problem solving in professional dialogue are prerequisite conditions, challenge coaching often evolves from other coaching approaches. (p. 21)

Source: Garmston, 1987.

The use of resources such as background reading and other materials (CD-ROM, videotapes) can enhance the coaching experience and program (Mello, 1984). Mello advocates a team approach to coaching in the "collegial interaction process," in which a team reviews a videotape of a teaching episode and records the events in writing; then the teacher whose class was videotaped conducts her own analysis of the teaching segment.

A Case Study

After reviewing data from the statewide testing program, Mr. Myers, principal of Dunwoody Elementary School, consults with the instructional coordinator, Mrs. Lucille, to decide how to tell the third-grade teachers that a majority of their students scored below average in key areas, mainly reading comprehension.

Because teachers at this grade level have been enthusiastically involved in peer coaching for three years, Lucille and Myers believe that challenge coaching could assist teachers as they examine their instructional practices in the area of reading comprehension.

♦ Outline a process to move into challenge coaching and then outline what challenge coaching would look like. What would teachers need to do to challenge-coach the problem of low reading comprehension scores?

♦ Develop a plan to present either to your colleagues in the class or at a board of education meeting.

Cognitive Coaching

Costa and Garmston (1994) developed the cognitive coaching model, based on the core beliefs that (a) everyone is capable of changing, (b) teaching performance is based on decision-making skills, which motivate skill development and refinement, and (c) teachers are capable of enhancing each other's cognitive processes, decisions, and teaching behaviors (Garmston, 1987).

The processes of cognitive coaching promote thinking, with the coach

♦ Applying rapport skills (body matching, intonation, language);

♦ Structuring (time, space, purposes);

♦ Posing reflective questioning (using positive presuppositions);

♦ Using silence (wait-time, listening);

♦ Paraphrasing (feeling, content, summary);

♦ Accepting (nonverbally, verbally);

♦ Clarifying (probing for details, values, meanings);

♦ Providing (data, resources). (Costa & Garmston, 1986, p. 5)

Creative use of technology and scheduling of personnel open a wide range of options for supporting peer coaching pairs or teams. Though school situations vary, a supervisor should seek ways to incorporate coaching into the overall supervisory program.

A Case Study

Gwendolyn Warren, principal of East Middle School, supported video-tape analysis as a tool for teachers to examine their classroom practices. During the summer she bought several video cameras and other materials so that each team would have their own equipment. When school opened, Gwendolyn delivered equipment to each team office. At a faculty meeting, she made known her expectation that teachers would use the equipment to videotape and analyze their teaching.

Immediately following the winter holiday, Gwendolyn asked each teacher to submit a video clip of a teaching episode for her to watch. Her teachers did not respond well, and several complained to her. Gwendolyn did not listen; instead, she fired off a memo that ended: "Any teacher who does not submit a video clip by next Friday will be admonished."

♦ As a leader, what has Gwendolyn communicated to her staff by the way she implemented and monitored the use of technology to enhance instruction?

♦ Will videotape analysis of teaching flourish in this school?

The Processes and Components of the Peer Coaching Model

Peer coaching affirms the sequential processes of the original clinical model of supervision (Pajak, 1993) and includes the preobservation conference, the extended classroom observation, and the postobservation conference. Figure 9.3 (on the next page) illustrates how coaches prepare for a classroom observation.

Figure 9.3. The Peer Coaching Model

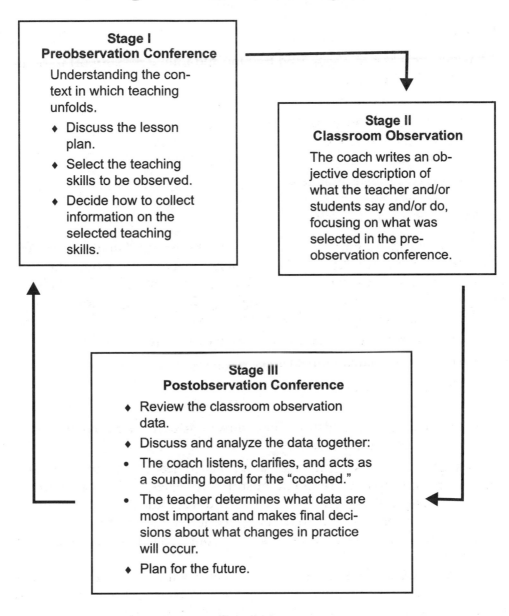

Stage I
Preobservation Conference

Understanding the context in which teaching unfolds.

- Discuss the lesson plan.
- Select the teaching skills to be observed.
- Decide how to collect information on the selected teaching skills.

Stage II
Classroom Observation

The coach writes an objective description of what the teacher and/or students say and/or do, focusing on what was selected in the preobservation conference.

Stage III
Postobservation Conference

- Review the classroom observation data.
- Discuss and analyze the data together:
- The coach listens, clarifies, and acts as a sounding board for the "coached."
- The teacher determines what data are most important and makes final decisions about what changes in practice will occur.
- Plan for the future.

Conditions for Successful Peer Coaching

Training

As peer coaches, teachers need training and follow-up support to refine coaching skills in the areas of

- Human relations and communication;
- Clinical supervisory processes: preobservation conference, the extended classroom observation, and the postobservation conference; and
- Data collection techniques.

Trust

Change means leaving "what we are" and becoming "what we are not" (Barott & Raybould, 1998, p. 31). It can be unnerving to leave behind the comfortable and step into the unknown. Fullan (1982) believes that "all real change involves loss, anxiety, and struggle" (p. 25). Not surprisingly, educators tend to resist change; the reasons may include

- The perception that change is a personal or professional attack;
- The loss associated with change;
- The history of change in the school or district;
- Community or district reaction to change; and
- The possibility of added individual responsibility and accountability as a result of change.

Change also means admitting that a practice needs to be modified, extended, or implemented. Teachers must trust coaches, colleagues, and administrators, as well as themselves. Whether development takes the form of mentoring, peer coaching, or reflection, teachers must trust that feedback will be constructive, based on best practice, grounded in research, and not in any way a personal attack.

Trust is essential for success in any form of coaching or mentoring. Costa and Garmston (1994) identify three key areas in which a coach must build trust: (a) in self, (b) between individuals, and (c) in the coaching process.

Trust in Oneself Trust in oneself is a prerequisite for developing trust in any other area. A person must have a firm sense of his own values and beliefs. Being consistent, open and accessible, nonjudgmental, and freely admitting one's own mistakes are all characteristics of trust in oneself (Costa & Garmston, 1994).

Teachers must develop a measure of objectivity when reflecting on their own practices. Artifacts such as journals, videotapes, and portfolios lose their effectiveness when teachers cannot be honest with themselves.

Trust in Each Other   Secondly, trust must exist between individuals. This trust is established by knowing what is important to others, how others process information, and what are their current thoughts and concerns. Teachers must be able to trust their coaches. What occurs in a coaching session is sacred and should not be made public information. If supervisors coach teachers, what emerges in the classroom and the conferences must not be used as a basis for a summative evaluation.

Trust in the Process   If peer coaching is to endure, teachers need to trust that peer coaching will be a collaborative effort, not tied to teacher evaluation. Teachers need to feel safe and secure with one another and the process. In part, safety is "having things regular and predictable for oneself" (Gage & Berliner, 1988, p. 337). If teachers are not certain that they can share their ideas without fear of personal criticism or that what is observed in the classroom is confidential (between the teacher and coach), they will be wary of investing themselves in the process or the efforts needed to make changes in practice.

Trust must be forged between teachers and administrators. Blase and Blase (2000) offer that for leaders (both teachers and administrators) to develop trusting relationships, they need to

- Listen with respect;
- Be a model of trust;
- Help others to communicate effectively;
- Clarify expectations;
- Celebrate experimentation and support risk; and
- Exhibit personal integrity. (p. 36)

Teachers will not readily accept administrative support unless trusts exist; coaching will not endure without a basis of trust, respect, and good intentions. Trust is the brick and mortar of coaching.

Extended Reflection

In your opinion, should a teacher on a formal plan of improvement (also referred to as a remediation plan) be involved in peer coaching activities while on the plan of improvement?

Administrative Support

Every person who formally supervises and evaluates teachers (e.g., assistant principal, principal, department chair, instructional lead teacher) holds a position with many responsibilities. Some items in the job description, such as supervising the instructional program and its personnel or evaluating certified and noncertified personnel, cannot be delegated. In the early years of the evolution of differentiated supervision, Glatthorn (1984), thought to be the originator of the concept, believed that teachers were more than capable of engaging in activities that situated them as responsible for their own learning and promoted collegial relationships between teachers. However, Glatthorn (1984) also believed that implementing differentiated approaches to supervision would free the busy supervisor from providing day-to-day instructional supervision to all teachers. The intent was really to clear time in the schedule so the administrator could work with teachers who needed more intensive assistance (e.g., teachers on a plan of improvement, struggling first-year teachers).

Fieldwork

In the school system where you work, obtain job descriptions for the following positions: assistant principal, principal, department chair, instructional lead teacher, instructional coordinator (or any other positions that require the supervision of instruction or the instructional program).

What items in the job descriptions explicitly address the supervision and evaluation of teachers or other certified or noncertified staff?

Where do these items appear in the job description (toward the top, middle, bottom)?

Also obtain any information such as forms that evaluate the overall performance of the people who serve as principals, assistant principals, department chairs and any other positions in which you were able to locate job descriptions.

What percentage of the overall evaluation plan is related to the supervision and evaluation of teaching and the overall instructional program?

What else do you notice in comparing the two sets of documents?

Coaching, regardless of its form, can indeed free up time in the administrator's day; however, administrators must still provide leadership and support before and during the implementation of a peer-coaching program.

Gingiss (1993, p. 82) believes, "Principals can provide informal encouragement, formal endorsement, personal involvement, and resource designation."

Given the complex nature and specific context of each school, the type of administrative support needed to develop, implement, and assess the overall value of a peer coaching program will vary. For coaching to flourish, principals must

- *Allocate resources:* Provide substitute teachers to cover classrooms while coaches coach; schedule release time for teachers to coach each other and conduct pre- and postobservation conferences; procure professional development materials on techniques under construction; obtain funds to develop a professional library for teachers (journals, videos).

- *Arrange for initial and ongoing training:* Coaches will need training in the processes of peer coaching; follow-up training might be needed depending on how the program evolves.

- *Provide emotional support and encouragement:* Any time teachers try new practices, they need support and affirmative feedback to keep the momentum going.

Starting a coaching program means a great deal of upfront work for the supervisor. Upfront tasks include building momentum for such a program, involving the faculty in its design, garnering support from the central administrative office, and scanning the environment for potential obstacles.

Fieldwork

Given the context in which you work, develop a strategy to begin a peer-coaching program. Identify what would be involved in each of the following upfront tasks.

- Building momentum

- Involving the faculty in the design of the program

- Garnering support from the central administrative office and others

- Scanning the environment for potential obstacles

Develop a PowerPoint presentation to share your thoughts with the class.

As a peer-coaching program evolves, needs will change and so must the program. In time, the supervisor might even be able to step back and let teachers run the program. Letting go empowers both the supervisor and the peer coaches, but it does not obviate the need for ongoing support and some oversight. Some school systems support teacher leadership by appointing a teacher leader to manage the logistics of the program. Effective supervisors continually seek such opportunities to empower teachers and build collegiality.

Connecting Peer Coaching to Other Forms of Supervision

Peer coaching offers one way to differentiate instructional supervision. Peer coaching can extend the model of clinical supervision in several ways, most notably by including action research and portfolio development. Although action research is examined in Chapter 10 and portfolio development in Chapter 11, peer coaching as it relates to these two differentiated forms of supervision is briefly discussed here.

Through action research, teachers develop a question or a problem of practice to investigate and then gather data from a variety of sources such as instructional artifacts (e.g., lesson plans) and classroom observations. Peer coaches can help teachers make sense of their practice by giving feedback from classroom observations. The original model of peer coaching centered on skill transfer from professional development opportunities. Coaches can examine lesson plans, observe classrooms (with one eye on the teacher and the other on student responses), and give feedback on the application of skills and techniques. Coaching keeps action research alive, as data related to classroom practices and outcomes guide further observations and coaching sessions.

Extending the coaching process to portfolio development can also enhance adult learning. In fact, combining action research with portfolio development and peer coaching yields an even more powerful iteration and extension of the clinical model of supervision. Teachers can construct, examine, reexamine, and refine their teaching portfolios (along with their practice) based on the observations of peer coaches who give feedback on the artifacts chosen and the reasons for including them in the portfolio.

The reader is encouraged to consult Chapters 10 (*Action Research*) and 11 (*Portfolio Supervision*) for further discussion.

Summary

Peer coaching can enhance supervision by situating teachers at the center of their own learning. Coaching in any form breaks the isolation found in most K-12 schools and promotes collegiality. Peer coaching supports teachers as they implement new strategies and amplifies the benefits of other differentiated forms of supervision such as action research and portfolio development.

Administrative support is essential to peer coaching efforts. More importantly, peer coaching as a tool for teachers to examine their practices in ways that make sense to them will not flourish until teachers feel valued and supported in their efforts to improve instruction. Effective supervisors focus their attention here.

Suggested Activities

From Theory to Practice

Visit a school with a peer-coaching program to see the program in practice. Interview the principal or another administrator to find out how the program began, who was involved in developing the program, and how the program was implemented. If a teacher leader runs the peer-coaching program, interview this person as well. From what you learned from this site visitation and from reading this chapter, design a peer-coaching program model for the school where you work.

Group Processing

In a small or large group, develop a rationale for implementing a peer-coaching program. Include the benefits for teachers, students, and the school system. Prepare a 15-minute PowerPoint presentation that your group will present to a local board of education. Be prepared to field questions from other members of the class who will assume the role of members of the school board and/or members of the community attending the meeting.

Reflection

As a journal entry, respond to the following statement: Teachers on a plan of improvement for weaknesses in some aspect of their teaching should not be involved in a peer-coaching program.

References

Ackland, R. (1991). A review of the peer coaching literature. *Journal of Staff Development, 12*(1), 22–27.

Bandura, A. (1986). *The social foundations of thought and action.* Englewood Cliffs, NJ: Prentice-Hall.

Barott, J., & Raybould, R. (1998). Changing schools into collaborative organizations. In D. G. Pounder (Ed.), *Restructuring schools for collaboration: Promises and pitfalls* (pp. 27–42). Albany, NY: State University of New York Press.

Blase, J., & Blase J. (2000). *Empowering teachers: What successful principals do* (2nd ed.). Thousand Oaks, CA: Corwin Press.

Costa, A. L., & Garmston, R. J. (1994). *Cognitive coaching: A foundation for renaissance schools.* Norwood, MA: Christopher-Gordon.

Costa, A. L., & Garmston, R. J. (1986). Student teaching: Developing images of a profession. *Action in Teacher Education, 9*(3), 1–7.

Fullan, M. (1982). *The meaning of educational change.* New York: Teachers College Press.

Gage, N., & Berliner, D. (1988). *Educational psychology* (4th ed.). Dallas, TX: Houghton Mifflin.

Garmston, R. J. (1987). How administrators support peer coaching. *Educational Leadership, 44*(5), 18–26.

Gingiss, P. L. (1993). Peer coaching: Building collegial support for using innovative health programs. *Journal of School Health, 63*(2), 79–85.

Glatthorn, A. (1984). *Differentiated supervision.* Alexandria, VA: Association for Supervision and Curriculum Development.

Joyce, B., & Showers, B. (1995). *Student achievement through staff development: Fundamentals of school renewal* (2nd ed.). White Plains, NY: Longman.

Joyce, B., & Showers, B. (1982). The coaching of teaching. *Educational Leadership, 40*(2), 4–10.

Joyce, B., & Showers, B. (1981). Transfer of training: The contribution of "coaching." *Boston University Journal of Education, 163*(2), 163–172.

Mello, L. T. (1984). *Peer-centered coaching: Teachers helping teachers to improve classroom performance.* Indian Springs, CO: Associates for Human Development. (ERIC Document Reproduction Service No. ED274648)

Pajak, E. (1993). *Approaches to clinical supervision: Alternatives for improving instruction.* Norwood, MA: Christopher-Gordon.

Wood, F. H., & Killian, J. (1998). Job-embedded learning makes the difference in school improvement. *Journal of Staff Development, 19*(1), 52–54.

10

Action Research

In This Chapter...

♦ Action research defined

♦ Models of action research

♦ The processes and components of action research

♦ Reflection

♦ Connecting action research to instructional supervision

Introducing Action Research

Action research can transform the ways teachers work and learn with and from one another while improving their classroom practices. The results of action research can inform school systems and can aid in formulating and reformulating goals related to school improvement. Action research can enhance a peer-coaching program (Chapter 9) and can be an integral part of developing a professional portfolio (Chapter 11).

Action research (undertaken by teachers) is research that occurs in conjunction with, and often concurrently with, day-to-day classroom or school activities. As an extension of instructional supervision, action research assists a teacher's inquiry into classroom practices. Integrating aspects of action research with processes of supervision yields a more powerful and seamless form of learning.

Action research can broaden the clinical model of supervision by focusing attention more specifically, but over an extended period, on a practice or a dilemma the teacher wants to examine. Through inquiry, teachers as active learners seek to make discoveries about their practices. Dewey's (1929) beliefs about the value of discovery provide the rationale for action research as a means to extend instructional supervision: "The discovery is never made; it is always making" (p. 74), and "each day of teaching ought to enable a teacher to revise and better in some respects the objectives aimed at in previous work" (1929, p. 75).

Action Research Defined

Action research is a method of inquiry "undertaken by educators in order to better understand the education environment and to improve practice" (Grady, 1998, p. 43). Hopkins (1985) describes action research as "self-reflective inquiry undertaken by participants in order to improve the rationality of (a) their own practices, (b) their own understanding of these practices, and (c) the situations in which these practices are carried out" (p. 32).

Teachers make quick decisions every day, both in and out of the classroom environment—teaching a lesson, interacting with students, and handling situations that pop up. Such split-second decisions provide little time to stop, analyze, and reflect on the data underlying them. Good decisions are based on data. Better decisions are made after collecting and examining data, reflecting on alternatives, and getting feedback from another person.

Action research engages teachers in their own intentional actions of collecting, analyzing, reflecting, and then modifying practice. The clinical supervision model can embrace action research if teachers can take advantage of numerous cycles of the clinical model (preobservation, extended observation, postobservation conference). The same applies to peer coaching (Chapter 9), with colleagues engaged in repeated rounds of coaching.

Extended Reflection

What are the links between supervision, professional development, and teacher evaluation?

How does a supervisor ensure that these links are made?

How can action research be incorporated as a form of supervision and professional development?

Through the clinical model of supervision, teachers engage in discussion with the supervisor (perhaps a peer coach) during the pre- and postobservation conferences. During the observation, the supervisor or peer coach collects data related to the focus, and in the postobservation conference, these data enable the teacher to reconstruct the events of the classroom related to the focus.

Like peer coaching and supervision, action research can position teachers to search "for answers to questions relevant to educators' immediate interests, with the primary goal of putting the findings immediately into practice" (McKay, 1992, p. 18). Johnson's (1993) explanation of action research points to its cyclical nature:

> Action research is deliberate, solution-oriented investigation that is group or personally owned and conducted. It is characterized by spiraling cycles of problem identification, systematic data collection, reflection, analysis, data-driven action taken, and, finally, problem redefinition. The linking of the terms "action" and "research" highlights the essential features of this method: trying out ideas in practice as a means of increasing knowledge about and/or improving curriculum, teaching, and learning. (p. 3)

As job-embedded learning, action research enables teachers to

♦ Examine real-life practices and experiences in the very place in which these practices and experiences occur—the classroom;

♦ Use a systematic approach (which may become a cyclical and continuous vehicle for ongoing action research);

♦ Develop deeper meanings about their practices with the assistance of a colleague;

♦ Experiment with their practices based upon extended reflection and analysis of data; and

♦ Implement change.

Models of Action Research

Numerous models of action research exist, with slight variations that distinguish them from each other. Figure 10.1, on the next page, offers the processes that all models of action research have in common.

Figure 10.1. The Processes of Action Research

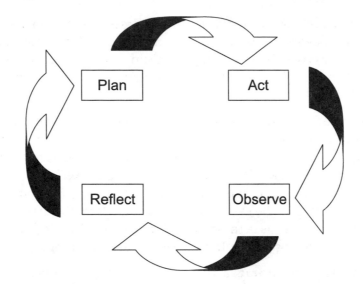

Source: Dick, 1999. Used with permission.

Marshak (1997) characterizes action research as a methodology in which teachers systematically

- ♦ Form a research question that is central to their own professional practice;
- ♦ Devise methods of collecting data pertinent to that question;
- ♦ Collect data;
- ♦ Analyze the data;
- ♦ Articulate findings and conclusions that inform teaching practice; and
- ♦ Change teaching in ways indicated by the research findings and conclusions. (p. 107)

Similarly, Glanz (1998, 1999) outlines four basic stages with substeps to guide the processes of action research (Figure 10.2, next page).

Figure 10.2. Glanz' Stages to Action Research

Stage 1: Selecting a focus

    (a) know what you want to investigate

    (b) develop questions about your chosen area

    (c) establish a plan to answer the chosen questions

Stage 2: Collecting data

    (a) organize the data to be shared with others

Stage 3: Analyzing and interpreting data

    (a) describe or summarize data clearly

    (b) search for consistent patterns or themes among the data

    (c) answer the question and/or prove the hypothesis

Stage 4: Taking action

    (a) continue the practice as originally established, or

    (b) discontinue the practice, or

    (c) modify the practice.

Source: Glanz, 1999, pp. 22–23.

A Case Study

Tiffany Scott, a fourth-grade math teacher at Phillip's Elementary School, strongly supports guided practice and independent practice after teaching and demonstrating a concept. Still, she notices that no matter how much guided practice she provides, more than half her students do not fare well when it comes time to apply concepts during independent practice. She wonders why. Her lessons are complete; her teaching includes lectures, worksheets, and manipulatives when appropriate.

Perplexed, Tiffany consults John Weber, a fellow fourth-grade teacher, for some ideas. John suggests that Tiffany try action research to pursue a solution. John agrees to work with Tiffany, and they meet several times. The action research steps that John and Tiffany follow appear in Figure 10.3 (on the next page).

Figure 10.3. Action Research Steps

Focus	Examine sequence of lecture, guided practice, and independent practice	Time frame 3 months	Process
Data collection	1. Examine lesson plans.	Ongoing	
	2. John observes Tiffany as she teaches lessons that include guided practice and independent practice.	2 months	Once every other week—both formal and informal observations.Postobservation conferences. John tracks instructional activities and the uses of manipulatives.
	3. Teacher-generated worksheets and guides.	3 months	Match skills with activities—levels of application in both guided and independent practices.
Analyzing and interpreting data	Observation notes, worksheets, student work, postobservation notes, lesson plans.	Ongoing	Comparison of patterns over time. Tiffany examines and reexamines the intents of her lessons against the data from classroom observations.
Taking action	Tiffany discovers that she uses manipulatives in most of her instruction but that during guided and independent practice, students are required to give concrete answers.	Ongoing	Modify activities so that application of knowledge matches instruction.Revisit the problem of practice and the focus—refocusing.

The Processes and Components of Action Research

Action research engages teachers in

- Raising questions about classroom practices;
- Developing a plan (methods for collecting data);
- Analyzing data (with or without the assistance of others);
- Reflecting on data and the implications for practice; and
- Experimenting with new practices.

Action research is an iterative process that can lead teachers to a better understanding of what happens and why. A lockstep approach to action research discourages the spontaneity to experiment with data as they emerge. Throughout the dialogue with peer or supervisor, the analysis of data, and the modification or creation of strategies, the teacher as action researcher needs the latitude to recast practices in light of new discoveries.

In most of its forms, action research involves participation by others, such as peer coaches and mentors; however, action research may be a solo venture. Action research can explore both qualitative and quantitative data. Data from multiple sources enrich the opportunities for interpretation and analysis. Figure 10.4 provides sample sources of data to examine. The only criterion for a useful data source should be whether it makes sense to include the information.

Figure 10.4. Possible Data Sources for Action Research

Possible data sources to consult include, but are not limited to:

- Classroom observation notes
- Test results from both standardized and nonstandardized instruments
- Student-generated artifacts such as a final essay, project, and aggregated responses to a particular test question or a subset of questions
- Lesson plans, including objectives
- Portfolios
- Videotape and/or audiotape of teaching and/or student performance
- Journal entries
- Type and frequency of office referrals and student infractions
- Grade distributions on a test or quiz
- Patterns in types of questions asked during a lecture or on a test or quiz

Action research without follow-up is counterproductive. Follow-up provides opportunities for teachers to reflect on their observations, analyze multiple sources of data, revisit practices, and plan changes based on their discoveries. Perhaps the quintessential strategy of action research is reflection—examining practices that are real.

Reflection

Throughout the processes of action research, teachers flex their intellectual muscles. Reflection is one of the key skills of action research. Reflection encourages teachers to

♦ Return to experience by recalling or detailing salient events.

♦ Attend to or connect with feelings, which has two aspects: using helpful feelings and removing or containing obstructive ones.

♦ Evaluate experience, which involves reexamining experiences in the light of new knowledge. It also consists of integrating new knowledge into practice. (Jeffs & Smith, 1999)

Reflection can be private or public—or a combination of the two; Stevenson (1995) asserts that reflection occurs "privately as an individual action or internal dialogue with oneself or publicly in dialogue and reflection with others" (p. 201, emphasis in the original).

Teachers who reflect effectively gain new perspectives on the dilemmas and contradictions inherent in classroom practices, improve judgment, and increase their capacity to take purposeful action based on the knowledge they discover. Shulman (1987) describes reflection as

> what a teacher does when he or she looks back at the teaching and learning that has occurred, and reconstructs, reenacts, and/or recaptures the events, the emotions, and the accomplishments. It is that set of processes through which a professional learns from experience. (p. 331)

A synthesis of reflective tools as described by Huntress and Jones (2000) appears in Figure 10.5 (pages 251–253).

(Text continues on page 253.)

Figure 10.5. Reflective Tools

Reflective Tool	Description and Source
Photo albums	Through a structured procedure, teachers and administrators describe their practice in terms of behavior, cause/effect relationship, rationale, and the like. These multiple descriptions create a "photo-album" of actions that are the focus of reflective discussion. Killion, J. P., & Todnem, G. R. (1991). *A process for personal theory building. Educational Leadership, 80*(3), 14–16.
Video study groups	Teachers tape lessons and then use these tapes as a springboard for collaborative reflections upon practice by a peer study group. Hassler, S. S., & Collins, A. M. (1993, April). Using collaborative reflection to support changes in classroom practice. Paper presented at the annual meeting of the American Educational Research Association, Atlanta, GA.
Action research	Classroom-based studies, initiated and conducted by teachers, form the basis of action research. Action research affords teachers the opportunity to collect, analyze, and then reflect on the meaning of data. Bennett, C. K. (1994). Promoting teaching reflection through action research: What do teachers think? *Journal of Staff Development, 15*(1), 34–38.
Thinking frameworks	Thinking frameworks provide a common language and basis from which reflection can occur. Cook writes that models of thinking, such as Gardner's Multiple Intelligences and Martinello and Cook's Habits of Mind can aid in the inquiry process of clinical supervision by providing common understandings from which to work. Cook refers to such models as a "variety of lenses to view the world of the classroom and gain new insights into its workings" (p. 50). Cook, G. E. (1996). Using clinical supervision to promote inquiry. *Journal of Staff Development, 17*(4), 46–50.

(Figure continues on next page.)

Dewey's reflective framework	Teachers move through Dewey's five-step problem-posing process: 1. Felt difficulty 2. Location and definition 3. Suggestions of possible solution 4. Development by reasoning of the bearings of the suggestion 5. Further observation and experimentation leading to its acceptance or rejection. After going through the five-step process, teachers can better reflect upon classroom experiences while generating solutions to problems of practice. Yusko, B. P. (1997, February). Planning and enacting reflective talk among interns. What is the problem? Paper presented at the annual meeting of the Association of Teacher Educators, St. Louis, MO.
Journals	Teachers make journal entries focused on beliefs, knowledge, observations, and actions related to teaching. Kasten, B. J., & Ferraro, J. M. (1995, April). A case study: Helping pre-service teachers internalize the interconnectedness of believing, knowing, seeing, and doing. Paper presented at the annual meeting of the American Educational Research Association, San Francisco, CA.
Dialogue journals	Teachers/interns keep journals to record classroom experiences, ideas, and questions. Mentors respond through commentary, or "dialogue," within these journals. Krol, C. A. (1996, February). Pre-service teacher education students' reflective writing and teachers' comments. Paper presented at the annual meeting of the Association of Teacher Educators, St. Louis, MO.
Think alouds	Mentors model reflection-in-action as they talk through a lesson. As the lesson progresses, mentors articulate their decision-making framework. Loughran, J. (1995, April). Practicing what I preach: Modeling reflective practice to student teachers. Paper presented at the annual meeting of the American Educational Research Association, San Francisco, CA.

(Figure continues on next page.)

Zen	Mentor teachers practice the "mindful awareness of the present moment" to encourage reflection-in-action among pre-service teachers.
	Tremmel, R. (1993). Zen and the art of reflective practice in teacher education. *Harvard Educational Review, 63*(1), 443–58.
Cognitive coaching	Cognitive coaching is a plan designed to "stimulate collaborative efforts" (p. 5) in the analysis of practice. Thought clusters, such as metacognition and dissonance, are used to help teachers become more aware of the thinking upon which their teaching is based.
	Costa, A. L., & Garmston, R. J. (1994). *Cognitive coaching: Foundation for Renaissance schools.* Norwood, MA: Christopher-Gordon.
Teaching dialogues	This staff development model is structured to engage four or five participants in inquiry, reflection, and discussion on a scheduled basis. Creative restructuring of the school day provides time for teacher dialogues.
	Arnold, G. C. (1995). Teacher dialogues: A constructivist model of staff development. *Journal of Staff Development, 16*(4), 34–38.
Critical incidents	Teachers write autobiographies describing their own experiences of school, then write about a "critical incident" from daily practice in their own teaching experience. In follow-up discussions, participants compare the two documents to discover their assumptions about teaching.
	Kennedy, R. L., & Wyrick, A. M. (1995, April). Teaching as reflective practice. Paper presented at the annual meeting of the Mid-South Educational Research Association, Biloxi, MS.

Source: Huntress & Jones, 2000.

If embedded in the workday, the processes annotated by Huntress and Jones can assist supervisors to help teachers reflect on their practices and the impact of these practices on student learning. Reflection does not occur automatically; teachers must engage in activities that promote it. Further, they need coaching as they learn how to reflect on practice in a way that leads to growth and development. Consider Bryan, Abell, and Anderson's (1997) insights:

Coaching reflection, like reflection itself, is a nonlinear process. There are no prescribed, specified series of steps one takes in order to coach someone to develop reflection skills. Learning to observe and analyze one's own teaching; learning to isolate, frame, and reframe problems of practice; and learning to take action and interpret that action—all of these skills take time and practice to develop.

Connecting Action Research to Instructional Supervision

Action research is an approach to professional development in which teachers systematically study and reflect on their work and then make informed changes in their practices. Action research can be incorporated throughout processes of the clinical and peer coaching models of supervision. Action research linked to supervision and peer coaching can provide a focal point for dealing with the "messiness and complexities of reality" while finding solutions to problems of practice (Avery, 1990).

A Case Study

The teachers at Birmingham High School have engaged in peer coaching for the past two years, and several were interested in action research as a way to extend coaching. Tom Dorsey, the assistant principal for instruction, thought this was a great idea, and he organized a meeting with the coaches. Before the meeting, Tom purchased a set of books about action research and made a few calls to see if any other schools in the district were using action research. Tom also met with a few of the coaches who had originally suggested action research as a possibility. He asked these teachers to run the meeting.

At the meeting, the teachers considered the idea of action research and brainstormed a few ideas about getting started. They asked for more resources and a release day to develop a working model. Tom provided these, making clear that the model they developed belonged to them. Within a few weeks, the teachers presented the model to Tom, and he indicated that he would examine their work and get back to them.

Six weeks later, Tom sent a memo listing 9 or 10 changes that had to be made to the plan. For example, Tom noted, "District policy would not support any type of data collection that included student-generated work," and he indicated that it would be ridiculous to include a survey for students to complete—that students would not take such an activity seriously and the data from their perspectives could never be stable enough to support changes.

- ◆ Analyze Tom's work and approach to working with his teachers.

- ◆ Identify the issues as they relate to supervisory behavior.

The supervisor's role in action research can range from intensive involvement (highly directive), involvement as an equal (collaborative), or support as a resource or occasional facilitator (nondirective). Supervisors may guide the focus for investigation, assist in interpretive processes, facilitate recommended action, or simply let peers work with peers.

Action research can take many forms; however, most action research involves teachers observing each other, providing feedback, and coaching each other to learn new skills. Figure 10.6, on the next page, illustrates how the clinical model of supervision can include the principles of action research.

Figure 10.6. Clinical Supervision and Action Research

Clinical Supervisory Phases	Action Research Processes	Data Collection Methods
Preobservation conference	Identification of a problem or issue.	Data collection based on the observation focus.
Observation	Data collection.	Observer notes, audio- or videotapes a teacher in action.
Postobservation conference	Analysis and interpretation of data.	Follow-up observation and examination of artifacts.
	Refocusing for ongoing observations (data collection).	
	Reflection on results.	
	Taking action based on what is discovered. Action could include modifying, continuing, or discontinuing a practice.	

Figure 10.7 offers a range of tools that can complement action research and supervision.

Figure 10.7. Tools to Extend and Complement Action Research and Supervision

Peer classroom observations	Peers observe one another while teaching and collect data purposefully linked to a question of practice.
Videotape or audiotape	Teachers collect data about their own practices with a video or audio recorder, or an instructional aide or colleague tapes the lesson. Later, the teacher can review the tape alone or with a colleague.
Auditing	Auditing can take many forms, but essentially the teacher collects data, examines them as an accountant would audit financial records, and draws conclusions.
Portfolio development	Teachers can track changes in practices with artifacts serving as the data. As action research, portfolio development chronicles changes in practices and the data underlying those changes.

Summary

Avery (1990) asserts, "learning is a messy, mumbled, nonlinear, recursive, and sometimes unpredictable process" (p. 43). Action research can help teachers sort out classroom events and make sense of their practices. Action research supports the developmental aspects of supervision particularly in light of its emphasis on reflection. Through extended cycles of supervision or coaching, teachers can examine practices and problems in the very context of the classroom. The power of action research lies in the fact that data inform practice, and that the model presents an ongoing, cyclical tool for individual and schoolwide growth.

Suggested Activities

From Theory to Practice

Identify a teaching colleague whom you feel secure working with and conduct action research in your own classroom. Consult Figure 10.2 (page 247), Glanz' Stages to Action Research, to guide this action research project. Track the processes and the conclusions you draw from the experience. Stepping out of the role of teacher as action researcher, reflect on the types of support teachers need as they conduct action research.

Group Processing

The school system where you work is considering action research as a form of professional development and a way to extend clinical supervision and peer coaching. As prospective building-level supervisors, develop a plan to implement action research. This plan should include needed resources, training, and supervisory support.

Reflection

Quigley and Kuhne (1997) report, "action research widely shared offers the promise of real empowerment and professional development for long-term impact" (p. 39). From your perspective, can action research be empowering?

References

Avery, C. S. (1990). Learning to research/researching to learn. In M. W. Olson (Ed.), *Opening the door to classroom research* (pp. 32–44). Newark, NJ: International Reading Association.

Bryan, L. A., Abell, S. K., & Anderson, M. A. (Last updated October 2, 1997). *Coaching reflective practice among preservice elementary science teachers.* Retrieved June 30, 2001, from http:/ /www.ed.psu.edu/CI/Journals/96pap27.htm

Dewey, J. (1929). *Sources of science education.* New York: Liverisht.

Dick, B. (1999). *What is action research?* Previously available at http://www.scu.edu. au/schools/gcm/ar/whatisar.html

Glanz, J. (1999). Action research. *Journal of Staff Development, 20*(3), 22–25.

Glanz, J. (1998). *Action research: An educational leader's guide to school improvement.* Norwood, MA: Christopher-Gordon.

Grady, M. P. (1998). *Qualitative and action research: A practitioner handbook.* Bloomington, IN: Phi Delta Kappa.

Hopkins, D. (1985). *A teachers' guide to classroom research.* Milton Keynes, England: Open University Press.

Huntress, J., & Jones, L. (2000, April). *Reflective process tools.* A presentation made at the annual meeting of the Association for Supervision and Curriculum Development for the Instructional Supervision Network. New Orleans, LA.

Jeffs, T., & Smith, M. K. (1999). *Informal education: Conversation, democracy and learning.* Ticknall, UK: Education Now Books (pp. 49–50). Retrieved September 18, 2000, from http:/ /www.infed.org/foundations/f-refl.htm

Johnson, B. (1993, March). *Teacher-as-researcher.* Washington, DC: Office of Educational Research and Improvement. (ERIC Document Reproduction Service No. ED355205)

Marshak, D. (1997). *Action research on block scheduling.* Larchmont, NY: Eye On Education.

McKay, J. A. (1992). Professional development through action research. *Journal of Staff Development, 13*(1), 18–21.

Quigley, B. A., & Kuhne, G. W. (1997). Understanding and using action research in practice settings. In B. A. Quigley and G. W. Kuhne (Eds.), *Creating practical knowledge through action research: Posing problems, solving problems, and improving daily practice* (pp. 23–40). San Francisco, CA: Jossey-Bass.

Shulman, L. S. (1987). Knowledge and teaching: Foundations of the new reform. *Harvard Educational Review, 57*(1), 1–32.

Stevenson, R. B. (1995). In S. E. Noffke & R. B. Stevenson (Eds.), *In educational action research: Becoming practically critical* (pp. 197–209). New York: Teachers College Press.

11

Portfolio Supervision

In This Chapter...

♦ What is a portfolio?

♦ Extending clinical supervision through portfolio development

♦ A model of portfolio supervision

♦ Essential skills: Reflection, goal setting, and decision making

♦ The portfolio as a framework to extend supervision

Introducing Portfolio Supervision

The portfolio has a rich history as a form of student assessment; in the past 10 years, the use of the portfolio by adults has emerged as a viable way to chronicle more holistically adult growth and development. In an era of high-stakes accountability, teacher performance is based almost exclusively on student performance on such formalized and quantifiable measures as standardized test results. As the era of accountability moves forward, school systems run the risk of losing sight of what teachers do each day and the gains in learning—for both students and teachers—that cannot be measured through standardized assessments. Perhaps the portfolio is a way to examine what teachers learn from their work. As a way for teachers to assess their learning, portfolios

> ...are messy to construct, cumbersome to store, difficult to score, and vulnerable to misinterpretation. But in ways that no other assessment method can, portfolios prove a connection to the contexts and personal histories that characterize real teaching and make it possible to document the unfolding of both teaching and learning over time. (Shulman, 1988, p. 36)

Portfolios have been used in preservice education programs to chronicle growth through coursework and clinical experiences before entering teaching. The portfolio has been used to evaluate teacher performance (summative evaluation) and as part of the application process for National Board certification. Moreover, in some districts the portfolio forms part of the job application process. Many universities and colleges accredited by the National Council for Accreditation of Teacher Education (NCATE) require students seeking initial or ongoing certification to develop a professional portfolio.

Whether in preservice, evaluation, or professional development, the intents of the portfolio are to chronicle growth and development—to capture learning through artifacts that are representative of practice. Educators who use the portfolio to extend clinical supervision and peer coaching believe that people engage in more meaningful learning when they learn in the company of others and when they can concretely see the results of modifying practice. Portfolio supervision supports the ongoing study of the teaching process by the individual teacher, alone or with collegial or supervisory support.

Developing a portfolio involves numerous processes—collecting artifacts, analyzing their meaning, reflecting on practice—and each requires certain skills. Portfolio development can be linked to supervision, professional development, and evaluation, and the processes that these embrace as best practice—reflection, feedback, and goal setting—lead to learning.

The portfolio is gaining a foothold as a tool to chronicle professional growth, an authentic way for teachers to reflect on their impact on student learning while assessing their own performance. Constructing a portfolio is an interactive process; ideally, a peer (coach or mentor) or a supervisor provides data, feedback, and encouragement. Feedback helps the teacher not only to think about the artifacts, but also to examine their meaning as part of the portfolio.

What Is a Portfolio?

Campbell and associates assert that

> A portfolio is not merely a file of course projects and assignments, nor is it a scrapbook of teaching memorabilia. A portfolio is an organized, goal-driven documentation of your professional growth and achieved competence in the complex act called teaching. (1997, p. 3)

For veterans, just as for first-year teachers, a portfolio is a work in progress that allows teachers to chronicle teaching practices (including changes made over time), attainment of short- and long-term goals, and knowledge gained through constructing artifacts.

A Case Study

Several teachers at Benton High School have been developing professional portfolios for almost an entire school year. Holly Young, a veteran teacher, serves as the mathematics department chair, and Lois Astor, an assistant principal, evaluates all members of the Mathematics Department. At Benton, department chairs are required to provide instructional supervision and complete two full cycles of supervision (preobservation conference, an extended classroom observation, and a postobservation conference), and the administrator who oversees and evaluates teachers in the department conducts one classroom observation (with a pre- and a postobservation conference). The department chair is to provide ongoing support but not to be involved in the summative evaluation of teachers—this is the work of the members of the administrative team.

Teachers at Benton receive a rating at the end of the year (E = excellent; G = good; S = satisfactory; or U = unsatisfactory).

Laurel Patton, a geometry teacher, received an "S" rating at the end of the year, based on the perception that she assessed student learning exclusively through end-of-chapter tests. She challenged this rating. In a meeting after receiving her rating, Laurel presented her portfolio to Lois Astor. Laurel complained that Lois had not examined her portfolio—which contains artifacts demonstrating that she uses a variety of assessment techniques—after observing her classroom.

Lois Astor did not examine the contents of Laurel Patton's portfolio because its intended use was to extend the formative aspects of teacher development and growth (the work of the department chair).

There appears to be a disconnection between the work of the department chair and assistant principal. A greater issue, however, is the boundary between supervision and evaluation. Lois decides that she and Holly need to meet.

Develop an agenda for the meeting.

Doolittle (1994) believes that "a teacher portfolio is a document created by the teacher that reveals, relates and describes the teacher's duties, expertise and growth in teaching" (p. 1). The portfolio's strength lies in the opportunity for teachers to collect artifacts over an extended time—an entire school year, even from year to year. The ongoing nature of portfolio development makes it a natural way to enhance clinical and peer-mediated forms of supervision (e.g., coaching), focus mentoring activities, and provide data for action research.

Extended Reflection

How can a portfolio be used as a form of action research?

What role could a peer coach play in the development of a portfolio?

Wolf (1991) indicates that a portfolio "represents an attitude that assessment is dynamic, and that the richest portrayals of teacher…performances are based upon multiple sources of evidence collected over time in authentic settings" (p. 129). The assessment of teaching is an ongoing process; this assessment will hold meaning for teachers only if they are active in

♦ Developing goals;

♦ Selecting artifacts that offer rich portrayals of teaching;

♦ Receiving feedback on the artifacts as they relate to teaching practice;

♦ Reflecting on the impact of the artifacts through data collected in classroom observations; and

♦ Chronicling changes in practice based on accumulating artifacts over time. (Zepeda, 2002)

Meanings are derived from the processes of collecting, examining, and reflecting on the portfolio contents. Thus, portfolio development is a process and a product. The product is the portfolio itself. The process is the way artifacts are selected, what is done with them after they are placed in the portfolio, and what changes in practice occur as a result of these efforts.

The Contents of a Portfolio

Although opinions vary on what to include in a portfolio, only one rule should dictate the decision—the purposes or goals targeted by the teacher (Sanborn & Sanborn, 1994). Goal setting is discussed extensively in Chapter 7. Items in a portfolio might include written documentation (e.g., targeted student work, lesson plans, results of tests, curricular outlines, formal evaluations, letters from parents) and other artifacts such as photographs, diagrams, and audio and videotapes.

> ## Extended Reflection
>
> A caution on including videotape footage of classroom events in the portfolio is warranted. Many school systems prohibit videotaping without prior consent from authorities and a signed release from the parent or guardian of any child who will be in the video clip. Before beginning a formal professional growth opportunity that requires either videotape or audiotape, the supervisor should consult policy and district-level personnel. Union agreements also should be considered.

Although Wolf (1990) initially had strong reservations about the use of videotaped evidence (e.g., classroom intrusion, time-consuming evaluation, access to equipment), he reported: "A review of the portfolios suggested that the videotape, along with the teachers' descriptions of the events on the tape, was one of the most important pieces of evidence" (p. 132).

This finding makes sense; videotape analysis of classroom events has proved its worth as a means for teachers to examine their teaching practices (Ponticell, 1995; Storygard & Fox, 1995). In a case study, Storygard and Fox (1995) report, "teachers can reflect on their practice through analysis of their videotapes. Reflecting with other teachers enriches this process" (p. 25). As with any effective practice, "teachers developed a common language for analyzing videotapes…participants were encouraged to base their comments on what they saw on the tapes, and [to look] for evidence to support their observations" (p. 26).

In the realm of supervision, videotape analysis of classroom events is one way to promote autosupervision, a self-directed and self-guided way for teachers to examine their own instructional practices (Zepeda, Wood, & O'Hair, 1996). Videotape analysis does not have to occur in isolation; a peer or a supervisor can readily view a teaching episode and then guide the teacher in analyzing the teaching segment.

Zepeda and Mayers (2000) indicate that the professional teaching portfolio might include artifacts from a range of topical areas

- ♦ Personal (e.g., statement of beliefs concerning teaching);
- ♦ Curricular (e.g., sample lesson plans and tests);
- ♦ Classroom (e.g., samples of student work);
- ♦ School as a learning community (e.g., committee work, interdisciplinary lesson artifacts); and
- ♦ Professional growth (e.g., career goals, journals, videotapes). (p. 168)

Once parameters regarding the contents of the portfolio have been agreed on, an organized approach facilitates their selection. The key ingredient is time; a primary responsibility of the supervisor is to find time for teachers to work on their portfolios, consult with others, and reflect on the meaning of the portfolio and its artifacts.

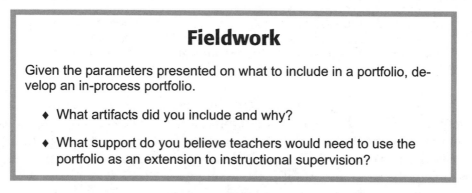

Fieldwork

Given the parameters presented on what to include in a portfolio, develop an in-process portfolio.

♦ What artifacts did you include and why?

♦ What support do you believe teachers would need to use the portfolio as an extension to instructional supervision?

Parameters for Selecting Portfolio Contents

Bird (1990) suggests that portfolio artifacts should center on broadly defined clusters of teaching tasks (e.g., planning and preparation, teaching the class, student evaluation, professional exchanges). To get at the crucial question—"So what?"—Van Wagenen and Hibbard (1998) propose an interrelated process, as illustrated in Figure 11.1.

Figure 11.1. What, So What, and Now What?

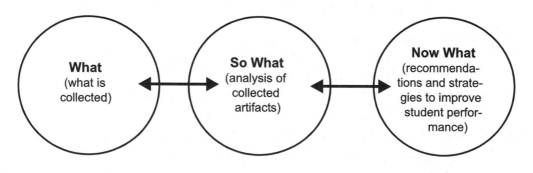

Source: Van Wagenen & Hibbard, 1998.

Krause (1996) suggests three processes: collection, selection, and reflection. Krause maintains that if the process stopped with collection, the model would stagnate, but if the portfolio contained "reflections exploring the

Extending Clinical Supervision Through Portfolio Development

Each cycle of the clinical supervision model rests on the triad of the preobservation conference, extended classroom observation, and postobservation conference. The intent of the original clinical model called for more than one complete cycle of supervision through the year. Incorporating portfolio development into the clinical model of supervision supports extended learning.

Setting overall goals, the teacher chooses an area to explore for the year; under optimal conditions, all classroom observations focus on the teacher's progress toward these established goals. Artifact selection can link to the data gathered in the classroom observation. The analysis of artifacts can inform and enrich the postobservation conference. The next section of this chapter presents a model of portfolio supervision (Zepeda, 2002).

Portfolio development is both developmental and differentiated. Teachers select artifacts at their current developmental level and then grow professionally through reflective analysis on the portfolio contents. The supervisor, peer coach, or mentor works with the teacher in any of several ways. Portfolio supervision by the supervisor or colleague may be structured (direct) or more collaborative (indirect), or the process can be self-directed with the supervisor serving mainly as a facilitator. Career stages and principles of adult learning are addressed in Chapter 7, and the reader is encouraged to consult that chapter before examining the model presented in the next section.

A Model of Portfolio Supervision

Based on the research of Zepeda (2002) in an extended two-year case study of the practices of teachers in an elementary school, a model of portfolio supervision evolved. Figure 11.2, on the next page, illustrates the model and shows how portfolio development can become part of the clinical supervisory process.

Figure 11.2. Portfolio Supervision

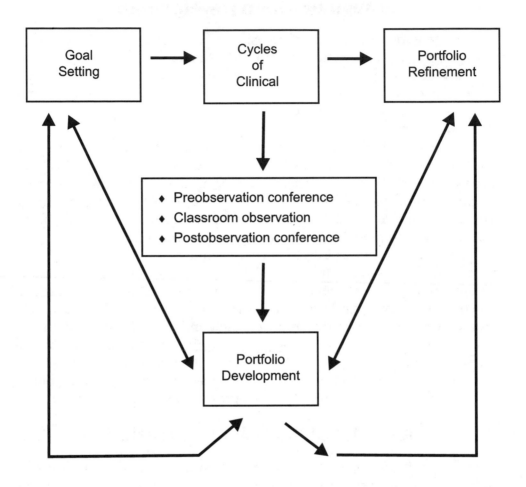

In this model, all activities—goal setting, observation focus, data collection, and artifact collection, selection, and analysis—are embedded in the preobservation conference, the extended classroom observation, and the postobservation conference. This model assumes that the skills needed for effective portfolio development are parallel (perhaps even identical) to those needed to conduct meaningful classroom observations and pre- and postobservation conferences.

Essential Skills: Reflection, Goal Setting, and Decision Making

Portfolio development as a complement to clinical supervision demands three essential skills:

1. Reflection about portfolio development and design;
2. Goal setting; and
3. Self-analysis.

Figure 11.3 portrays the interplay of skills when the portfolio is used to complement clinical supervision. Each skill does double duty as teachers explore their practices while constructing knowledge from examining and re-examining the artifacts in the portfolio.

Figure 11.3. Skills Inherent in Portfolio Supervision

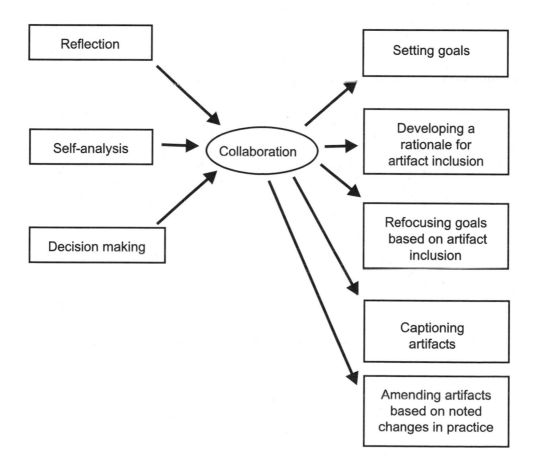

Reflection

All the portfolio models reported in the literature cite reflection as the primary skill involved; the "power of a portfolio is found in its ability to become a tool for an individual to reflect on the real tasks" involved in teaching and learning (Murray, 1994, p. 14). Whether through viewing videotapes, captioning artifacts, or keeping reflective logs or journals, reflection determines whether the portfolio becomes a useful tool or "simply a receptacle for disposable paper" (Murray, p. 9). To review processes that promote reflection, see Figure 10.5 (pages 251–253).

Self-Analysis

It is through self-analysis that a teacher can reflect on practice, make a change in practice, and begin to develop or refine practice. It is through self-analysis that meaning is derived from the process of developing a portfolio.

Decision Making

Decision making is central to portfolio development. The teacher, as an empowered professional, is constantly tinkering with artifacts, making decisions about artifacts to feature or cull, and identifying practices that have changed or will change. Decision making under these conditions signals thinking, and thinking signals growth and development.

The Portfolio as a Framework to Extend Supervision

As a process, the portfolio can serve as a framework to extend supervision by

- Establishing instructional and other closely related goals (e.g., classroom management, student assessment procedures);
- Encouraging ongoing self-assessment and evaluation of goals;
- Refining goals and targeted activities needed to accomplish goals;
- Fostering collaboration between professionals, whether it be peers serving as mentors, or administrators leading teachers through more formalized supervision and evaluation;
- Creating the conditions to examine practice through other complementary processes such as action research (e.g., tracking student achievement on standardized tests based on frequency of

instructional strategies and multitiered student assessments designed by the teacher);

- ◆ Pinpointing needed professional development within the learning context of the classroom and relevant to short and long-term goals; and

- ◆ Assessing the impact of professional development activities (e.g., professional development initiatives, professional readings, and lessons learned in graduate courses).

Summary

The portfolio will endure as a means to extend clinical supervision only if teachers are encouraged to think outside the box as they develop portfolios that reflect the knowledge they gain by refining their practices. With the advent of sophisticated technology, teacher portfolios can be stored on school home pages available for teachers and even parents to view. Discussions among teachers can be posted using electronic mail.

Teacher choice drives the portfolio process. Supervisory involvement can range from directive to more collaborative approaches that place teachers at center stage. Few models of differentiated supervision enable such concentrated study over extended periods with such an accurate and immediate portrayal of the teaching and learning situation—the classroom. This is the power of the portfolio.

Suggested Activities

From Theory to Practice

Work with a student teacher or a first-year teacher to develop a portfolio linked to extending the clinical model of supervision. What lessons from practice did you learn?

Group Processing

In a small group, develop a long-term plan to implement portfolio supervision. Present this plan to the class.

Reflection

How does a supervisor find the time to implement portfolio supervision?

References

Bird, T. (1990). The schoolteacher's portfolio: An essay on possibilities. In J. Millman, & L. Darling-Hammond (Eds.), *The new handbook of teacher evaluation: Assessing elementary and secondary school teachers* (2nd ed., pp. 241–256). Newbury Park, CA: Sage Publications.

Campbell, D. M., Cignetti, P. B., Melenyzer, B. J., Nettles, D. H., & Wyman, R. M. (1997). *How to develop a professional portfolio: A manual for teachers.* Needham Heights, MA: Allyn & Bacon.

Doolittle, P. (1994). *Teacher portfolio assessment.* Washington, DC: Clearinghouse on Assessment and Evaluation. (ERIC Document Reproduction Services No. ED385608)

Krause, S. (1996). Portfolios in teacher education: Effects of instruction on preservice teachers' early comprehension of the portfolio process. *Journal of Teacher Education, 47*(2), 130–138.

Murray, J. P. (1994, February). *The teaching portfolio: The department chairperson's role in creating a climate of teaching excellence.* Paper presented at the Third Annual International Conference for Community College Chairs, Deans, and Other Instructional Leaders, Phoenix, AZ.

Ponticell, J. A. (1995). Promoting teaching professionalism through collegiality. *Journal of Staff Development, 16*(3), 13–18.

Sanborn, J., & Sanborn, E. (1994). A conversation on portfolios. *Middle School Journal, 26*(1), 26–29.

Shulman, L. S. (1988). A union of insufficiencies: Strategies for teacher assessment in a period of educational reform. *Educational Leadership, 46*(4), 36–41.

Storygard, J., & Fox, B. (1995). Reflection on video: One teacher's story. *Journal of Staff Development, 16*(3), 25–29.

Van Wagenen, L. V., & Hibbard, K. M. (1998). Building teacher portfolios. *Educational Leadership, 55*(5), 26–29.

Wolf, K. (1991). The schoolteacher's portfolio: Issues in design, implementation, and evaluation. *Phi Delta Kappa, 73*(2), 129–136.

Zepeda, S. J. (2002). Linking portfolio development to clinical supervision: A case study. *The Journal of Curriculum and Supervision, 18*(1), 83–102.

Zepeda, S. J., Wood, F., & O'Hair, M. J. (1996). A vision of supervision for 21st century schooling: Trends to promote change, inquiry, and reflection. *Wingspan, 11*(2), 26–30.

Zepeda, S. J., & Mayers, R. S. (2000). *Supervision and staff development in the block.* Larchmont, NY: Eye On Education.

12

Mentoring
and Induction

In This Chapter...

♦ The multifaceted and complex nature of mentoring

♦ Examining qualities, skills, and functions of mentors

♦ Selecting, training, and assigning mentors

♦ Mentoring in an era of accountability

♦ Induction: Where mentoring matters most

♦ Formative assistance: The link to supervision

Introducing Mentoring and Induction

In the next decade and beyond, the needs of the changing corps of teachers already in the profession and those who join the ranks will demand that school systems elevate mentoring to new levels.

The literature on mentoring and induction abounds with descriptions of program designs, definitions, mentoring roles, and the apparently positive results of research conducted in school systems that incorporate induction and mentoring as part of the schoolwide professional development program. The benefits of cohesive mentoring and induction programs will be elusive until school systems build supportive environments that encourage learning while creating an ethos of care and concern for all its members.

Mentoring programs that benefit only new teachers slight an even larger percentage of teachers already in the profession, and there is increasing evidence that mentors themselves grow and develop through mentoring (Ganser, 1995). Perhaps school systems need to examine mentoring as an integral complement to supervision, peer coaching, professional development, and action research.

The Multifaceted and Complex Nature of Mentoring

The rationale for mentoring and induction programs in K–12 schools derives from

- The high number of teachers who leave the profession within the first three years of teaching;
- The proliferation of alternatively certified teachers;
- The high number of teachers who enter or reenter after being out of field;
- The number of teachers who are teaching out of their fields; and
- The varying contexts in which teachers teach (e.g., urban, suburban, rural).

Mentoring can ease the transition from the college experience to the teaching profession. "Beginning teachers benefit from assistance from colleagues and that assistance needs to be individualized to meet a wide variety of needs" (Huffman & Leak, 1986, p. 22).

Defining the term mentoring is difficult because the work mentors do is bound within the context of the workplace, and as Cross states, "Mentoring is a slippery concept" (in Daloz, 1999, p. 4). The various roles, functions, and contexts associated with the act of mentoring make it almost impossible to generalize a definition (Merriam, 1983).

Extended Reflection

How many first-year teachers have been hired over the past two years in the school district where you work? How many in the building where you work?

Discuss the opportunities afforded to first-year teachers at the district level and at the site where you work.

Do the supervisors in your building supervise first-year teachers differently than teachers with more experience?

What are your thoughts about the supervision first-year teachers need?

For the purposes of this chapter, *"mentoring* generally is used to denote a professional relationship in which a more experienced teacher assumes responsibility for assisting a less experienced teacher in making the transition from preservice teacher training to actual teaching" (Pellicer & Anderson, 1995, p. 163, emphasis in the original). Figure 12.1 provides some commonly accepted definitions of mentoring based on the roles mentors assume. Note the metaphoric value placed on the work that mentors do.

Figure 12.1. The Defining Features of Mentoring

Definition		Metaphor (task-related)	
Kay (1990)	"comprehensive effort directed toward helping a protégé develop the attitudes and behaviors (skills) of self-reliance and accountability within a defined environment" (p. 27).	Gehrke (1988)	"guide, sponsor, coach"
Odell (1990)	Believes that mentors guide the new teacher along the journey of professional development.	Gehrke (1988)	"developer of talent, opener of doors, protector"
		Daloz (1999)	"journey"
Sweeney (2001)	"Mentoring is a process of accomplishing a series of developmental tasks while creating a confidential, supportive, and mutual relationship" (p. xi).	Anderson & Shannon (1988)	"befriending, encourager, sponsoring, nurturer, role model"

The journey of mentors and their protégés can have profound effects on the culture of the school. "Mentoring is a journey strategy for gradually creating a learning community, two people at a time, by practicing collaborative learning one conversation at a time" (Sweeney, 2001, p. 18). A school that promotes mentoring as a form of support creates the conditions in which learning communities flourish.

Mentoring is a form of social learning in which knowledge is gained and integrated through action. Learning is enhanced through the relationship and the interaction between the mentor and the protégé; according to Gehrke (1988), "Relationships cannot be one-sided; the relationships have to be comprehensive, involving the mentor in the protégé's total life, not just work" (p. 44). Effective mentoring programs promote reciprocal learning between the mentor and protégé. Mentors can foster a more collegial atmosphere in the school by providing rich exchanges of knowledge, ideas, questions, and expertise.

Extended Reflection

Can a mentor learn from a protégé?

What does reciprocal learning mean?

Examining Qualities, Skills, and Functions of Mentors

In an early study, Lambert and Lambert (1985) identified the qualities, skills, and functions of mentors. Mentors were givers of support and encouragement, providers of developmentally appropriate learning opportunities, and champions of peer-mediated assistance (e.g., coaching). Figure 12.2, on the next page, presents the work and range of skills that mentors need to be effective in their work.

Fieldwork

In a school that has a formal mentoring program for beginning teachers, informally interview two or three first-year teachers who are working with mentors. Ask them to identify and describe the qualities that make, in their opinion, their mentors effective. Ask further, about

♦ The types of support the mentors provide.

♦ How often they meet with their mentors.

Examine documents that describe the mentoring program. How does the system match the mentors with the first-year teachers?

Does the program undergo any type of formal or informal evaluation to assess the quality of mentoring? If the program does undergo formal or informal assessment, it might be helpful to interview the person who oversees the assessment of the mentoring program. The objective of discussing the assessment is to gain insight on how the mentoring program has evolved from the lessons learned.

Figure 12.2 Skills Needed for Effective Mentoring

Effective Mentors

- Demonstrate strong collegial skills—including critique, support, and reciprocity.
- Understand and communicate knowledge of effective teaching.
- Provide solid experience as a context for examining ideas and actions.
- Demonstrate flexible learning style with skills in convergent and divergent thinking.
- Serve as a model adult learner.
- Understand persuasion, facilitation, and change processes.
- Demonstrate strong commitment to personal growth and development including continued learning, self-reflection, analysis, and critique.
- Demonstrate flexibility by knowing when to be a teacher, facilitator, listener, and inquirer.
- Demonstrate skills as an action researcher.
- Evidence capacity for mutual trust and regard.
- Orchestrate dissonance and consonance through such approaches as questioning, feedback, and coaching.
- Foster self-direction in others by encouraging independence and self-analysis.
- Understand the stages of mentoring relationship, altering the interaction in response to growing autonomy.

Source: Lambert & Lambert, 1985, p. 29.

Mentors provide learning opportunities for their protégés through action research, peer coaching, critique and analysis, reflective dialogue, and listening to and supporting the efforts of teachers. Mentoring is a nurturing process. The mentor serves as a role model by fulfilling five functions: (a) teaching, (b) sponsoring, (c) encouraging, (d) counseling, and (e) befriending (Anderson & Shannon, 1988).

Extended Reflection

Can a supervisor fulfill the five mentoring functions: teaching, sponsoring, encouraging, counseling, and befriending (Anderson & Shannon, 1988)?

Is there a conflict in store for the supervisor who tries to fulfill these roles?

A mentor's work depends on the context of the school, the roles of mentor and protégé, and the relationships that form between them. A mentor's numerous responsibilities include socializing newcomers to the profession and imparting a sense of belonging through formal and informal induction activities. Mentors also help their protégés examine their practices and find the personal resources to build on existing skills. Effective mentors give constructive feedback and provide ongoing opportunities for reflective and analytical discussions.

Selecting, Training, and Assigning Mentors

The overall effectiveness of a mentoring program begins with selecting, training, and assigning mentors. Preparing mentors to work with the newest members of the learning community requires administrative support and attention to detail. The goal is to develop more fully functioning and competent beginning teachers who can be self-directed and autonomous in their learning.

A Case Study

Carvin Elliot, a first-year teacher, and Judy Romano, his assigned mentor, were just not clicking. When they met, Judy provided information (how to request a substitute teacher), but Carvin does not believe that Judy has invested in him as a person.

♦ Should mentors and protégés be a forced pair?

♦ Are there alternatives for pairing mentors and protégés?

♦ If you were Carvin's supervisor and he came to you with concerns about his mentor, what would you do?

"Mentoring, like good teaching, should be defined by those who will carry it out" (Wildman, Magliaro, Niles, & Niles, 1992, p. 212). The literature describes a variety of approaches to mentor selection and assignment. For example, Clemson (1987) suggests that mentors should self-select to participate in mentoring activities. Forced pairings can hamper relationship building between mentor and protégé. Janas (1996, p. 3) favors "no fixed rule" in the selection of mentors and their pairing with protégés. In the typical school, teachers could easily get lost in the shuffle, and principals could put mentoring and induction on the back burner, creating what Zepeda and Ponticell (1998) refer to as the practice of benign neglect.

Any program is only as solid as its foundation. A mentoring or induction program must build on the values and beliefs of teachers, administrators, parents, students—all the members of the learning community. Although the work of mentors might be "magical" (Daloz, 1999), there is no magic formula for a mentoring or induction program. Supervisors must not only assess their own beliefs about the support (all) teachers need, but also hear the beliefs that teachers voice about their needs.

Sweeney's (2001) long-term work in assisting schools across the country to establish mentoring programs has led to the following assertions:

1. Leaders want to see mentors who model the excitement of learning every day, openly, and in front of their peers. They want to see mentors with a drive to find even better ways to help their students and their colleagues succeed.

2. With this kind of mentoring, beginning teachers become models of continual learning, and do so openly, in front of their students. Leaders want to see beginning teachers whose passion is finding ever better and more effective ways of ensuring their students' success.

3. Leaders need this kind of beginning teacher, because they know it is the best way to help students become lifelong learners and collaborative workers who are open to learning from each other, always searching for better and more effective ways to achieve their own goals. (p. 3)

To promote the type of learning that Sweeney describes, teachers must be empowered to model positive relationships that are "developmental," "reciprocal," and "ongoing" (Anderson & Shannon, 1988; Clemson, 1987; Gehrke, 1988; Healy & Welchert, 1990). What lifetime skills should mentors model to protégés? Reflective practice, the art of inquiry, risk-taking—perhaps these skills and more.

If mentors are to emerge as leaders, they need training in

- Effective communication;
- Problem solving;
- Peer coaching;
- Working with not only beginning teachers, but also other teachers who are being mentored (experienced teachers new to the school system, teachers wanting to learn or update skills); and
- Group development.

Because each school has its own context, training must be home grown; teachers and others within the system take the lead. The principal's job is to provide tangible resources and intangible support, such as encouragement for learning efforts. Research suggests that mentors learn as much as protégés, and Ganser (1997) reports:

> Veteran teachers frequently characterize working closely with beginning teachers as a source of fresh, new, cutting-edge ideas about curriculum and teaching. Mentors often characterize what they learn from new teachers as more immediately accessible and useful in their work than much of what they learn through graduate courses or typical in-service activities and workshops. In many cases, mentors and beginning teachers function as peer coaches as they simultaneously implement innovative strategies in their respective classes. (pp. 4–5)

Given their own learning opportunities, mentors can learn valuable lessons from the very help and support they give to beginning teachers. Further, mentors can mentor each other. To foster learning among mentors, the principal can

- Provide release time for mentors to communicate with each other;
- Extend training opportunities for mentors;
- Acknowledge the expertise of mentors by expanding their leadership opportunities (e.g., training new mentors, evaluating the effects of the mentoring program); and
- Be available to troubleshoot with mentors.

Support must be offered in a way that makes sense within the context of the school and the community it serves. However, support will be limited or ill conceived without evaluation. Evaluation of program efforts can track the benefits to beginning teachers and the school and help mentors make adjustments in the work they do. In this age of accountability, the stakes are high; the mentoring of beginning teachers must become a high-stakes priority for schools.

Montgomery Elementary School is part of a rural system with an elementary school (grades 1–5), a junior high school (grades 6–8) and a high school (grades 9–12). The district employs approximately 150 teachers. Superintendent Jack Kaufman wants to develop a mentoring program. During the weekly meeting with the principals, he asks each principal to name three teachers from their buildings to serve on a districtwide committee. Jack then reports the research that supports mentoring and describes some successful programs.

Lloyd Taylor, principal of Montgomery Elementary School, objects to forming a committee to examine mentoring because "not one single new teacher was hired in the past five years, and no one is expected to retire in the next five years." Lloyd further states, "All teachers live in the community—our teachers have a history in our town—they don't need any more mentoring."

♦ If you were Superintendent Jack Kaufman, how would you respond to Lloyd's statements?

♦ What issues might arise in a rural system that would be different from those in a suburban or urban setting?

Mentoring in an Era of Accountability

The New Teacher Center's Web site (http://www.newteachercenter.org/NTCoverview.html) offers a wealth of information and tools for educators. The New Teacher Center (NTC), housed at the University of California, Santa Cruz, is a national resource dedicated to teacher development and the support of programs and practices that promote excellence and diversity in America's teaching force. The NTC addresses the pressing national need for new teacher induction programs.

Ellen Moir, executive director for the New Teacher Center and an advocate of induction and mentoring, has been part of an initiative to bring accountability and standards to induction practices for beginning teachers. In the spring 2001 issue of *Reflections*, the NTC newsletter, Dr. Moir raises some interesting issues related to standards and accountability for the induction of new teachers. Dr. Moir's column is presented in Figure 12.3.

(Text continues on page 281.)

Figure 12.3. Formative Assessment

Formative Assessment as a Strategy for Growth
by Ellen Moir, NTC Executive Director

High stakes assessments. Data and accountability. This is the language that surrounds our classrooms and our schools, particularly this time of year. The pressure that accompanies the mandates for increased testing is taking its toll on both our new teachers and their veteran colleagues.

In this climate of intense pressure and public scrutiny, it becomes especially important for us to step back from the rhetoric and remind ourselves of the central role assessment plays in our ability to deliver effective instruction as well as provide high quality beginning teacher support.

Assessment has terrific importance for teaching and learning. Fine classroom teachers everywhere use an array of assessment tools and strategies to better understand their students' academic needs, to target their instruction, to guide next steps, and then to document their students' achievement. Assessment data informs our instruction and ensures that our teaching is responsive to the needs of all our students. Good teachers know this and seamlessly connect learning and assessing.

After years of working with beginning teachers, we have come to recognize that mentors and new teacher support providers need a variety of ways to **assess** their new teachers if they are to provide the most essential guidance and impact their new colleagues' learning. The challenge facing our induction programs and our mentors is to make sure that our formative assessment strategies support the mentor–new teacher relationship and teacher development.

One of the most important lessons we can teach our new teachers is the power of good assessment as a teaching and learning tool. What a loss if beginning teachers come to believe that assessment has little connection to their classroom practice or that it is comprised of hurdles for their students and themselves.

If we are to support beginning teachers in understanding the inherent value of assessment for both the teacher and the learner, then we have to carefully examine how we use assessment in the context of our teacher induction programs.

There are a number of questions we might want to ask ourselves: Are the tools we use assisting the novice in improving practice? Is the assessment data we collect relevant? Do our structures link teaching and learning? Are they embedded in the day-to-day work of professional growth and classroom practice? After induction, will our beginning teachers continue to seek and analyze data about their classroom instruction and their students' learning and assess their professional practice and their growth over time? Will they rely on assessment data to move to more ambitious levels of teaching? Do our beginning teachers use assessment data to clearly articulate their growth and achievement?

If we are not able to answer yes to the majority of these questions, then we have lost an incredible opportunity to help the next generation of educators develop the habits of mind essential to quality instruction. What a loss if our beginning teachers see assessment only for accountability's sake and come to believe that it has little connection to their teaching and their students' learning.

All of us know the essential ingredients of successful formative assessment: helping new teachers set meaningful goals informed by professional and student content standards; collecting and analyzing performance data to assess progress; using student work as data to guide instruction; and committing to personal accountability for professional growth.

In these times of high stakes testing and increased public accountability, we can help new teachers embrace relevant and meaningful assessment strategies that inform their teaching. Only then can they set standardized test data in the broader context of their students' academic growth.

We can model curiosity and inquiry. We can make our formative assessment strategies relevant and responsive. We can, as mentors, use data to guide our own mentoring practice and support strategies. We can avoid making the assessment a burden for the new teacher learner.

The teaching profession is at an important crossroads. Hundreds of thousands of new colleagues are entering America's classrooms this coming decade. We veterans have an enormous responsibility to induct them into the profession in ways that create a new status quo. This new way of being in schools will support all of us in becoming collaborative inquirers into the art and practice of teaching professionals who are able [to] use assessment data related to our own practice as well as the achievement of our students.

The stakes are high for all of us, and the opportunity is one we cannot let pass. I am excited to be a part of this great statewide, and nationwide, community of educators who are dedicated to helping new teachers. Let's make sure that effective, relevant, meaningful assessments guide our work. (pp. 1–2)

Source: Moir, 2001. Used with permission.

Moir's message is clear. Beginning teachers need ongoing and sustained assistance from the very moment they are hired. Ongoing and formative efforts occur over time, not just at the end of the year when very little can be done. Moreover, first-year teachers need to construct and reconstruct meaning from the experience of what happens in their classrooms. Mentoring embedded in an organized induction program appears to make most sense.

Induction: Where Mentoring Matters Most

In response to a national teacher shortage, our schools face the prospect of hiring more than two million teachers in the next five years. Those beginning teachers and the schools where they will work need formalized induction programs, and such programs often include mentoring as a key component. First-year teachers need induction and mentoring not only to survive the realities of the classroom at the beginning of their careers, but also to ensure longevity and continued development. Stansbury (2001) believes that:

> The purpose of induction programs is to provide logistical, emotional, and teaching support to ease a new teacher's transition from student to professional. Anticipated effects include the strengthening of teaching practice and increased retention rates. (p. 1)

During a period of transition, "new teachers need supervision and support to adjust to their new roles" (Blair-Larsen & Bercik, 1992, p. 25). Huling-Austin (1990) asserts that for a beginning teacher program, regardless of its intents, to be considered an induction program, it "must contain some degree of systematic and sustained assistance, and not merely be a series of orientation meetings" (p. 536).

Why do schools need mentoring and induction programs for beginning teachers? First-year teachers (a) are often unfocused workers, unable to think of appropriate ways to improve their teaching; (b) are highly motivated and coachable; and (c) tend to be idealistic, with their expectations often exceeding what they can reasonably achieve (Young, Crain, & McCullough, 1993).

Regardless of the structure (formal or informal) of the induction process, "if the intent of teacher induction programs is to persuade newcomers, particularly those with the greatest academic talent, to stay in the profession and contribute productively," then schools should provide first-year teachers with the following experiences:

- Initial teaching assignments that place them neither in the most difficult schools nor with the most difficult students.

- Discretion and autonomy to make important classroom choices with information about options and possibilities gained through opportunities to participate in decision making with colleagues and administrators.

- Clear goals set by administrators, colleagues, and beginners themselves toward which they should initially strive.

- Clear, frequent, and helpful feedback from administrators and colleagues about the progress they are making with suggestions to help them improve.

- Regular encouragement and acknowledgment of their efforts by building administrators and colleagues.

- A school ethos that explicitly encourages them to ask for advice when needed and to feel nonthreatened when others offer theirs.

- Opportunities to talk frequently with colleagues that are more expert about teaching problems and possibilities, to observe them at their work, and to be observed by them.

- Encouragement to continuously experiment with new teaching ideas and to enjoy colleagues who do likewise.

- Schoolwide standards for student conduct that beginners can be helped to enforce consistently.

- Opportunities for beginners to participate in school efforts that involve parents in their children's learning and that keep parents regularly informed. (Rosenholtz, 1989, p. 29)

Formative Assistance:
The Linkage to Supervision

Given this examination of mentoring and induction, how can supervisors assist first-year teachers? This question is not easily answered. Regardless of the approach, all learning opportunities need to be formative, or ongoing in nature. The induction program itself must be part of a larger system that provides human support programs.

Formative Approaches

Supervisors can adapt the following approaches to fit the context of the school.

Frequent Contact First-year teachers need frequent contact with mentors, supervisors, and other adults who can provide encouragement, reassurance, and resources. Supervisors can make informal classroom observations early in the year to assess the types of support needed by first-year teachers. Mentors and supervisors can plan informal opportunities for beginning teachers to interact with one another before the first week of school. Some supervisors in the field make it a point to confer with the "new kids on the block" on the first day of school.

Balanced Supervision Informal and formal classroom observations should begin within the first weeks of school. Formative supervision is ongoing, and the beginner needs open-ended assessment of instructional effectiveness from the start of the year.

Goal Setting Goal setting can begin within the first few weeks of school, as the teacher and supervisor or mentor (perhaps even both, to coordinate efforts) set goals based on the immediacy of the classroom environment.

Focused Classroom Observations Balanced supervision includes focused classroom observations based on an area identified during the preobservation conference. Formal classroom observations require both pre- and postobservation conferences. After the postobservation conference, the supervisor, coach, or mentor makes follow-up classroom observations.

Differentiated Approaches Differentiated approaches such as action research, portfolio development, and peer coaching enable beginning teachers to construct deeper meanings from their work. Data should drive the essential decision about which approach makes most sense for a particular beginning teacher and classroom. One example of differentiated supervision is videotape analysis of teaching (Figure 12.4, next page).

Figure 12.4. Videotape Analysis as Supervision

Video cameras offer teachers an invaluable tool for analyzing their teaching. By videotaping a class period, teachers can observe traffic patterns, verbal flow, and activities within the context of their own classrooms.

Reviewing the videotape, teachers can ask themselves the following questions:

♦ Do I achieve my objectives? How?

♦ What teaching behaviors support the answers to the above questions?

After viewing the videotape, teachers can identify areas for further development, set specific goals, and formulate a plan to accomplish them. Videotaping the same class period two or three weeks later allows the teacher to assess progress and reformulate plans.

When using videotape to capture classroom practices, teachers and supervisors should consider the following:

♦ The first videotape could be "unstable." Students curious about the undertaking might shift their attention from learning to the camera and the other person in the room. During subsequent videotaping, the novelty should diminish.

♦ Some people are nervous about seeing themselves on camera. Teachers might consider viewing the videotape several times to overcome this natural response.

♦ After viewing the videotape, teachers should be encouraged to watch the tape with a mentor and ask for feedback.

♦ Teachers can be paired and take turns videotaping, and giving feedback, to one another.

♦ Selected videotapes can form part of a professional portfolio.

Summary

Induction programs are crucial to the survival of teachers in their first year of teaching. Without such programs, many beginning teachers leave the profession. Human support systems must provide for the needs of all teachers as they proceed through distinct stages of their formal professional development.

Suggested Activities

From Theory to Practice

If your school does not have a mentoring program, organize a voluntary meeting for teachers interested in starting one. Develop a rationale for such a program and a description that includes how mentors would be selected and trained, resources needed for the first year, and the intended role of the supervisor.

Group Processing

School districts often provide a formalized induction program for new teachers. What must site-level supervisors do to customize induction activities and to align building-level work with the work of the central office?

Reflection

A first-year teacher in your building has asked not to have a mentor. How would you handle this request?

References

Anderson, E. M., & Shannon, A. L. (1988). Toward a conceptualization of mentoring. *Journal of Teacher Education, 39*(1), 38–42.

Blair-Larsen, S. M., & Bercik, J. T. (1992). A collaborative model for teacher education. *Education, 113*(1), 25–31.

Clemson, R. L. (1987). Mentorship in teaching. *Action in Teacher Education, 9*(3), 85–90.

Daloz, L. A. (1999). *Mentor: Guiding the journey of adult learners.* San Francisco: Jossey-Bass.

Ganser, T. (1997, April). *Promises and pitfalls for mentors of beginning teachers.* Paper presented at the Conference on Diversity in Mentoring, Tempe, AZ. (ERIC Document Reproduction Service No. ED407379)

Ganser, T. (1995). Principles for mentor teacher selection. *The Clearing House, 68*(5), 307–309.

Gehrke, N. J. (1988). On preserving the essence of mentoring as one form of teacher leadership. *Journal of Teacher Education, 35*(3), 43–45.

Healy, C. A., & Welchert, A. J. (1990). Mentoring relations: A definition to advance research and practice. *Educational Researcher, 19*(9), 17–21.

Huffman, G., & Leak, S. (1986). Beginning teachers' perceptions of mentors. *Journal of Teacher Education, 37*(1), 22–25.

Huling-Austin, L. (1990). Teacher induction programs and internships. In W. R. Houston (Ed.), *Handbook of research on teacher education* (pp. 535–548). New York: Macmillan Publishing.

Janas, M. (1996). Mentoring the mentor: A challenge for staff development. *Journal of Staff Development, 17*(4), 2–5.

Kay, R. S. (1990). A definition for developing self-reliance. In T. M. Bey and T. C. Holmes (Eds.), *Mentoring: Developing successful new teachers* (pp. 3–24). Reston, VA: Association for Teacher Educators.

Lambert, D., & Lambert, L. (1985, April-May). Mentor teachers as change facilitators. *Thrust,* 28–32.

Merriam, S. (1983). Mentors and protégés: A critical review of the literature. *Adult Educational Quarterly, 33*(3), 161–173.

Moir, E. (2001). Formative assessment as a strategy for growth. *New Teacher Center Reflections 4*(2), 1–2.

Odell, S. J. (1990). Support for new teachers. In T. M. Bey and T. C. Holmes (Eds.), *Mentoring: Developing successful new teachers* (pp. 25–42). Reston, VA: Association of Teacher Educators.

Pellicer, L. O., & Anderson, L. W. (1995). *A handbook for teacher leaders.* Thousand Oaks, CA: Corwin Press.

Rosenholtz, S. (1989). Workplace conditions that affect teacher quality and commitment: Implications for teacher induction programs. *Elementary School Journal, 89*(1), 421–439.

Stansbury, K. (2001). The role of formative assessment in induction programs. *New Teacher Center Reflections 4*(2), 1–3.

Sweeney, B. W. (2001). *Leading the teacher induction and mentoring program.* Arlington Heights, IL: SkyLight Professional Development.

Wildman, T. M., Magliaro, S. G., Niles, R.A., & Niles, J. A. (1992). Teacher mentoring: An analysis of roles, activities, and conditions. *Journal of Teacher Education, 43*(3), 205–213.

Young, T. A., Crain, C. L., & McCullough, D. (1993). Helping new teachers: The performance enhancement model. *The Clearing House, 66*(3), 174–176.

Zepeda, S. J., & Ponticell, J. A. (1998). At cross purposes: What do teachers need, want, and get from supervision? *Journal of Curriculum and Supervision, 14*(1), 68–87.

13

Confronting Marginal Teaching

In This Chapter...

♦ Marginal teaching

♦ Markers of marginal teachers

♦ Understanding the difficulties supervisors encounter while working with marginal teachers

♦ Confronting marginal teaching practices

♦ Working with the marginal teacher

♦ The plan for remediation

♦ When all else fails

Dealing with a marginal teacher is one of the most difficult situations a supervisor faces. Confronting marginal teaching will test the mettle of any administrator. Addressing marginal teaching is neither easy nor comfortable for the supervisor or the teacher. However, the reality is that there are teachers who are marginal, and in some cases, incompetent. It is difficult to know the numbers of marginal teachers in schools. Tucker (2001) asserts "expert opinion and empirical research indicate that 5 to 15 percent of the 2.7 million teachers in public school classrooms perform at marginal or incompetent levels" (p. 53). Not confronting marginal or incompetent teachers has a high cost: "The learning inequity created by incompetent teachers for millions of children each year cannot be ignored" (Tucker, 1997, p. 11).

Throughout this book, the formative aspects of working with teachers have prevailed using the baseline features (preobservation, extended classroom observation, and the postobservation conference) of the clinical model of supervision. More differentiated approaches, such as peer coaching (Chapter 9), action research (Chapter 10), and portfolio development (Chapter 11), were explored. And by reviewing the principles of adult learning and career stages (Chapter 7), and motivation (Chapter 8), it is the hope that supervision, regardless of its form, will be approached in a developmental and differentiated manner focusing the work of teachers and supervisors as a joint effort to ensure professional growth and increased competence.

All of these notions are still true in the work of a supervisor who is dealing with a marginal teacher; however, the supervisor's approach will more than likely need to be adjusted to more of a directive-control style (Glickman, 1990) of working with a marginal teacher (see Chapter 2 for detail). Bullock, Glatthorn, and Jones (2006) offer a balanced perspective on the issue of supervisory approach and marginal teachers:

> The best plan of assistance is the plan that produces the desired results. Although most marginal teachers have similar problems, improvement strategies should be individualized and grounded in the strengths and needs of the teacher. Some marginal teachers will be capable of directing their own improvement and could be successful using the nondirective approach; others will require the full intervention as described in the directive-control approach. (p. 68)

There is only one absolute about working with marginal teachers—intervention is needed. The interventions are guided by many factors including the following:

- The experience level of the teacher;
- The conceptual level of the teacher;
- The level of willingness on the part of the teacher (some people will not want to improve; some people are blinded by their weaknesses; some people just cannot improve);
- The willingness of the supervisor to work with a marginal teacher;
- The context of the school, including culture, norms of collegiality, and trust;
- The stance of the union or bargaining unit; and
- The history of supervision, evaluation, professional development, and the types of support given to struggling teachers in the past.

In the field of practice, one administrator indicated that she "takes off her supervisory hat" when dealing with a marginal teacher. She further elaborated that when dealing with a marginal teacher, she wears her "evaluator hat" so that "action can be taken to remove the teacher from the situation if marked improvements are not made." This administrator's words serve as a reminder to McGreal's (1983) perspective that "All supervisory roads lead to evaluation."

Within the scope of a chapter dedicated to the work of supervision, it is infeasible to detail the watershed about marginal teaching, the incompetent teacher, and all of the legal aspects surrounding teachers who are not performing to the detriment of student learning. The reader is encouraged to go beyond the scope of this chapter through extended reading, discussing the parameters of work within his or her school system, and, if necessary, seek the counsel of central office administration and legal counsel.

Marginal Teaching

A marginal teacher is one who manages to perform just well enough to keep his or her job to the detriment of student learning. Fuhr's (1996) characterization of marginal teachers is probably a universally accepted one, "Marginal teachers will pass evaluations required by the state, but flunk in the classroom" (p. xi).

There are many warning signs and manifestations of marginal performance. Lawrence, Vachon, Leake, and Leake's (1993) description of a marginal teacher focuses on lackluster instruction, and the assertion that "a marginal teacher is an individual who is consciously or unconsciously losing faith in the belief that every child can learn" (p. 5). They indicate that marginal teachers typically engage "in boring, uninspiring, and ineffective instruction" (p. 5).

Manatt and Sweeney (1984) indicate that "A marginal teacher is one who appears to have sufficient command of subject matter but whose lack of classroom management skills gets in the way of student learning" (p. 25). In unhealthy, toxic cultures, marginal teachers blame students for failure (Deal & Peterson, 1999). Marginal teachers take their toll on students, teachers, and the community in which the school resides.

Fuhr (1990) identifies three general types of marginal teachers: (a) those with inadequate teaching skills, (b) those with personal problems, and (c) those with attitude problems. Henderson-Sparks, Ehrgott, and Sparks, (1995) believe that marginal teachers have two types of problems—problems "that are *internally* driven (directly related to teaching competence and/or conditions within a school), and that are *externally* driven (rooted in conditions outside the school that have a negative effect on a teacher's competency of attitude)" (p. 33, emphasis in the original).

McEwan (2005) refers to marginal teachers as "instructionally challenged," and she encourages leaders to respond in a timely manner because instructionally challenged teachers have a deleterious affect on students and the school because they

1. Adversely affect the ability of students to learn, which, in turn, impacts their test scores, the quality of their effort and work, discipline referrals, and parent and student complaints;

2. Contaminate the culture of your school and inhibit school improvement efforts; and

3. Jeopardize your effectiveness as an instructional leader. (pp. 124–125)

Working with a marginal teacher requires skills in supervising and evaluating performance; working with a marginal teacher will take efforts away from working with other teachers; working with a marginal teacher diverts attention from school-based improvement efforts. Moreover, think of the marginal teacher at the high school level who teaches 150 students a year. The number of students a marginal teacher will teach in a 30-year career is 4,500 students. More than likely, this number is greater than the total enrollment of the entire school.

Markers of Marginal Teacher Performance

There are no absolute markers of marginal teaching; there are, however, patterns that mark ineffective (marginal) teaching from effective teaching competence. Lawrence et al. (1993) share that indicators of marginal teaching include "disproportionate disciplinary referrals; excessive student failure; and numerous complaints from students, parents, and even colleagues in the building (p. 5). Sawa (1995) reports the work of Dennis (1990) that marginal teachers show excessive patterns across areas including

◆ Excessive lack of preparation;
◆ Excessive deficiencies of teaching skills;
◆ Excessive problems of student control;
◆ Excessive manifestations of poor judgment; and
◆ Excessive absence from school.

The principal must confront excessive behaviors. In the final analysis, the principal is accountable for the instructional program and all who deliver it. If the principal has been actively engaged in formal and informal classroom observations in addition to tracking the artifacts of teaching and learning (e.g., test scores, lesson plans), he will have a frame of reference for the instructional behaviors of the marginal teacher. This frame of reference can only be complete through firsthand knowledge gained through classroom observations, examination of artifacts (student referrals, test data), and ongoing discussion with the marginal teacher.

What would an administrator see in the classroom of a marginal teacher? From examination of the literature on marginal and incompetent teachers, an administrator would enter the world of disjointed instruction, students not being challenged in constructive ways, and more than likely chaotic student behavior (Bridges, 1986; Bullock et al., 2006; Henderson-Sparks et al., 1995; Jackson, 1997; Lawrence et al., 1993). Figure 3.5 (pages 60–61), Criteria for Talking About Teaching, offered guidance for the supervisor to engage teachers in the talk of teaching. This information will be used now to help the supervisor see possible negative indicators of teacher performance by providing a distillation of the behaviors of marginal teachers (Figure 13.1, next page).

Extended Reflection

In the school system in which you work, how pervasive is marginal teaching? If you were asked to develop a plan for working with marginal teaching, what would be your priorities for working with this cadre of teachers? What types of support would be needed to forward this plan of support?

(Text continues on page 296.)

Figure 13.1. Markers of Marginal Teaching

Criterion	Possible Indicators
Knowledge of subject matter	◆ Shows no transfer of content/concepts to everyday life. ◆ Does not relate content to prior and future information. ◆ Does not communicate content in a logical and sequential manner. ◆ Does not use words and content appropriate to subject area and students' abilities. ◆ Does not demonstrate depth of subject knowledge. ◆ Does not actively pursue lifelong learning, especially in subject area.
Effectiveness of instructional strategies	◆ Uses limited instructional approaches often relying on one or two strategies regardless of what is being taught. ◆ Cooperative groups are poorly organized and member roles are not specified. ◆ Wait time is limited. ◆ Yes and No responses are sought. ◆ Student comments are not used to further lecture contents. ◆ Drill is a predominant instructional strategy.
Classroom management	◆ Routines are not evident. ◆ Rules and procedures are not posted. ◆ Rules and procedures are not enforced. ◆ Beginning and ending class procedures are not in place. ◆ Teacher does not monitor student behavior. ◆ Rewards and consequences are not in place. ◆ Physical environment is not conducive to orderliness. ◆ Teacher does not ensure a safe environment.

(Figure continues on next page.)

Variety of assessment methods	◆ Written, verbal, and nonverbal assessment do not include variety such as
	• tests/quizzes/written exams
	• teacher observation
	• participation
	• portfolios
	• feedback
	• projects
	• checking for continued understanding and application are absent
	◆ Assessments are infrequent.
	◆ Assessment instruments are not teacher-/student-driven.
	◆ Accommodations are not made for alternative assessments and individualized where needed.
	◆ Assessments are not based on curriculum objectives.
High expectations for all students	◆ Teacher has not established expectations for success.
	◆ Does not give varying opportunities for success.
	◆ Does not encourage each student to function at an appropriate level.
	◆ Does not begin instruction at level of the learner and does not plan for cognitive growth.
	◆ Does not provide enrichment opportunities as well as remediation.
Teacher/student rapport	◆ Is more teacher- than student-centered.
	◆ Closed climate.
	◆ Interactions with students are not positive.
	◆ Teacher does not demonstrate tact, patience, and understanding and does little to foster growth in student self-esteem.
	◆ Does not use specific praise; uses harsh criticism and sarcasm.
	◆ Does not demonstrate enthusiasm.
	◆ Does not generate excitement for learning.

(Figure continues on next page.)

Technology	◆ Does not use technology as a learning tool but rather as reward.
Communication	◆ Does not use standard English in written and spoken communication.
Gender, race, and culture	◆ Does not reflect learning styles and levels of functioning.
	◆ Teacher is not sensitive to students' cultural backgrounds and their effect on learning.
	◆ Communication (oral and written) is not free of bias. Female and male students are not treated equally relative to calling patterns and other practices.

It is important to note that marginal teachers often stay off the radar because they can put on the "dog-and-pony" show for yearly evaluations and that marginal teachers are not necessarily marginal in all areas. The key is to stay in contact with the instructional program as it unfolds in classrooms. The value of principals being visible in classrooms cannot be stressed enough.

Understanding the Difficulties Supervisors Encounter While Working with Marginal Teachers

Complexities abound surrounding the work supervisors encounter while working with marginal and/or incompetent teachers. McEwan (2005) reports that many principals "tolerate ineffective teaching because they know that confronting them will be cognitively demanding, emotionally draining, and physically exhausting" (p. 120). It is indeed demanding work especially for supervisors who may be new to a building and discover that there are marginal or incompetent teachers in their buildings. Complexities include

◆ Preparation and background of the supervisor (Fuhr, 1996)

◆ Perception about present and past site leadership (Bridges, 1990; Fuhr, 1996)

◆ Lack of support from central office (Blacklock, 2002; Bridges, 1990)

◆ Time constraints (Blacklock, 2002; Bridges, 1990; Fuhr, 1996; McEwan, 2005)

◆ Psychological stressors (Bridges, 1990; Fuhr, 1996; McEwan, 2005)

Preparation and Background of the Supervisor

Not all preparation leading to the principalship or a supervisory position is equal. As Fuhr (1996) reports, "Unfortunately, few schools of higher education prepare school administrators for the challenges of remediating marginal performers" (p. xi–xii). Although most preparation programs include a basic course in instructional supervision and/or teacher evaluation, it is doubtful that much time, depth, or breadth about the marginal or incompetent teacher is afforded to these topics. Likewise, school law courses deal with the procedural aspects of due process and termination. However, working with marginal and/or incompetent teachers requires sustained work. Supervisors can take a proactive stance in their development by consulting with other building-level supervisors, enrolling in specialty courses that deal with supporting teachers with issues, engaging in professional development, reading books, and asking central office to provide ongoing training and support for the work needed to assist in learning the skills needed to work with marginal teachers.

Perception about Present and Past Site Leadership

There is not a single principal who likes the idea of having a marginal or incompetent teacher present in the school. Generally speaking, teachers who are marginal or incompetent did not just suddenly become marginal or incompetent. The markers of marginal teaching have more than likely been evident for some time and have been able to keep off the proverbial radar. Fuhr (1996) reports that marginal teachers have learned to "become experts at putting on a 'show' before the evaluator" (p. 22).

Discovering a marginal teacher who has been in the building for some time, might in that principal's eyes cast a shadow on credibility. Many principals believe that if such a teacher is discovered, they will be viewed negatively by their immediate supervisors. A principal new to a building who discovers a marginal teacher, might be in a difficult situation bringing this information to light especially if the former principal was revered by the faculty and the central office administration. This would be especially true if the former principal was in a central office position. Once a marginal teacher is put on a plan of improvement or a remediation plan (discussed later in this chapter), news will spread throughout the faculty. Fellow teachers could doubt the accuracy of the principal's assessment of the marginal teacher.

There could be instances where a teacher is assigned to teach a class in an area closely related to credential (e.g., geography or world history) or outside of the teacher's formal area of preparation. This teacher might struggle to close the gaps in formal preparation. These instances of marginal teaching are serious and need supervisory attention, but these instances are not as difficult to manage as the teacher who is just plain marginal in multiple areas, such as management of students, learning objectives, and the learning environment.

Principals who do not confront marginal teaching face losing credibility with the faculty. Competent teachers really do not want to work alongside marginal teachers who have been able to stay off the radar. The perspectives of Fuhr (1996) add to this discussion:

> Principals don't like to talk about the marginal or incompetent teacher, or admit that such teachers are in their schools. The reason is obvious. It makes the management team look bad. Meanwhile, parents, students and the effective teachers wonder why marginal teachers are allowed to continue teaching without something being done to improve their skills (p. 1)

Lack of Support from Central Office

Although it might seem like a lonely journey for a principal working with a marginal teacher, there is a need for others to be involved. The marginal or incompetent teacher is not easy to confront without the support and backing of the central office (Blacklock, 2002; Fuhr, 1996). Blacklock (2002) reports:

> The principal can't do it alone. Making decisions of this magnitude, developing an improvement process that is fair for the teacher, and remaining focused on improvement until the evidence is unequivocal requires the full support and involvement of central office administrators. (p. 27)

This support is critically important especially in instances where remediation efforts do not yield favorable results—a teacher must be dismissed. The amount of time, resources, and possible intervention from those outside of the school or system warrant support. Once a principal detects and substantiates marginal performance, the central office should be consulted (e.g., director of personnel, director of elementary, secondary, or high school education, assistant superintendent) to gain perspective, garner support for confrontation, learn procedures, and any other information that will help the principal confront and work with the marginal and/or incompetent teacher.

Time Constraints

The amount of time a supervisor will spend working with a marginal or incompetent teacher is immense. Fuhr (1996) writes, "Managing the marginal teachers will involve extra time needed for reading reports, planning, consulting with experts, and arranging conferences" (p. 8). More time, however, will be spent observing the teacher informally and formally, and in following up with feedback.

Depending on the specifics of the plan of remediation, there could be other tasks such as arranging for the teacher to observe other teachers, arranging for the teacher to participate in professional development, and then committing these activities and the outcomes of efforts to writing. The principal will spend a great deal of time communicating not only with the marginal teacher but also with central office personnel. Although the dismissal of a tenured teacher is rare (Bridges, 1990), the paper trail needed to move toward dismissal must be substantial and detailed, and these tasks take time and energy. Lawrence et al. (2005) state, "The documentation must show that an intensive assistance plan was established and implemented for the teacher using school and district resources and that the teacher was given a reasonable length of time to improve performance" (p. 74). In the case of movement toward dismissal related to incompetence, "Each dismissal charge statement must be supported by 'airtight' documentation. You must prove that the teacher failed to improve teaching performance, thereby hindering student achievement and learning opportunities in the classroom" (Lawrence et al., 2005, p. 78).

Psychological Stressors

Working with marginal or incompetent teachers is stressful in addition to being "cognitively demanding, emotionally draining, and physically exhausting" (McEwan, 2005, p. 120). Bridges (1990) states that this work evokes "powerful emotions—fear, self-doubt, anger, and guilt" (p. 57). No administrator wants to have to confront a teacher for subpar performance. There are the human factors involved. The teacher might very well be a good person, have a family to support, or experienced personal events that are tragic but that, unfortunately, have affected performance. However, marginal performance must be confronted.

The principal who confronts marginal teaching or incompetence might feel vulnerable especially if this is a new school for the principal. The new principal (or even the veteran principal new to a building assignment) has not had the opportunity to establish credibility and trust with the faculty. Bridges (1992) speaks of the "criticism" factor. The criticism factor is a two-way street for both the principal and the teacher. Bridges (1992) reports,

"The most important personal factor is the deeply seated human desire to avoid conflict and unpleasantness which often accompany criticism from others" (p. 20). Kaye (2004) reports another aspect of potential conflict—the conflict where teachers and administrators might have to choose sides—the side of the administrator who has confronted marginal performance and the side of some teachers who want to support teachers regardless. Kaye (2004) describes this conflict like this: "The implementation of compensatory and covert disciplinary responses to marginality by administrators has placed teachers and teaching in a context in which the conflict between rightness and fairness is not easily resolved" (pp. 254–255).

Confronting Marginal Teaching Practices

What should a principal do once marginal teaching has surfaced? As Platt, Tripp, Ogden, and Fraser (2000) suggest, confront marginal teaching. They report that many principals prefer to play it safe, and they rely on other strategies, including transferring the teacher referred to in practice as "passing the trash" or the "dance of the lemons," moving high-maintenance students, and tailoring classes and the master schedule so the mediocre teachers does less harm. These are ineffective strategies in that the problem of lackluster teaching still exists, and the teacher is still marginal.

Before confronting marginal teaching, the principal must examine many aspects of the situation before proceeding. This examination will take time. Some things that the principal should seek to uncover and understand include

- *The teacher's history in the building and district.* How many years has the teacher been in the field? In the building? In the district? How many times has the teacher been transferred from one school to another?

- *What have prior reports on the teacher's performance indicated?* Are there areas that have been noted as unsatisfactory in the past, and what has been done to remediate these weaknesses? Who has written these reports? Have these reports been sent to the personnel office? How recent are these reports?

- *What has brought to your attention this teacher's performance?* Student, parent, teacher, central office complaints?

- *Sudden shifts.* Has there been a shift in school demographics, abrupt changes in the teacher's assignment as in the case of moving to a different grade level, teaching a new subject area? (Henderson-Sparks et al., 1995)

- *Other*. How often has this teacher been observed (both formal and informal classroom observations)? Who has observed this teacher? What has been the follow-up to classroom observations? What other types of data are available including, for example, student test scores, discipline referrals, remediation plans, letters from parents, students, others?

Once this type of information is known and you have observed firsthand the teacher suspected of being marginal, it is time to confront the marginal teacher. DuFour and Eaker (1998) offer a caveat: "Confrontation is not, however, synonymous with personal attack" (p. 113). DuFour and Eaker cite Maxwell's (1995) seven guidelines for confrontation:

1. Conduct the discussion as soon as possible.
2. Focus on the behavior or action, not the person.
3. Be specific.
4. Give the person an opportunity to respond and grant the benefit of the doubt.
5. Avoid sarcasm and words such as "always" and "never."
6. Attempt to develop a mutual plan to address the problem.
7. Affirm the person. (pp. 113–114)

But who wants to hear a negative message about teaching? No teacher wants to hear that his or her performance is subpar. Bridges (1986) in his discussion of incompetent teachers details the defensive reactions as such:

> When confronted with criticism of their teaching effectiveness, incompetent teachers often are defensive and antagonistic. The defensiveness and antagonism are expressed in several ways. The teachers who are under fire may deny the validity of the administrator's criticisms, may launch counter attacks, or may acknowledge their difficulties, but blame them on factors beyond their control. (p. 51)

Bridges (1986) furthers our understanding with the perspective that defensiveness is in some instances justifiable given that most teachers "in trouble" "have been receiving satisfactory evaluations for several years. This misleading information, combined with a strong tendency of poor performers to attribute their difficulties to external causes, is a breeding ground for resistance and defensiveness" (p. 53).

It is the defensiveness and other reactions that will stand in the way of supervisors "to provide a foundation for needed changes or improvements" (Jackson, 1997, p. 29). However, the principal must work past the defensive response and help the teacher get to the point of understanding the issues.

The editors of *Communication Briefings* (2005) offer these tips for confronting marginal work:

- Start by *defining acceptable performance* and specifying how the employee's work falls below that standard.

- *Remove emotion from the discussion.* Don't grimace, fidget, or look sad or angry when you level with the worker. Maintain a neutral demeanor and adopt a clear, businesslike tone.

- *Stay on track.* If the employee tries to change the subject, stick to the main issue. Deflect blame-shifting. Example: "We're not here to talk about other people's roles in this. We're here to focus on what you can do to improve."

- *Solicit a commitment to change* from the employee. Examples: Ask "How will you apply what we've talked about here?" or "What will you do to solve this problem?" (emphasis in the original)

Extended Reflection

Time to return to the discussion of the Johari Window as described in Chapter 4 (The Preobservation Conference) and Chapter 6 (The Postobservation Conference). How could knowledge about the Open, Hidden, Blind, and Unknown Panes assist the supervisor who must confront marginal teaching?

The research of Trimble, Davis, and Clanton (2003) yielded three classifications in which they characterize marginal teachers as being either a "Contrite Teacher, a "Cocooner Teacher," or a "Coaster Teacher." These images do not build a positive image of the teachers within each category; however, the descriptions and possible reactions to confronting marginal teaching may be of benefit.

Contrite: The Contrite marginal teacher meekly asks, "What did I do wrong?" They are generally well-meaning people who have a real desire to do their job. They are either unable to take directions or lack the skills to do the job.

Cocooner: This type of ineffective teacher projects the attitude of "Trying to trap me? Just come and try to get me." They feel no system, person, or process should constrict their behaviors. They are offended by criticisms and respond in a confrontational manner.

Coaster: The coaster exemplifies the ostrich with its head in the sand, responding to any comment about the need to attend to neglected duties, with the innocent remark, "Really? I was supposed to do that?" They put forth minimum effort that may originate in a lazy, don't care attitude; burnout; or other causes. (pp. 36–37)

Once marginal teaching has been confronted, it is time to move forward to start the work of assisting the marginal teacher. Again, there may be resistance; however, the work is necessary and warranted. The principal will need to outline the issues with very specific language, giving detail to bring to light the seriousness of the marginal teacher's work. Consider the information presented in Figure 13.2 on the next page.

Extended Reflection

Smith (2005) asserts, a marginal teacher

- Lacks "bell to bell" instruction.
- Does not teach to the curriculum in general and to specific objectives in particular.
- Students become easily distracted and are off-task.
- Lacks enthusiasm for students and teaching.
- Doesn't provide meaningful and timely feedback to students.
- Has poor personal relations with students.
- Exhibits poor teaching skills.
- Unorganized classroom and lessons.
- Does not establish expectations for student behavior, and thus discipline is usually a major problem.
- Lacks knowledge of the subject matter. (p. 213)

If you observed a teacher with many of these areas of concern, how would you begin a discussion with this teacher?

Figure 13.2. Outline of Issues
Related to Marginal Performance

Classroom Management

Mr. Jones' lack of classroom management skills interferes with students being able to learn. Mr. Jones has referred over 50% of his students to the assistant principal for coming to class unprepared and for not handing in homework.

Parental Concerns

Five parents have called requesting that their children be transferred from Mr. Jones' class. Two parents have written letters to the superintendent indicating that their children were not able to concentrate during class because of the noise level, that quiz, test, and homework had not been returned, and that small-group work is the staple of the class period.

Faculty Concerns

Two teachers have complained that they have difficulties teaching near your classroom because of the noise; the department chair spoke with you about the situation on September 12 and then on October 13, 2006.

Classroom Observations

Informal classroom observations have yielded key suggestions to consider related to classroom management. These suggestions have included the following:

♦ Develop classroom routines for the beginning and ending of the periods (take attendance as students are walking in the door; have materials ready to begin class once the bell rings; develop a point system for students who do not have homework; have extra pens and pencils for students who do not have supplies [the office provided a box of pens and pencils and paper]).

♦ Cease small-group work until classroom routines are established.

♦ Observe Mrs. Maxie. A substitute teacher was provided on two occasions (September 17 and October 20); however, you chose not to take advantage of this opportunity, citing that grades were due soon and you needed this time to work on grading student papers.

Formal Classroom Observations—Two extended classroom observations were conducted (September 6 and October 4, 2006). During the post-observation conference, we targeted three areas to concentrate efforts: (1) classroom routines, (2) the overuse of small-group activities that consumer approximately 90% of 55-minute-long classroom periods, and (3) the noise level.

Follow-up informal classroom observations have yielded less than satisfactory implementation of suggestions or movement toward implementing classroom procedures to keep students focused on learning, implementing more than small-group work, and returning student work.

Working with the Marginal Teachers

After confronting marginal teaching practices and having very specific information about the unacceptable aspects of the teacher's work, comes the work. The principal is encouraged to do three things before proceeding further.

1. *Study district policies and procedures* for the plan of remediation and develop a time line according to the policies and procedures outlined in district documents. Examine the history of how the union or bargaining unit gets involved with personnel issues (grievances).

2. *Consult with your immediate supervisor* (a central office director) or the director of personnel who can give you guidance on how to proceed. Because there are many legal issues surrounding working with marginal teachers, frequent communication with central administration is vitally important, especially if a marginal teacher is not making the mark. No one likes surprises. In addition to providing legal counsel, the central office administration might also provide valuable resources to assist the principal work with marginal teachers.

3. *Remember that issues of confidentiality* will prevent you from discussing the issues with anyone except your immediate supervisor, the director of personnel, or the superintendent, and possibly, legal counsel. This is important to remember in that the

"grapevine" will leak that a teacher is on a plan of improvement. Some teachers will want to affirm that you are doing the right thing and some teachers will want to find out what is going on because of their allegiances with the marginal teacher.

Fieldwork

Ask a Supervisor...

Make an appointment to speak with a supervisor about working with a marginal teacher. Focus your discussion on the following:

♦ How did you feel the first time you had to confront a teacher about marginal teaching?

♦ Did you develop a formal plan of remediation with the teacher? If so, what lessons did you learn about the experience?

♦ Was there any backlash that you experienced from putting a teacher on a plan of remediation? Please describe the backlash and how you handled it.

What insights did you learn from this fieldwork? Share these insights either in small group or formally in writing with your instructor.

Working with a marginal teacher is more than a written plan of remediation discussed in the next section of this chapter. The amount of assistance that a marginal teacher will need is dependent primarily on the degree of marginality. Some teachers will need more intensive types of assistance than others. There are many factors to consider. It is often knee-jerk reaction to assist a teacher "more" if there are complaints from students, parents, or other teachers. Although these complaints might put the marginal teacher "on the radar," there are instances where there are no complaints yet marginal performance exists and must be dealt with equal to the marginal teacher who is receiving complaints.

There are many ways in which a principal can work with a marginal teacher. These methods include

♦ Peer coaching (Chapter 9)

♦ Mentoring programs (Chapter 10)

♦ Focused professional development (Chapter 14)

♦ College courses

- Frequent formal observations (with pre- and postobservation conferences) (Chapters 4, 5, and 6)
- frequent informal classroom observations (with postobservation conferences) (Chapter 3)
- Observing the classrooms of exceptionally strong teachers
- Participation in districtwide support programs

Whatever types of assistance offered, the priority should be given to working with teachers to engage them in the process, not just the work of improving performance. Without involvement, it is unlikely there will be much success. Just think of the expression "Make Me" while thinking through the type of assistance provided. Again, some teachers will resist remediation and openly rebuke efforts of assistance; however, other teachers will welcome the support. Each case is different, and Blacklock (2002) suggests that "principals can help provide low-performing teachers with knowledge, strategies, and skills that translate into improved classroom instruction and management" (p. 28).

Formal Plan of Remediation

Developing, implementing, and monitoring a plan of remediation (often called a plan of improvement or a professional development plan) is time intensive and requires an eye to detail. Depending on progress, a teacher on a plan of remediation could be recommended for termination. Tucker (2001) explains that principals need to be actively involved in supporting teachers and that they:

> have an ethical obligation to do so because successful remediation affects many people....For teachers, remediation reflects the school system's concern for its teachers' professional development. Dedicated school administrators know that whole-school improvement won't happen unless everyone performs well, and helping each teacher do so is an integral part of an instructional leader's role. (p. 53)

The intent of any plan of remediation should be the growth and development of the teacher who is experiencing difficulty in the classroom. The intent is for the teacher and the principal to work as a team so that deficiencies can be removed. Sometimes this is easier said than done. When a principal observes consistent problems and patterns of behavior that interfere with student learning, it is the time to move toward a formal plan of remediation. Most school systems have different levels of remediation from in-house to more intensive levels of remediation. Most plans of remediation include the basic information found in Figure 13.3 on the next page.

Figure 13.3. Components of a Plan of Remediation

♦ Identification of the problem or areas of concern. A description of the areas of concern must be available. The description should also include artifacts that chronicle the areas of concern.

♦ Communicating the problem or areas of concern to the teacher both orally and in writing.

♦ Developing strategies to remediate the marginal performance. Strategies must be specific with the end in mind. Specific teacher behaviors must be specified with expected levels of performance included.

♦ Time lines must be included in the plan of remediation: when the plan begins, the frequency in which the teacher's performance will be evaluated, and by whom.

♦ Progress toward the goals of improvement must be documented. Both the teacher and the principal (and in the case where a school system includes others in the process) include reports on progress.

♦ Documentation of the process of the plan of remediation, including meetings with the teacher, strategies offered, progress made (or lack of progress), resources offered to assist the teacher, and time lines.

McGrath (2006) offers that a plan of remediation must address the following seven questions:

1. What specific conduct or behavior must improve?

2. What resources will be provided to address the directed change (e.g., workshops, counseling, mentoring, retraining, written technical assistance)?

3. What measures will be used to determine if the individual has been successful in meeting the directive(s) for change?

4. Is it appropriate to give a warning that disciplinary action will be taken if the behavior does not improve?

5. How will the administrator and the employee know if the requirements have been satisfactorily met?

6. When will the administrator communicate again with the employee to check progress?

7. Has the administrator listed any pertinent attachments, such as letters from parents or copies of previous memos to the individual on the behavior/conduct/incident to focus? (p. 261)

Figure 13.4 (pages 309–310) offers a very basic sample plan of remediation form. Again, every school system has its own way of communicating information, and the leader is encouraged to become familiar with the types of formal documentation, policies, and procedures for developing a formal plan of remediation.

Figure 13.4. Sample Plan of Remediation Form

Teacher _____ Date of Initial Meeting _____

Documentation of the process of the plan of remediation, including meetings with the teacher, strategies offered, progress made (or lack of progress), resources offered to assist the teacher, and timelines.

SECTION 1: AREAS OF CONCERN

Area 1:

Description of Current Status

Artifacts:

Area 2:

Description of Current Status

Artifacts:

Area 3:

Description of Current Status

Artifacts:

SECTION II: STRATEGIES TO MEET IMPROVEMENT

Area 1 Strategies to Meet Improvement:

Area 2 Strategies to Meet Improvement:

Area 3 Strategies to Meet Improvement:

SECTION III: SUPPORT AND RESOURCES

Area 1 Support and Resources:

Provided By:

(Figure continues on next page.)

Area 2 Support and Resources:

Provided By:

Area 3 Support and Resources:

Provided By:

<table>
<tr><td colspan="5">SECTION IV: MONITORING THE PLAN</td></tr>
<tr><td>Area of Concern</td><td>Strategies to Meet Improvement</td><td>Support and Resources</td><td>Provided By and Date</td><td>Markers of Achievement</td></tr>
<tr><td></td><td></td><td></td><td></td><td></td></tr>
<tr><td></td><td></td><td></td><td></td><td></td></tr>
<tr><td></td><td></td><td></td><td></td><td></td></tr>
<tr><td></td><td></td><td></td><td></td><td></td></tr>
<tr><td></td><td></td><td></td><td></td><td></td></tr>
<tr><td></td><td></td><td></td><td></td><td></td></tr>
</table>

This plan spans from _____ to _____ (dates).

Written and Oral Feedback will be given formally on _____, _____, and _____ (list dates).

Principal Signature _____ Date _____

Teacher Signature_____ Date _____

The principal needs to be in a position to offer both assistance and at the same time, to be in a position to take corrective actions beyond the plan of improvement if the teacher has not made progress.

When All Else Fails

Dismissal, if it becomes necessary, rests in the domain of the principal working in tandem with the central office. For teachers with inadequate teaching skills, traditional supervisory processes and professional development strategies can help assist the marginal teacher to improve performance. In some cases, however, a specific plan of improvement that identifies skills to improve and strategies for achieving needed improvement will fail regardless of the efforts of the principal and the teacher.

If the issue with a marginal teacher is a personal problem, the principal can enlist others who can provide a range of assistance (e.g., employee assistance program). When the personal issue is resolved, the marginal teacher's performance usually returns to an acceptable level (Fuhr, 1990). Perhaps the most difficult type of marginal teacher to assist is the teacher with an attitude problem that compounds instructional and classroom management issues. If the attitude problem does not improve negatively impacting classroom performance and dismissal becomes necessary, the principal must take the lead in the process. Taking the lead in the dismissal process is a double-edged sword. On the one hand, teachers know who the marginal teachers are in the building. Competent teachers have little professional respect for marginal teachers because they take away from the strength of the group. Parents and students make generalizations about the competency of all teachers based on their experiences with marginal teachers. Marginal teachers, because they are able to get away with substandard teaching, erode teacher morale, and if gone unchecked, competent teachers begin to lose faith in the administration and the system that allows marginal teachers to continue without remediation.

On the other hand, nothing will send shock waves through a school system more than when a principal confronts a marginal teacher. Often, the very teachers who may complain to the principal about the lack of performance of a marginal teacher will be the ones who will be listening to the marginal teacher "pop-off" about what a principal is doing to remediate the situation. In school cultures that promote learning and development and in which the principal has established trust, the marginal teacher will have an audience limited to the confines of the faculty lounge. It is unsettling when a teacher is put on a plan of remediation, and it is possible that teachers will become stressed about the presence of an administrator in a classroom conducting formal and informal observations. Although teachers do not like to work in the company of marginal teachers, they will form a safety net around their members.

Above all else, remain cautiously optimistic while working with marginal teachers.

Summary

Morally, we owe it to our profession and to the children entrusted to our care to confront marginal teaching enduring the discomfort associated with this work. Not confronting marginal teaching will erode teaching and learning in a school. Several approaches to confronting marginal teaching are offered in this chapter. The supervisor must consider many items before confronting marginal teaching: the experience level of the teacher, the teacher's past performance, and the magnitude of the situation are just a few of the items to understand. The supervisor will need to enlist the support of the central office and perhaps others when working with a marginal or an incompetent teacher. Familiarity with district policies and procedures and an understanding of the dynamics of the union or bargaining unit are important.

The supervisor should remain cautiously optimistic when working with a marginal teacher. A plan of remediation helps to spell out what the issues are, provide targets for improvement, detail the support that the teacher will receive and by whom, and give a time line for assessing improvement. Although optimism is important, it is a reality that not all teachers will be able to make the mark. In these instances, dismissal might be warranted. Legal counsel and the central office will provide guidance in these instances.

Suggested Activities

From Theory to Practice

Go to the Web site of the local department of education to see if marginal or incompetent teaching and teachers are addressed. Also, review local district documents to see how marginal or incompetent teaching is addressed. What does this documentation reveal? Based on what information is available, what would be needed to develop a plan of remediation? Who would be involved, and what procedural considerations would need to be considered?

Group Processing

In role-play fashion, practice confronting a marginal teacher's performance. Give feedback to the supervisor who is confronting the marginal performance.

Reflection

There are many reasons why administrators do not want to confront marginal teaching performance, and there are reasons why administrators do not try to push the envelope by confronting teachers who are, as one student shared with the author, "sorry, incompetent" teachers. What factors do you believe deter administrators from confronting incompetence? How do administrators cope with this struggle?

References

Blacklock, K. (2002). Dealing with an incompetent teacher. *Principal, 81*(4), 26–28.

Bridges, E. M. (1986). *The incompetent teacher: The challenge and the response*. Philadelphia: Falmer Press.

Bridges, E. M. (1990). *Managing the incompetent teacher* (2nd ed.). Eugene, OR: ERIC.

Bridges, E. M. (1992). *The incompetent teacher: Managerial responses* (Revised and extended). London: The Falmer Press.

Bullock, A. A., Glatthorn, A. A., & Jones, B. K. (2006). Working with marginal teachers. In R.D. Clouse (Ed.), *Developing highly-qualified teachers* (pp. 64–73). Thousand Oaks, CA: Corwin Press.

Confronting a sub-par worker (2005). Retrieved August 13, 2006, from http://as01.ucis.dal.ca/hrd/hrd_2592_3199.html

Deal, T. E., & Peterson, K. D. (1999). *Shaping school culture: The heart of leadership*. San Francisco, CA: Jossey-Bass.

DuFour, R., & Eaker, R. (1998). *Professional learning communities at work: Best practices for enhancing student achievement*. Bloomington, IN: Solution Tree.

Fuhr, D. (1990). Supervising the marginal teacher: Here's how. *National Association of Elementary Teachers, 9*(2), 1–4.

Fuhr, D. L. (1996). *No margin for error: Saving our schools from borderline teachers*. Dubuque, IA: Kendall/Hunt.

Glickman, C. D. (1990). *Supervision of instruction: A development approach* (2nd ed.). Boston, MA: Allyn and Bacon.

Henderson-Sparks, J. C., Ehrgott, R. H., & Sparks, R. K., Jr. (1995). Managing your marginal teachers. *Principal, 74*(4), 32–35.

Jackson, C. M. (1997). Assisting marginal teachers: A training model. *Principal, 77*(1), 28–30.

Kaye, E. B. (2004). Turning the tide on marginal teaching. *Journal of Curriculum and Supervision, 19*(3), 234–258.

Lawrence, C. E., Vachon, M. K., Leake, D. O., & Leake, B. H. (1993). *The marginal teacher: A step-by-step guide to fair procedures for identification and dismissal*. Newbury Park, CA: Corwin Press.

Lawrence, C. E., Vachon, M. K., Leake, D. O., & Leake, B. H. (2005). *The marginal teacher: A step-by-step guide to fair procedures for identification and dismissal* (3rd ed.). Thousand Oaks, CA: Corwin Press.

Manatt, D., & Sweeney, J. (1984). A team approach to supervising the marginal teacher. *Educational Leadership, 41*(7), 25–27.

McEwan. E. K. (2005). *How to deal with teachers who are angry, troubled, exhausted, or just plain confused.* Thousand Oaks, CA: Corwin Press.

McGrath, M. J. (2006). Dealing positively with the nonproductive teacher. In J. H. Stronge (Ed.) *Evaluating teaching: A guide to current thinking and best practice* (2nd ed) (pp. 253–267). Thousand Oaks, CA: Corwin Press.

McGreal, T. (1983). *Effective teacher evaluation.* Alexandria, VA: Association for Supervision and Curriculum.

Platt, A. D., Tripp, C. E., Ogden, W. R., & Fraser, R. G. (2000). *The skillful leader: Confronting mediocre teaching.* Acton, MA: Ready About Press.

Sawa, R. (1995). *Teacher evaluation policies and practices.* Retrieved December 1, 2002, from http://www.ssta.sk.ca/research/instruction/95–04.htm

Smith, R. E. (2005). *Human resources administration: A school-based perspective* (3rd ed.). New York: Eye on Education.

Tucker, P. (2001). Helping struggling teachers. *Educational Leadership, 58*(5), 52–55.

Tucker, P. D. (1997). Lake Wobegon: Where all teachers are competent (Or, have we come to terms with the problem of incompetent teachers?). *Journal of Personnel Evaluation in Education, 11*(2), 103–126.

Trimble, S., Davis, E., & Clanton, M. T. (2003). Working with ineffective teachers. *Principal Leadership, 4*(3), 36–41.

14

Professional Development

In This Chapter...

♦ Standards for professional development

♦ Planning for professional development

♦ Identifying professional development needs

♦ Job-embedded learning—finding time for professional development

♦ Making the connection between instructional supervision and professional development

♦ Using ELCC Standards to place supervision and professional development in a context

The structures to support teachers include supervision, professional development, and teacher evaluation. However, some schools, and perhaps by extension the systems in which they reside, fail to connect these support structures to create seamless learning opportunities for teachers. For professional development to make a difference, there is a need to bundle multiple learning opportunities to work in complementary ways.

The defining features of such efforts would include learning opportunities embedded in the workday replete with opportunities for reflection, dialogue, and collaboration. Without a school culture that supports collaboration, these efforts will yield few lasting results.

Professional development plays an integral part in the overall supervisory plan of the school. In Chapter 1, the notion of coherence was introduced. Essentially, the basic premise is that instructional supervision, professional development, teacher evaluation, and other efforts form a seamless web to support the work of teachers. Refer to Figure 1.7 (page 14) to see the seamless nature of these processes. This chapter explores professional development that supports supervisory efforts. Professional development is a natural complement to instructional supervision given that during the postobservation conference, the final question should be what types of professional development can support teachers to improve teaching?

Supervisors who connect the dots between supervision, teacher evaluation, and professional development

♦ Assist teachers in identifying professional development targets that point to improved classroom practices.

♦ Provide the resources that can be accessed by the teacher.

♦ Empower teachers to build their own learning plans

♦ Work with teachers co-monitoring the results by frequently returning to the place where instruction unfolds—the classroom.

This chapter examines some ideas about professional development, national perspectives and standards for professional development, the process of planning for professional development, and approaches to framing professional development within the context of the school.

There is a relationship between accountability, improved teaching, and support that teachers need from those who supervise the instructional program. Accountability systems have essentially created a ripple effect between what students and teachers do. Recognizing this effect, the National Association of Elementary School Principals (NAESP) reports:

> We've learned that it's meaningless to set high expectations for student performance unless we also set high expectations for the performance of adults. We know that if we are going to improve learning, we must also improve teaching. And we must improve the environment in which teaching and learning occurs. (2001, p. 2)

Standards for Professional Development

In its publication, *Professional Learning Communities: Strategies that Improve Instruction* (n.d.), the Annenberg Institute for School Reform (AISR) reports:

> Effective professional development to improve classroom teaching also concentrates on high learning standards and on evidence

of students' learning. It mirrors the kinds of teaching and learning expected in classrooms. It is driven fundamentally by the needs and interests of participants themselves, enabling adult learners to expand on content knowledge and practice that is directly connected with the work of their students in the classroom. (p. 1)

AISR also asserts that "research findings have repeatedly confirmed that a significant factor in raising academic achievement is the improvement of instructional capacity in the classroom" (p. 1) and that professional development that achieves these ends has four "critical factors." Professional development is

♦ Ongoing

♦ Embedded within context-specific needs of a particular setting

♦ Aligned with reform initiatives

♦ Grounded in a collaborative, inquiry-based approach to learning (p. 1).

Wiggins and McTighe (2006) provide insight about learning that can be applied to professional development. Figure 14.1 details these insights.

Figure 14.1. Insights about Professional Development that Supports Adult Learning

Learning promotes...

♦ Fluency and flexible transfer to immediate and long-term situations;

♦ Value and worth in the application of knowledge;

♦ Transfer of skills;

♦ The power of ideas in the work to be accomplished;

♦ Practical applications;

♦ Clear priorities;

♦ Multiple opportunities for continuous feedback;

♦ Opportunities for reflection, self-assessment, and opportunities to apply and reapply prior knowledge to new situations;

♦ Personalization for the learner.

Source: Adapted from Wiggins and McTighe (2006).

Just as there are standards of practice and preparation for educational leaders (see Chapter 1), there are standards for professional development. In 1995, the U.S. Department of Education published a report, *Building Bridges: The Mission and Principles of Professional Development*. This report provides a broad-based set of principles for effective professional development practices (Figure 14.2.).

Figure 14.2. Mission and Principles of Professional Development

Professional development...

♦ Focuses on teachers as central to student learning, yet includes all members of the school community;

♦ Focuses on individual, collegial, and organizational improvement;

♦ Respects and nurtures the intellectual and leadership capacity of teachers, principals, and others in the school community;

♦ Reflects the best available research and practice in teaching, learning, and leadership;

♦ Enables teachers to develop further expertise in subject content, teaching strategies, uses of technologies, and other essential elements of teaching to high standards;

♦ Promotes continuous inquiry and improvement embedded in the daily life of schools;

♦ Is planned collaboratively by those who will participate in and facilitate that development;

♦ Requires substantial time and resources;

♦ Is driven by a coherent long-term plan;

♦ Is evaluated ultimately on the basis of its effects on teacher instruction and student learning, and uses this assessment to guide subsequent professional development efforts.

Source: U.S. Department of Education (1995). *Building bridges: The mission and principles of professional development.* Retrieved August 20, 2006, from http://www.ed.gov/G2K/bridge.html

In 1995, the National Staff Development Council (NSDC) developed the *Standards for Staff Development* and since then has revised them to reflect changes in the field. The 12 NSDC *Standards for Staff Development* are available for review at http://www.nsdc.org/index.cfm. These standards are positioned across context, process, and context standards (see http://www.nsdc.org/standards/index.cfm).

For each standard, NSDC offers the rationale for each and an extensive bibliography. For many of the citations in the annotated bibliography, documents available on the web include the URL address. Figure 14.3, on the next page, presents the National Staff Development Council *Standards for Staff Development*.

Figure 14.3. National Staff Development Council *Standards for Staff Development*

Standard Focus Area	The Standard
Learning Communities	Staff development that improves the learning of all students organizes adults into learning communities whose goals are aligned with those of the school and district.
Leadership	Staff development that improves the learning of all students requires skillful school and district leaders who guide continuous instructional improvement.
Resources	Staff development that improves the learning of all students requires resources to support adult learning and collaboration.
Data-Driven	Staff development that improves the learning of all students uses disaggregated student data to determine adult learning priorities, monitor progress, and help sustain continuous improvement.
Evaluation	Staff development that improves the learning of all students uses multiple sources of information to guide improvement and demonstrate its impact.
Research-Based	Staff development that improves the learning of all students prepares educators to apply research to decision making.
Designs and Strategies	Staff development that improves the learning of all students uses learning strategies appropriate to the intended goal.
Learning	Staff development that improves the learning of all students applies knowledge about human learning and change.
Collaboration Skills	Staff development that improves the learning of all students provides educators with the knowledge and skills to collaborate.
Equity	Staff development that improves the learning of all students prepares educators to understand and appreciate all students, create safe, orderly, and supportive learning environments, and hold high expectations for their academic achievement.

(Figure continues on the next page.)

| Quality Teaching | Staff development that improves the learning of all students deepens educators' content knowledge, provides them with research-based instructional strategies to assist students in meeting rigorous academic standards, and prepares them to use various types of classroom assessments appropriately. |
| Family Involvement | Staff development that improves the learning of all students provides educators with knowledge and skills to involve families and other stakeholders. |

Source: National Staff Development Council. http://www.nsdc.org/standards/index.cfm

These focus areas and standards provide a framework in which professional development can be situated as an integral part of the instructional supervision program that supports adult learning.

Extended Reflection

Consult the state department of education Web site in the state in which you work. Identify the standards for professional development. What professional development standards does your state promote?

Then access the Web site of the formal organization to which you belong (e.g., National Council of Teachers of Mathematics) that sets standards for teaching and accountability in your field (e.g., English = National Council of Teachers of English). Do these organizations have their own standards for professional development? If so, identify the commonalities across the standards.

Planning for Professional Development

Instructional leaders who are visible in classrooms and in other settings in which teachers meet (grade level or department meetings) are in an advantageous position to identify professional development needs and to provide the follow-up support teachers need to implement new skills or to refine existing skills into their daily practices. The supervisor plans for professional development on two levels.

♦ The first level is planning for professional development to meet global or large-scale needs of the faculty related to school improvement plans.

- The second level is planning professional development that meets individual teacher needs as identified during classroom observations and working with teams of teachers (e.g., grade level, subject matter, departments).

In a perfect world, the first and second levels will meet. More often than not, however, large-scale needs for various reasons often take center stage to meeting individual and targeted group needs.

The supervisor can begin thinking about professional development by asking some general questions:

- What professional development is needed and by whom is it needed?
- What planning for professional development needs to be completed?
- What resources are needed to provide professional development?
- What follow-up activities are needed to support the application and extension of skills learned during formal professional development?
- How can the overall impact of professional development on student and teacher learning be evaluated?

The answers to these questions can serve as a guide for framing professional development.

Knowing and understanding the history of professional development in the school and the district is important, and consulting with the district professional development contact person will help to acquaint the principal with the district's vision of professional development.

In the Field

Visit with the person responsible for professional development in the system in which you are employed. Ask this person how No Child Left Behind has influenced professional development in the system for teachers across career stages. Are there any unique professional development programs in place across the system to address accountability standards to ensure teachers are Highly Qualified?

Examining artifacts such as descriptions of professional development offerings will help the principal discover when professional development is offered (during the year, summer), who offers professional development (outside consultants, districtwide personnel), and where professional development is conducted (at site buildings, central office, college/university campus).

- ♦ At the site level, the principal needs to uncover:
- ♦ Who conducts professional development?
- ♦ Who decides what professional development should be made available?
- ♦ Does professional development align with site-level goals?
- ♦ Are there processes in place for teachers to request professional development?

The answers to these questions will help the principal understand the history of professional development at both the site and district levels and to gain insight how and if professional development between these two levels align.

Identifying Professional Development Needs

Methods of identifying professional development needs include informal discussion (e.g., during planning periods, over lunch), formal discussions (e.g., faculty meetings, department, team, or grade level meetings), faculty surveys, and classroom observations. The tracking sheet offered in Figure 14.4, on the next page, can assist in tracking identified professional development needs, making connections between identified needs and, identifying strategies to meet those needs.

Figure 14.4. Tracking Professional Development Needs

Need	Teacher(s) Requesting/ Needing	In-House Resources	Strategies
Cooperative Learning	Temple, Vanderhoof, Witt	Ms. Patton	Two workshops, model teaching unit by Ms. Patton, and classroom observations
Classroom Management	All-district mandated	Assistant principal Smith	Workshop on district classroom management policy; individual meetings with each grade-level/team/department member; classroom observations; follow-up meetings
Integrating Technology	Denton, Watson, Younger	Dr. Vardaman (Computer Science Teacher)	Workshop, modeling teaching unit by Dr. Vardaman; follow-up meetings with each teacher

Perhaps nothing is more hurried than the schedule of a PreK-12 teacher. Therefore, making every minute count becomes a necessity, and principals need to learn how to scan the environment, looking for opportunities for teachers to learn. However, before developing learning opportunities for adults, principals need to know what needs to be learned and by whom. Opportunities abound for principals to talk with teachers and to include time during planning periods and lunch periods to engage teachers in discussion about teaching. In the relaxed atmosphere of the faculty lunchroom, teachers tend to be more comfortable participating in candid discussions about teaching. During informal discussions, the principal can work as a prospector, searching for hidden "nuggets" that can be further examined through more formal discussions in a department, grade level, or team meeting or become a focus in future classroom observations.

The principal can purposefully link supervision and professional development through classroom observations. Needs can also be identified through more formal means such as informal and formal classroom observations, and this is the value of making classroom observations a priority. Through analysis of data collected and the discussion that occurs during the pre- and postobservation conferences, the principal can assist teachers to identify techniques that can help enhance strategies already in use in the classroom as well as to identify new strategies or potential problem areas that need attention.

Because much of the planning for professional development occurs before each school year begins, some schools distribute surveys so teachers can formally indicate what they want and need to learn. Ideally, there is alignment between site-level goals and the professional development offered at the site. Figure 14.5 offers a sample questionnaire.

Figure 14.5. Professional Development Questionnaire

Developmentally Appropriate Middle School

Name: _____ Date: _____

1. Considering our school goals in the areas of assessment, technological applications, and integrated learning, are there specific areas within these goals that you would like to explore next year and for which you feel you would benefit from involvement in professional development activities?

2. What kinds of activities (workshops, collaborative meetings, planning time, in-the-classroom support, formal coursework, etc.) do you feel would most benefit you in your support of the school goals?

3. Are there other areas in which you are interested—classroom management, specific projects, curriculum materials, idea exchanges, discussion groups, etc.?

4. Are there areas in which you have been working and in which you have developed proficiency to be a leader and resource for other teachers in the school or district?

Teacher Expertise—A Rich Resource for Learning

As professional development needs are identified, strategies to meet those needs should be taking form. Often, district and site professional developers look immediately to outside facilitators to support their professional development programs. In the process, resources within the district or site are overlooked. At the beginning of the school year, principals are encouraged to "solicit" volunteers to assist with in-house professional development. Think of the potential in any given school. For the most part, teachers are lifelong learners, and they continually attend workshops, graduate school courses, and other specialized training opportunities to add to their repertoire of skills.

Teachers attend to their own learning during the school year and during the summer, and they often pay entirely or partially for these learning opportunities. Teachers return to the schoolhouse with new knowledge and new skills eager to implement in their classrooms. However, follow-up support and encouragement from those who plan professional development is often missing. Here are some sobering facts about learning and transfer of skills. Hirsh and Ponder (1991) conclude that on the strength of a workshop alone, only about 10 percent of teachers are able to transfer newly learned skills into daily practice, and according to McBride, Reed, and Dollar (1994), only 12.6 percent of teachers reported any meaningful follow-up to determine if skills learned in professional development workshops were being implemented in the classroom.

Extended Reflection

What can supervisors do to help teachers transfer knowledge from professional development to practice?

One of the ironies in the work lives of teachers is that they often do not have the opportunity to share with others what they have learned. Effective principals find opportunities for teachers to share their expertise with others. The first step in the process is to identify expertise among teachers, and this can be achieved by asking teachers to self-identify their expertise and willingness to share knowledge with others. Two strategies are

1. Developing a self-reporting faculty expertise survey distributed at the beginning of the school year (Figure 14.6, next page); and,

2. Tracking professional development, workshops, and university courses that teachers attend throughout the year (Figure 14.7, page 327).

Figure 14.6. Faculty Expertise Survey

Dear Colleagues:

Every year we update our Teacher Expertise Pool. Please take a few minutes to review the following areas and check those in which you have expertise and are willing to share your knowledge with others. Looking forward to hearing from you,

Paula

1. Peer Coaching_____
2. Phonics_____
3. Literacy_____
4. Math Our Way Series_____
5. Writing across the Curriculum_____
6. Big Book lesson planning_____
7. Authentic Assessment and Rubrics_____
8. Technology Applications_____
9. Portfolio Development____
10. At-Risk Children_____
11. Reluctant Learners____
12. Outdoor Education____
13. Science Fair_____
14. Music and Art Therapy____
15. Conflict Resolution____
16. Other:_____

Name:_____ (optional)

A second way to track teacher expertise is to keep a record of what professional development teachers attend throughout the school year and summer. Often, school systems pay teachers to attend professional development during the year and summer, and teachers need to request funds and substitute teachers to attend workshops and seminars. Teachers by their very nature are lifelong learners and many pursue advanced degrees, add-on certificates (e.g., ESOL, Gifted and Talented, Special Education), and they prepare for National Board Certification. A database (Figure 14.7, next page) can assist with tracking this information.

Figure 14.7. Database—
Teacher Professional Development

Teacher	Conference or Workshop	Dates	Date of follow-up presentation made to the faculty (meeting date)	Resources needed for follow-up
Arnold	Cooperative Learning for Special Needs Students	10/23/06	11/09/06	Preview video series on cooperative learning; purchase workbooks for teachers; possible full day in-service for staff—check with central office for funding.
Asher	Managing Aggression in Students	03/24–27/07	04/11/07; 04/14/07 (PTA presentation)	Schedule a meeting with counselors and social workers in the school cluster; books recommended by Asher

Job-Embedded Learning:
Finding Time for Professional Development

The notion of job-embedded learning is critical to professional development. In Chapter 15, the job-embedded nature of instructional supervision concludes this text. For now, the discussion of job-embedded learning and professional development are examined. Sparks and Hirsh (1997) write that

> Job-embedded learning...links learning to the immediate and real-life problems faced by teachers and administrators. It is based on the assumption that the most powerful learning is that which occurs in response to challenges currently being faced by the learner and that allows for immediate application, experimentation, and adaptation on the job. (p. 52)

Job-embedded learning means that professional development is a continuous thread that can be found throughout the culture of a school. There are three attributes of successful job-embedded learning: (a) it is relevant to the individual teacher, (b) feedback is built into the process, and (c) it facilitates the transfer of new skills into practice.

First, because job-embedded learning is a part of the teacher's daily work, it is, by its very nature, relevant to the learner. Job-embedded learning addresses professional development goals and concerns of the individual teacher. In addition, job-embedded learning occurs at the teacher's job site. Therefore, the teacher's learning becomes an integral part of the culture of the classroom and by extension the school.

Second, through job-embedded learning, feedback is built in. Processes that can generate feedback include mentoring, peer coaching, reflection and dialogue, study groups, videotape analysis of teaching and discussion about the events on tape, and journaling. Teachers can use these tools to chronicle implementation of new instructional skills, to provide artifacts for assessing transition from one learning activity to the next, or to use as material to frame future initiatives.

Third, job-embedded professional development facilitates the transfer of new skills into practice. When ongoing support through the tools of job-embedded professional development is linked with instructional supervision, transfer of skills into practice becomes part of the job.

There are four essential conditions to ensure successful implementation of job-embedded professional development.

- *Learning needs to be consistent with the principles of adult learning:* learning goals are realistic; learning is relevant to the teacher, and concrete opportunities for practice of skills being learned are afforded;

- *Trust in the process, in colleagues, and in the learner him-/herself:* For learning to occur on the job, teachers must be able to trust the process (e.g., peer coaching, videotape analysis), their colleagues, and themselves. Teachers need to know that feedback will be constructive, not personal;

- *Time within the regular school day needs to be made available for learning:* Traditionally, professional development takes place after hours, usually at some remote site. Job-embedded learning requires time to be available within the context of the normal working day at the teacher's school site; and,

- *Sufficient resources must be available to support learning:* Providing release time for teachers' professional development requires the creative use of human resources. In addition, outside facilitators are sometimes needed to assist teachers in learning new skills. Funding must be made available to meet these costs (Zepeda, 1999).

Time for learning regularly built into routine school days is needed and the principal can consider two strategies for extending learning time into the regular school day by

♦ *Rearranging existing time:* Planning time for teachers is rearranged to create extended time for teacher learning and planning; and,

♦ *Creating additional time:* Planning time, in addition to the traditional daily planning period, is provided for collaborative learning.

In the best of all worlds, teachers would have extended periods for collaborative planning and learning without having to sacrifice any of their traditional planning time. In the elementary arena, some principals have discovered that by multiplying the school site's workers through innovative use of outside volunteers, this dream can be realized. The varied and complex nature of the curriculum in the secondary arena creates an ideal setting for enlisting the assistance of outside experts. Because district and state attendance mandates, as well as curricular requirements, confine the frequency with which students may be released, schools can multiply their workers through volunteers to provide time for teacher learning. The key is the recruitment of enough volunteers to make release of the teaching faculty for a half-day or full day of learning and planning possible. Volunteers to support this effort could come from parents, patrons of the district, and local business and professional people, especially those who look to the local school district to produce the best possible workforce.

Most schools hold faculty meetings—some weekly, some bi-weekly, and some monthly. Regardless of the faculty-meeting configuration, faculty meetings provide opportunities for professional development opportunities and the promotion of staff collaboration. Much of the information that is shared during faculty meetings can easily be distributed by memo, e-mail, or in a faculty bulletin. Principals are encouraged to work with their teachers to design and implement strategies for using faculty meeting time for providing learning opportunities for teachers.

The faculty meeting can become a powerful forum for professional development when teachers who attend workshops and seminars paid for by the school system "present" what was learned. Again, this goes back to the notion that teachers are the most important resource—they bring expertise to their work. The following suggestions can assist framing faculty meetings as a learning opportunity.

♦ Introduce the teacher and the name of the conference or seminar the teacher attended.

- Publicize the topic and presenters in the weekly memo, send an all-school e-mail, or use the meeting agenda.
- Allow sufficient time by asking the teacher to project how much time is needed.
- Include time for teachers to ask questions, discuss implications, or to work in small groups.
- Videotape the presentation and keep a copy of the presentation in the library. By the end of the year, there should be a sizable collection of learning materials. These materials will be helpful for newcomers to the staff in subsequent years.
- Assist teachers with developing a handout about the content of the seminar (or be ready to provide secretarial support to reproduce materials from the seminar) before the faculty meeting.
- Follow-up after the faculty meeting with a summary of the discussion. Seek additional learning materials for faculty based on needs or interest generated during the faculty meeting. Consult with district staff to obtain additional resources.

One way to transform faculty meetings into learning opportunities is to develop a planning committee that would help to shape the focus of faculty meetings throughout the year. The professional development planning committee could meet a few weeks before the school year begins to plan. The committee could include the lead teacher, the instructional coordinator, or one or two grade-level leaders or department chairs in addition to either the principal or the assistant principal. Much of the configuration of the committee will depend on the level—elementary, middle, or high school.

The names of the individuals on the planning committee could be published in a staff bulletin or memo, so that all of the teachers can give their ideas to one of the individuals on the professional development planning committee. The key is to get teachers talking about their professional development needs.

After professional development needs have been identified, a yearlong agenda with a time line based on the consensus of the teachers' professional development needs can be developed. Once the agenda of topics is identified, leadership among the members of the professional development committee can be shared—lining up teachers to present or conduct the professional development, with the principal or a teacher (or both) acting as facilitator, timekeeper, or recorder during faculty meetings or in-service days. The agenda and focus of the professional development can be varied. For instance, some topics may deal with faculty interests, while others may relate more to district initiatives or school goals. Sometimes, simply sharing a specific teaching technique makes for a stimulating professional development topic. Figure 14.8 offers a summary form of in-house professional development human resources.

Figure 14.8. In-House Professional Development Resources

Teacher	Subject(s) Taught	Areas of Expertise/Interest
Allison	Mathematics	Integrating technology in instruction
Clay	Mathematics	Classroom management
Jay	Science	Modifying instruction for diverse learners
Patton	Social Studies	Cooperative learning; Socratic seminars
Rascoe	English	Calling patterns as a classroom management tool

This form will expand as expertise and willingness to share expertise grows. In addition to potential workshop facilitators, the process of identifying "in-house" professional development expertise might also assist principals to locate faculty members with expertise and interest in various professional development and supervision models such as peer coaching, action research, reflection, and portfolio development. Other sources of professional development support include regional service centers, area universities, and state departments of education.

Identifying professional developers inside and outside of the district or site is just the first step in planning for professional development. Because workshops alone do not adequately support teacher growth, a comprehensive plan that promotes continuous learning is needed. Although no "magical formula" for planning and conducting professional development exists, some general strategies that help to promote ongoing learning include establishing the initiative, developing a follow-up plan, and creating a method for assessing the initiative.

Planning for Professional Development: Pulling the Pieces Together

There are numerous processes and steps to be taken in the planning for professional development, and the scope of this book does not allow for full coverage of each process. Figure 14.9, on the next page, offers planning considerations for large-scale site professional development.

Figure 14.9. Planning Considerations
for Professional Development

1. Identify the objectives and goals of the plan.
2. Identify the target population (e.g., first-year teachers, fifth-grade math teachers, high school English teachers).
3. What are the needs of the teachers and staff who will be the benefactors of the professional development?
4. How were needs determined?
5. Who will be involved in the planning of the program?
6. How will these people be involved in planning?
7. What resources are needed? What are the costs of thee resources?
8. Detail the workings of the plan: What will be involved? What will teachers be doing (hopefully, more than just listening to someone)? What activities are planned for teachers? Identify the types of learning activities that will be embedded in the day-to-day work of teachers and how these activities will be embedded.
9. What types of ongoing support will be provided for teachers? How will this support be given and by whom?
10. How will the plan be monitored?

By working through these questions and processes with others (such as a planning committee, discussed earlier), the principal will be in a solid position to plan and to deliver professional development that is responsive to the needs of the teachers at the site.

Making the Connection Between Instructional Supervision and Professional Development

Earlier in this chapter, the second level of planning for professional development that meets individual teacher needs as identified during classroom observations and working with teams of teachers (e.g., grade level, subject matter, departments) was identified as a goal. The informal and formal classroom observations and the discussions during pre- and postobservation conferences provide windows of opportunities to connect that work with professional development. Through the purposeful interactions, the supervisor can seek to discover

◆ Skills teachers are implementing in practice

◆ Skills that teachers are struggling to implement

◆ What is working in practice—how, why, or why not

◆ The ongoing support and resources that teachers need

- Follow-up activities needed to support implementation
- Teachers who would be willing to let others observe their teaching

Through peer coaching, action research, and the use of the portfolio, the clinical model of supervision can be extended to include teachers working with teachers in addition to the supervisor. Professional development can be personalized for each teacher and be based on the data collected during classroom observations and teachers' sense of what is most important to examine. The value of connecting supervision and professional development is the tailored nature of learning for adults.

Summary

Learning expends resources and a through a seamless approach of connecting supervision, professional development, and evaluation, the principal takes a step in the right direction of unifying efforts to promote teacher growth and development. To provide appropriate learning opportunities, the principal understands the career stages of teachers, the principles of adult learning, and the vital importance of sustained "teacher talk" over time, and coaching. In addition to professional development conducted outside of school hours, teachers need learning opportunities that are a part of their daily work. Fulfilling this need requires time during the day. Through job-embedded learning techniques such as peer coaching, study groups, and action research, the principal situates the teacher as the "doer" in their own learning.

Using ELCC Standards to Place Supervision and Professional Development in a Context

From Theory to Practice

In Chapter 1, the Educational Leadership Constituent Council Standards (ELCC) for Advanced Programs in Educational Leadership for Principals, Superintendents, Curriculum Directors, and Supervisors were introduced. In short, the ELCC Standards that relate to supervision and professional development are summarized in Figure 14.10 on the next page.

Figure 14.10. ELCC FOCUS and Targets to Instructional Supervision and Professional Growth Plans

Standard 2.0: Candidates who complete the program are educational leaders who have the knowledge and ability to promote the success of all students by promoting a positive school culture, providing an effective instructional program, applying best practice to student learning, and designing comprehensive professional growth plans for staff.

2.4 Design Comprehensive Professional Growth Plans:

2.4a Candidates design and demonstrate an ability to implement well-planned, context- appropriate professional development programs based on reflective practice and research on learning consistent with the school vision and goals.

2.4b Candidates demonstrate the ability to use strategies such as observations, collaborative reflection, and adult learning strategies to form comprehensive professional growth plans with teachers and other school personnel.

As a culminating activity, conduct a complete cycle of clinical supervision in the field with a practicing teacher. The completed field project should include (a) a written report including a videotape of the preobservation and postobservation conference, (b) raw data collected using two data collection tools deemed appropriate based on the focus established in the preobservation conference, (c) an analysis of the school and classroom context including the characteristics of the students, (d4) a summary and analysis of what was shared with the teacher in the videotaped postobservation conference, (e) a detailed professional growth plan for the teacher based on career stage, principles of adult learning, and instructional improvement targets, and (f) a long-term plan for assessing the professional growth plan. This performance component is intended to go beyond knowledge and understanding to the doing and applying of skills to the practice of supervising teachers in a specific context.

The following are some highlights to help frame this culminating field project.

Section I: Profile: Establishing the Context and Characteristics

Narrative

1. *Profile of the teacher for whom the plan is being developed.* Include such information as: Number of years in teaching (beginning teacher, etc.); number of years at this school setting; highest degree held; professional development activities over the past two years; views about supervision in general.

Narrative

2. *Profile of the supervisory procedures in place in the setting.* Include a district or school description of the supervisory/evaluation process (appendix) and a copy of the evaluative forms used (appendix).

Narrative

3. *Profile of the school setting.* Identify the type of school (urban, suburban, rural, high school, elementary, middle school, public, private, parochial, military), and school demographics (size, number of students, number of teachers) and other areas that make the school context unique (e.g., theme school, charter school, block schedule, teacher attrition rates, socioeconomic status).

Section II: Preobservation Conference and the Classroom Observation

This section is to be videotaped, but there is also a writing component to this phase of the plan:

1. *Preobservation:* Conduct a preobservation conference with the teacher you are working with. In writing, identify the teacher's instructional concerns. Also, identify the supervisory focus and the data collection tools to be used during the observation. See Figure 4.2, page 71.

2. *Observation:* After conducting the preobservation conference, observe the teacher. The classroom observation should be at least 45 minutes long. This observation may or may not be videotaped (this will depend on the comfort level of the teacher, the availability of equipment, and/or school/district policies governing videotaping in the classroom). Work with the teacher to agree mutually on this aspect. Also, run this past the principal to determine his/her comfort level with videotaping. Remember that the videotape will only be viewed by you, the teacher with whom you are developing the plan, and perhaps your instructor.

At least two observation tools are to be used to collect data. See Chapter 5 for possible tools to use to collect data during the classroom observation.

Section III: The Postobservation Conference

1. Conduct a postobservation conference with the teacher you observe. This conference should be held in the classroom in which the teacher you observed taught the lesson. Present the data in such a way that the teacher can begin to orally reflect on his/her instruction. Remember to show data by using the tools learned in class *and* to address

the teacher's concerns (which were to be teased out during the preobservation conference).

2. The writing component. Submit a formal report of your observation and include the major points that were discussed with the teacher. Focus on the data that were collected, and how the teacher responded to the data.

Here are some additional questions to help you frame the written summary:

3. What data did you share with the teacher, noting strengths and future target areas for the teacher to focus?

4. What areas did the teacher want to focus on during the postobservation conference?

6. Assume there is truth to the statement "The more teachers talk about teaching, the better they get at it" (McGreal, 1983). What do you think the teacher learned about his or her own teaching through the experience?

Section IV: The Professional Growth Plan

Based on the preobservation conference (area of focus), the observation, and the discussion in the postobservation conference, develop a semester-long *detailed* professional growth plan *with* the teacher. Include areas for the teacher to explore, ways in which the teacher can explore these areas, and any other mutually agreed on aspect (e.g., what artifacts to include). Include how you and the teacher will mutually monitor the plan (e.g., markers of completion, time frame). Negotiate how you and the teacher will communicate about the plan once it is in place.

Start by writing a rationale including the need for the Professional Growth Plan. Remember, though, that this is not a Plan of Remediation.
Situate this plan within the context of the school or system in which the plan is being developed. Then proceed with the following components of the plan.

1. List the objectives and/or goals of the plan.

2. Identify the characteristics of the teacher (first-year, alternatively certified, veteran teacher).

3. What are the needs of the teacher based on your work and what the teacher identifies as needs?

4. How did you determine these needs? Or How would you determine the needs?

5. How did you involve the teacher in the planning, ongoing assessment, evaluation?

6. What resources are needed? What are the costs of thee resources?

7. Detail the workings of the plan: (a) What will be involved? (b) What will the teacher be doing (hopefully, more than just listening to someone)? (c) What activities are planned for the teacher? (d) Identify the types of learning activities that will be embedded in the day-to-day work of the teacher and how these activities will be embedded in the workday.

8. What types of ongoing support will be provided for this teacher? How will this support be given and by whom?

9. How will you monitor the plan?

Section V: Reflections on the Process and Summary

What insights have you gained about the process of working with teachers and your role as a supervisor? What have you learned? What are the "rough" spots? How does a supervisor overcome the rough terrain of working with teachers?

Bundle materials in such a way that the videotape and other artifacts do not get lost.

Highlights of what to include in this packet:

1. Profile of the teacher and the school context.
2. Preobservation (videotaped and notes).
3. Observation (videotape and/or raw notes).
4. Discussion of what data collection tool(s) you used and why (include raw notes).
5. Postobservation conference (videotaped and formal narrative report).
6. Detailed professional growth plan.
7. Reflections on the process and summary.

Self-Assessment of This Work

Each component of the Individual Teacher Supervisory Plan and the Comprehensive Professional Growth Plan Project can be assessed overall based on the following three criteria:

1. Completeness (Have all of the requirements for that component been completed?);

2. The degree to which the project provides a coherent image of a comprehensive teacher growth plan (Does the professional growth plan follow logically from the focus identified in the preobservation conference, the observational tool used, the data collected during the observation, and the report from the postobservation conference?); and,

3. The extent to which the student has demonstrated the ability to create an atmosphere of collaboration in the supervision process (Do the artifacts from the process demonstrate equal involvement on the part of the teacher and the supervisor?).

Rubric—Classroom Observation
(Preobservation Conference, Classroom
Observation, Postobservation Conference)

ELCC Standard	Elements of the Standard in Which Performance Is Assessed	Improvement Needed	Proficient	Exceptional
2.4b Candidates demonstrate the ability to use strategies such as observations, collaborative reflection, and adult learning strategies to form comprehensive professional growth plans with teachers and other school personnel.				
	1.1: Teacher Profile/School Context Narrative			

(Figure continues on next page.)

ELCC Standard	Elements of the Standard in Which Performance Is Assessed	Improvement Needed	Proficient	Exceptional
	Profile of the teacher for whom the plan is being developed	Information about the teacher is sketchy. Does not include discussion of the characteristics of the teacher relative to career continuum (beginning, mid-career, veteran); history of professional development lacks description.	Includes information about the teacher relative to career continuum but lacks key insights about needs of the teacher related to the key principles of adult development; lacks explanation and analysis of professional development activities.	Includes detailed information such as: Number of years in teaching (beginning teacher, etc.); details and discusses the principles of adult learning that characterize the teacher's needs; includes number of years at this school setting; highest degree held; staff development activities over the past two years and provides explanation of how these activities have promoted growth and development; views about supervision in general.

(Figure continues on next page.)

ELCC Standard	Elements of the Standard in Which Performance Is Assessed	Improvement Needed	Proficient	Exceptional
	Profile of the supervisory and evaluative procedures in place in the setting	Provides only rudimentary information and documents from within the system are not included as appendix material	Includes documents from within the system; provides some insight on how the supervisory and evaluative procedures "play out" in practice; makes some connections to how these processes promote teacher development.	Documents from within the system are included with detailed analysis of how these practices and procedures add to the development of teachers, especially the teacher with whom the student is working with during the current semester; analysis is provided detailing the specific points of the procedures and processes and how these processes support teacher development and growth. Distinction is made between the differences in summative and formative procedures within the supervisory and evaluative plans and procedures.

(Figure continues on next page.)

ELCC Standard	Elements of the Standard in Which Performance Is Assessed	Improvement Needed	Proficient	Exceptional
	Profile of the School setting including: ♦ Percentages of free and reduced lunch ♦ Demographic changes ♦ Unique and special programs in place to work with students, parents, community ♦ Emerging programs developed to meet needs ♦ AYP status ♦ Changes in personnel (principal, teachers) ♦ Instructional issues facing the school ♦ Districtwide initiatives ♦ School mission	The profile does not include a majority of detail to add texture to the context of the school setting; many profile factors are missing or only "covered" without detail on how each one of items contribute a full understanding of the context in which the teacher works.	The profile includes numerous descriptions of the context but full explanations are not offered showing deep understanding of how the context factors affect supervisor, evaluative, and professional development practices.	The profile of the school context includes all factors (see profile) with full discussion of how these factors contribute to providing supervision, evaluation, and professional development. Detail and analysis provide a full rendition of the "life" of the school and the policies and procedures in place that support or inhibit supervision, evaluation, and professional development.
	1.2: Supervisory Skills (Preobservation Conference)			

(Figure continues on next page.)

ELCC Standard	Elements of the Standard in Which Performance Is Assessed	Improvement Needed	Proficient	Exceptional
	Identification of classroom context, characteristics of the learners	Preobservation and video-clip show perfunctory discussion of the learning environment.	Preobservation and video-clip shows discussion but certain aspects of the learning environment are not included or barely discussed (e.g., culture, climate, and atmosphere).	Preobservation form and video-clip shows discussion of the classroom context including characteristics of students as learners and unique learning needs; details the culture and climate of the classroom with discussion of the atmosphere in the room and how students contribute.
	Learning objectives	Learning objectives do not give much detail about what students will learn and why; objectives are not teased out during discussion; incomplete information is given	Learning objectives are provided, namely a listing of learning objectives without full specificity	Learning objectives are discussed in relation to past learning and future learning objectives; shows detail about content of the lesson; how students will cue into what is being taught and why. Full explanation of what instruction will look and sound like given the content specifications and the learning objectives.

(Figure continues on next page.)

ELCC Standard	Elements of the Standard in Which Performance Is Assessed	Improvement Needed	Proficient	Exceptional
	Focus mutually identified between the supervisor and the teacher	Classroom observation focus is unclear	Classroom observation is clear but lacks some forms of specificity that could be achieved with follow-up and probing questions of the teacher during the preobservation conference.	Clear classroom observation focus developed with appropriate probes and follow-up questions to further define the classroom observation focus; teacher and observer develop the focus mutually with the teacher leading the discussion; observer asks probing questions so the teacher can define the focus.

(Figure continues on next page.)

ELCC Standard	Elements of the Standard in Which Performance Is Assessed	Improvement Needed	Proficient	Exceptional
	Discussion of which Data Tools Used and Why	No discussion of what tools will be used to collect data or discussion consists of merely identifying the types of data collection tools to be used without elaboration or explanation of the tools and what data will look like and significance of the types of data that can be collected and how this data will shed light on the agreed on focus of the classroom observation.	Moderate discussion of the tools to be used to collect data with some discussion on the types of data that can be collected using the tools.	Elaborate discussion related to the tools and identifies at least two data collection tools. Provides detail on the types of data that can be collected, shows value of the type of data that can be collected and how this data can be used to shed insight on classroom practices as identified in the observation focus.

ELCC Standard	Elements of the Standard in Which Performance Is Assessed	Improvement Needed	Proficient	Exceptional
	1.3: The Classroom Observation	Spends less than 45 minutes conducting the classroom observation; notes are sketchy and do not relate to the classroom observation focus; gaps in the notes do not afford the observer to frame for the postobservation conference.	Spends 45 minutes in the classroom observing the teacher; some gaps in observation notes make it possible but difficult to relate data to the classroom observation focus; data are not necessary related to classroom focus agreed on in the preobservation conference; overreliance on one data collection tool with the second tool only used in a cursory manner.	Spends 45 minutes or more conducting the classroom observation. The data collection tool was aligned with the discussion in the preobservation conference. Raw classroom observation notes detail what was observed—what the teacher was doing and what the children were doing; Notes show a composite of teaching and learning based on the lesson being taught, and the characteristics of the students; the data collected relate directly to the focus.

(Figure continues on next page.)

ELCC Standard	Elements of the Standard in Which Performance Is Assessed	Improvement Needed	Proficient	Exceptional
	1.4: The Postobservation Conference	Data are presented with the observer dominating the talk of the postobservation conference. Data are "listed" with some value judgments made by the observer.	Data are presented as factual, with the observer mediating the conversation with some opportunity for the teacher to extend thoughts. Questions are closed-nature not allowing dialogue to flow from the teacher presenting his or her point of view.	Observer presents data in a value-free manner; allows teacher to analyze and reflect "out loud" about the data; teacher is able to reconstruct the lesson. Ongoing plans are developed for follow-up. Concrete suggestions are developed based on the insights of the teacher moderated by the data collected during the classroom observation. The teacher owns data and has latitude to develop "next steps."

Rubric—Professional Growth Plan

ELCC Standard	Elements in Which Performance Is Assessed	Improvement Needed	Proficient	Exceptional
2.4a Candidates design and demonstrate an ability to implement well-planned, context-appropriate professional development programs based on reflective practice and research on learning consistent with the school vision and goals.				

(Figure continues on next page.)

ELCC Standard	Elements in Which Performance Is Assessed	Improvement Needed	Proficient	Exceptional
	1.1: Based on the preobservation conference (area of focus), the observation, and the discussion in the post-observation conference	The Professional Growth Plan is not connected to the needs of the teacher based on (a) knowledge of the teacher through classroom observation and postobservation dialogue, (b) the developmental level of the teacher (based on principles of adult learning and career stage theory), (c) the needs of the students as based on the context of the classroom.	The Professional Growth Plan is developed based on the needs of the teacher but lacks clarity based on data from the classroom observation and/or knowledge about the teacher's conceptual development. Plan is only partially developed with specificity.	The Professional Growth Plan is fully developed driven by data gleaned from the preobservation, the extended classroom observation, and the postobservation conference. The objectives and/or goals of the plan align with the principles of adult learning based on the needs of the teacher. Activities reflect needs of the teacher based on principles of adult learning and/or career stage theory, the context of the classroom, and the students who the teachers works with.

(Figure continues on next page.)

ELCC Standard	Elements In Which Performance Is Assessed	Improvement Needed	Proficient	Exceptional
	1.2: Detailed Professional Growth Plan includes areas for the teacher to explore, ways in which the teacher can explore these areas, and any other mutually agreed on aspect (e.g., what artifacts to include).	The Professional Growth Plan (activities) does not reflect a broad range of activities. Planning did not include the teacher in the process.	The Professional Growth Plan reflects a moderate number of activities; the teacher was involved to a limited degree in the development of the professional growth plan.	The Professional Growth Plan includes a wide range of activities focused on the needs of the teacher; the teacher was involved in planning, ongoing assessment of the professional growth plan. The detailed workings of the plan include specification related to (a) What will be involved? (b) What the teacher will be doing, (c) the activities planned for the teacher are explicit, (d) the types of learning activities that will be embedded in the day-to-day work of the teacher, and (e) how these activities are embedded in the workday are detailed.

(Figure continues on next page.)

ELCC Standard	Elements in Which Performance Is Assessed	Improvement Needed	Proficient	Exceptional
	1.3: Monitoring plan (e.g., markers of completion, time frame).	A monitoring plan exists but lacks specificity relative to who will provide support, what resources are needed, who will assist with the plan, and the time frame of the plan.	The monitoring plan exists with approximate needs identified, and a time frame is identified but not linked to the activities and resources identified in the plan. A certain amount of ambiguity creates a sense of too much room for interpretation about who will monitor the plan and when the monitoring will begin and end.	There is a detailed monitoring plan that includes both the supervisor and the teacher in the ongoing assessment and evaluation of the professional growth plan. Resources needed to deliver the professional growth plan are identified. The types of ongoing support and personnel needed are identified and plans are made to ensure that this support is provided for this teacher.

References

Annenberg Institute for School Reform (n.d.). *Professional learning communities: Strategies that improve instruction.* Providence, RI: Annenberg Institute for School Reform at Brown University.

Hirsh, S., & Ponder, G. (1991). New plots, new heroes in staff development. *Educational Leadership, 49*(3), 43–48.

McBride, R., Reed, J., & Dollar, J. (1994). Teacher attitudes toward staff development: A symbolic relationship at best. *Journal of Staff Development, 15*(2), 36–41.

McGreal, T. (1983). *Effective teacher evaluation.* Alexandria, VA: Association for Supervision and Curriculum.

National Association of Elementary School Principals. (2001). *Leading learning communities: Standards for what principals should know and be able to do.* Alexandria, VA: Author.

National Policy Board for Educational Administration (2002). *Educational Leadership Constituent Council Standards for advanced programs in educational leadership for principals, superintendents, curriculum directors, and supervisors.* Reston, VA: Author. Retrieved August 9, 2006, from http://www.npbea.org/ELCC/ELCCStandards%20_5–02.pdf

National Staff Development Council. Standards for staff development. Retrieved August 22, 2006, from http://www.nsdc.org/standards/index.cfm

Sparks, D., & Hirsh, S. (1997). *A new vision for staff development.* Oxford, OH: National Staff Development Council.

U.S. Department of Education (1995). *Building bridges: The mission and principles of professional development.* Retrieved October 13, 2002, from http://www.ed.gov/G2K/bridge.html

Wiggins, G., & McTighe, J. (2006). Examining the teaching life. *Educational Leadership, 63*(6), 26–29.

Zepeda, S. J. (1999). *Staff development: Building learning communities.* Larchmont, NY: Eye on Education.

15

Pulling It All Together

The journey of instructional supervision follows a winding and often up-hill path, but the instructional supervisor does not walk alone. Others who travel this road continue to refine such practices as peer coaching, action research, and portfolio development, extending the clinical model of supervision as a vehicle to enhance professional development. Along the way, supervisors guide teachers to discover strengths and identify opportunities for learning and growth.

Indeed, learning is the hallmark of a teacher's professional journey. Effective teachers do not merely direct their students' learning; rather, they grow and thrive through their own. At its best, adult learning arises from the workday and returns to enrich it. Sound instructional supervision supports this cycle. Fittingly, therefore, this book culminates with an exploration of job-embedded learning.

Job-Embedded Learning

Those who study professional development have discovered the outstanding efficacy of learning that is embedded in the workday and tailored to individual needs. McLaughlin and Oberman (1996) indicate that administrators and others responsible for professional growth need to "recognize the importance of embedding teachers' learning in everyday activities" (p. x).

Pajak (1993) offers several options for embedding supervision into the teacher's workday, including collegial supervision (peer coaching and cognitive coaching), self-directed supervision, informal supervision, and inquiry-based supervision (action research). Underpinning all these techniques is the conviction that teachers are professionals who can take responsibility for their own learning.

Attributes of Job-Embedded Learning: Applications to Supervision

Wood and Killian (1998) define job-embedded learning as "learning that occurs as teachers and administrators engage in their daily work activities" (p. 52). Among their findings is the conclusion that schools must

> restructure supervision and teacher evaluation so that they support teacher learning and the achievement of personal, professional, and school achievement goals....[B]oth supervision and teacher evaluation should be modified to focus on school and/or personal improvement goals rather than the district and state required observation forms. (p. 54)

Instructional supervision—supervision that seeks to guide growth and learning—reaches its fullest potential when woven into the everyday professional activities of teachers. Job-embedded supervision

- Enhances reflection;
- Promotes collegiality;
- Combats isolation;
- Makes supervision more relevant to each teacher;
- Increases transfer of newly learned skills;
- Supports the ongoing refinement of practice; and
- Fosters a common lexicon that facilitates dialogue and improvement.

Job-Embedded Supervision Enhances Reflection Reflection—serious thought about professional practice—thrives in an atmosphere where teachers are free to make decisions about their own instructional practices. Practices such as peer coaching and autosupervision remove the threat of evaluation and empower teachers to take risks. Peer coaching frames supervision as a process between equals—something that teachers do "with one another" rather than something that is done "to them" (Pajak, 1993, p. 223). Because these practices mirror the processes of clinical supervision, training and experience are essential to help teachers implement them effectively.

Job-Embedded Supervision Promotes Collegiality Job-embedded supervision flattens traditional hierarchies, breaks down barriers between teachers and supervisors, and makes their work more collaborative. Supervision that brings teachers and supervisors together in the classroom promotes collegiality. The work of the school is accomplished most efficiently when all members of the learning community work together as a team (Calabrese & Zepeda, 1997).

Job-Embedded Supervision Combats Isolation Compartmentalized into their separate cubicles of classroom and office, educators too often feel distant from one another. Lortie (1975) identified isolation as one of the most common problems teachers face. The feeling of isolation has been compared to treading water over one's head without a life preserver (Ganser, 1997). Supervision practiced by teachers and for teachers can transform a group of isolated individuals into a faculty of colleagues.

Job-Embedded Supervision Makes Supervision More Relevant to Each Teacher Adults seek learning opportunities that are relevant to their current situation (Dalellew & Martinez, 1988). When supervision is a part of the teacher's daily practice, learning opportunities are tailored to the teacher's specific learning needs.

Job-Embedded Supervision Increases Transfer of Newly Learned Skills The traditional model of professional development places learning in workshops and courses removed from the work environment. When supervisors embed professional development in the workday, learning becomes integral to practice. Teachers implement new techniques as they acquire them.

Job-Embedded Supervision Supports the Ongoing Refinement of Practice In the traditional clinical supervision model, time passes between observation and feedback. Unfortunately, the memory of events during the observation fades with time. Supervision embedded in the teacher's daily work adds immediacy to feedback, places reflection in the context of the classroom, and thus supports the ongoing refinement of practice.

Job-Embedded Supervision Fosters a Common Lexicon Combining traditional supervision with other practices embedded in the daily routine leads teachers and administrators to develop a common lexicon. This enhances dialogue, promotes reflection, and paves the way for improving instructional practices.

The educator who understands the principles of professional development, masters the practices of instructional supervision, and works with teachers with care and concern can make a difference. The stakes are high; the rewards, immense. Supervisors embarking on this journey can expect pleasures and pitfalls, frustrations and fulfillment, learning and growth. The journey awaits.

References

Calabrese, R. L., & Zepeda, S. J. (1997). *The reflective supervisor*. Larchmont, NY: Eye On Education.

Dalellew, T. & Martinez, Y. (1988). Andragogy and development: A search for the meaning of staff development. *Journal of Staff Development, 9*(3), 28–31.

Ganser, T. (1997). Gateways to experience: Similes for beginning teachers. *Kappa Delta Pi Record, 33*(3) 106–108.

Lortie, D. C. (1975). *School teacher: A sociological perspective.* Chicago: University of Chicago Press.

McLaughlin, M. W., & Oberman, I. (1996). *Teacher learning: New policies, new practices.* New York: Teachers College Press.

Pajak, E. (1993). *Approaches to clinical supervision: Alternatives for improving instruction.* Norwood, MA: Christopher-Gordon.

Wood, F. H., & Killian, J. (1998). Job-embedded learning makes the difference in school improvement. *Journal of Staff Development, 19*(1), 52–54.

Index